ROYCE'S SAILING ILLUSTRATED course

sailors helping sailors

Sixteen hours of sail lectures for our ACTI

Ten years preliminary concentrated testi
grew on its own in evening classrooms i
plus 1600 private sailing students full day
Final revision of the course and text began in 1984.

Sailing Illustrated required three full years to revise stem to stern to become the new basic text. The sail course was being developed at the same time, requiring more time to bring to the present status than I want to remember.

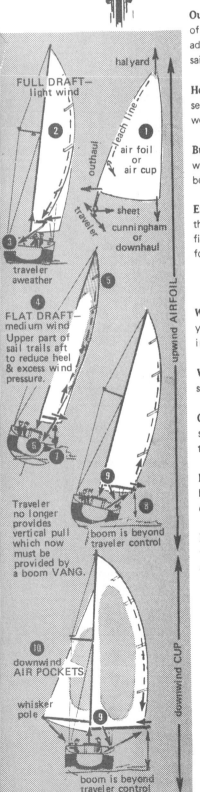

FULL DRAFT— light wind

halyard
leach line
air foil or air cup
outhaul
traveler
sheet
cunningham or downhaul
traveler aweather

FLAT DRAFT— medium wind. Upper part of sail trails aft to reduce heel & excess wind pressure.

upwind AIRFOIL

Traveler no longer provides vertical pull which now must be provided by a boom VANG.

boom is beyond traveler control

downwind CUP

downwind AIR POCKETS

whisker pole

boom is beyond traveler control

ISBN 0-911284-01-X

Our existing sail course was revised and expanded to help a larger variety of sailors. Many full page details of dinghies and cabin sailboats were added from IOR to lug rig, and a 1938 gaff rigger to add the foreign sailing standing and rigging language terms for familiarity.

Heritage sailing information kept expanding as more people begin to seek their heritage from the 1700s to 1900 for coastal sailing AND worldwide square rig weather sailing patterns.

But where is the lecture material my son asked. A lecuturer can read it word for word if desired, or study the content and sequence to provide better coverage for local sailing interests and needs.

Exposure is provided to endless basic sailing subjects. Students can learn the foreign sailing language while having exposure to how all the ideas fit into the overall pattern. from spinnakers to square rig. With this foundation students can expand their information any direction desired.

16 hours of lectures and eight or more hours of homework.

Weekly 2½ hour evening classroom lectures are the best method for yacht clubs, boat clubs, and community sailing programs, especially in snowbelt areas with limited on-the-water summer sailing.

Weekend seminars. It provides considerable flexibility for sailing schools, with considerable homework assigned in advance.

On the water instruction. It proved excellent to teach dinghy and cabin sailboat operation for my full day sailing lessons others can adapt to, assigning some homework beforehand.

High school, college, university sail programs. The information can be adapted to hour lectures with homework as regular curriculum or after school classes.

Fragmented sail courses— the competition. Existing ones are limited to small specialized sailing areas which is a handicap as the students are missing much of the fun and enjoyment of sailing. The best example is a large jigsaw puzzle for which you only have a few parts.

Thoroughness with flexibility seems the best way to summarize the first quality sail course designed for nationwide use, as well as our Canadian friends to the north, and sailing friends in Australia.

© 1993 by Patrick M. Royce
information also from—
© 1985 Sailing Illustrated
Homestudy Guide
© 1993 Sailing Illustrated
all by Patrick M. Royce

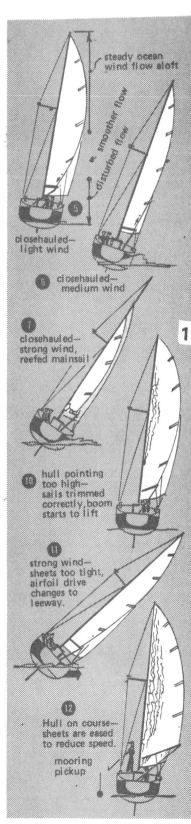

steady ocean wind flow aloft
smoother flow
disturbed flow
closehauled— light wind
closehauled— medium wind
closehauled— strong wind, reefed mainsail
hull pointing too high— sails trimmed correctly, boom starts to lift
strong wind— sheets too tight, airfoil drive changes to leeway.
Hull on course— sheets are eased to reduce speed.
mooring pickup

1

ROYCE'S SAILING ILLUSTRATED COURSE

MW00905679

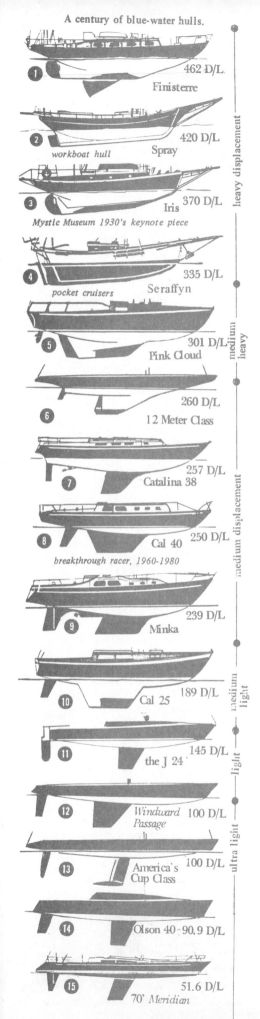

A century of blue-water hulls.

1 — 462 D/L.
Finisterre

2 — 420 D/L
workboat hull — Spray

3 — 370 D/L
Iris
Mystic Museum 1930's keynote piece

4 — 335 D/L
Seraffyn
pocket cruisers

5 — 301 D/L
Pink Cloud

6 — 260 D/L
12 Meter Class

7 — 257 D/L
Catalina 38

8 — 250 D/L
Cal 40
breakthrough racer, 1960-1980

9 — 239 D/L
Minka

10 — 189 D/L
Cal 25

11 — 145 D/L
the J 24

12 — 100 D/L
Windward Passage

13 — 100 D/L
America's Cup Class

14 — Olson 40 — 90.9 D/L

15 — 51.6 D/L
70' *Meridian*

heavy displacement | *medium heavy* | *medium displacement* | *medium light* | *light* | *ultra light*

The sport of sailing opens many new worlds to you.

Students interests vary considerably depending on personalities, goals, free time, and disposable income. Some may just enjoy reading sea stories and crewing. Others may choose it as a way of life with the yacht club racing world... to the low key, long-distance cruising sailor always on the move.

Most forms of transportation are no longer a thrill, but a means to go from one place to another in minimum time... with minimum discomfort.

This is reversed in sailing with the thrills and sensations of a boat under full sail, though only 5 to 7 knots with spray flying, quietly and efficiently using the forces of nature against each other. It can be for a peaceful afternoon sail, a lazy week vacation, or a month under sail out of sight of land.

Sailing is an emotional sport, one of few which offers something for everyone from nine thru 70. A new sport opens for women sailors as many universities give them letters, finding they can compete equally racing against men.

For most sailors it is the momentary escape back to nature from the artificial bureaucratic pressures of our political and economic worlds... to winning that hard fought race or series against the best competitors in your class.

For some sailors it is the goal to pull into a beautiful south seas anchorage at dusk after many days at sea to enjoy the new smells of land, flowers, and vegitation.

Returning to the dock and false security of dry land becomes a letdown. Sailors often become quiet until planning that next sail. Whether it will be a drifting match, or rails under with a double reef... is the unknown challenge.

The history of sail began way before recorded history.

Engineering involved in sailing probably follows that of mans interest to build homes to protect his family from the elements... and crude bridge building.

Sailing grew as the best method for inexpensive bulk cargo transportation. Leaders of many civilizations were actively involved in it: from boat building, to operation, plus making a profit buying a cargo in one port, to sell in another.

Half the worlds cargo tonnage was still under sail by 1880, when reaching its peak as a method of commercial transportation with minimum cost. Slowly, then rapidly sail was replaced by steamships using coal, then oil. Steamship costs were higher in the changeover period, with better arrival-date predictability.

It was the end of the sailing era for profit when square riggers, then large fore and aft commercial carriers disappeared from the oceans, though small sailing vessels were still hauling inter-island cargo in outlying areas of the world.

A new era slowly began to evolve which was sailing for pleasure. Growth of the wooden sailboat and canvas sails began slowly for recreational use, the exception being the wealthy with large professionally operated and maintained craft.

Middle class interest developed rapidly around 1960 with the introduction of fiberglass hulls, Dacron and nylon for sails and rope, aluminum masts and stainless rigging, plus the ability to maintain their smaller sailboats.

The change was best defined by a San Francisco sailor, "I loved my old wooden hull sailboat with canvas sails, and manila rope. The disadvantage for my one day of weekly sailing... was six hours maintenance for two hours operation on the water.

"I now spend 30 minutes washing my fiberglass sailboat in its slip, enjoying the rest of the day on the water sailing, or racing. Maintenance is fun as varnish trim and other details are taken care of on windless weekends".

What the future of sailing will be... is up to the new generation of sailors in your classroom. The instructor responsibility is to make coverage of the numerous technological subjects fun, practical, and with ample coverage for your students sailing interests and potentials.

> **The author found an average of three of five first owners... chose sailboats that didn't match their personalities.** Discussions of the 15 sailboats at left with their differences from cargo-carrying to racing, and the compromises between, will help sailors become more aware of sailboat personalities that match theirs. *All 15 are excellent sailboats...* IF the personalities of owners and their sailboats match the other to make it a happy combination.

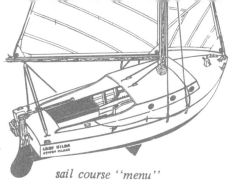

Background information for *ROYCE'S* **SAILING ILLUSTRATED** *COURSE*.

We bought our first sailboat in 1949, a 20' centerboard sloop with a cabin. We had 11 sailing books in our Brooklyn apartment. I couldn't understand any of the books covering the foreign technical language... without illustrations. The first mate recommended, "Why don't you draw the book on sailing you are looking for?" We finally published it in 1956 in Los Angeles.

The book was based on four years of east coast sailing on the Hudson River, and south side of Long Island. Sailing was limited to 4 months, often with rapidly changing weather conditions.

West coast sailing from Santa Barbara south to the Mexican border had good weather with up to 11 months sailing yearly, and easy westerly winds. I was soon teaching on a variety of sailboats from dinghies to forty footers. The more I relied on illustrations to explain sailing ideas starting with coming about and jibing, the more rapidly our students could learn to sail.

Overcome the foreign language barrier... the rest of sailing is easy.

The Long Beach Coast Guard Auxiliary wanted to start a sailing course in 1960. We prepared 30" by 36" charts and lecture material for their instructors which they used for ten years.

A similar interest developed in Newport Beach where we made reproductions of the large charts following the basic sequence used in this workbook. During a 5 minute break I overheard students saying, "I wish we had small copies of the charts to add notes during this lecture".

We supplied 8½ x 11 copies of all the charts in red ink for student use in the next lecture. Continual use found illustrations the key-- *when students write the foreign sailing terms such as lateener, sprit rig, pintles and gudgeons on the illustrations... the new sound becomes engraved in the mind with minimum wasted energy.*

We kept testing and improving the course materials and sequence in evening classes held locally for 10 years that were open to the public. We also tested the same material in full day sailing lessons on the water with over 1600 students. It was an interesting test laboratory with many of my east coast ideas falling apart in the first 3 years teaching on the water.

A workbook was required... plus word for word lecture material.

Our latest workbook had a final testing. It was printed in a similar format that grew thru the years, only greatly expanded to cover all kinds of sailing from dinghies to a variety of ocean-going sailboats.

Our Sail Course text was completed with word for word lecture material. Instructors can read the material... or expand on the information as desired. If an instructor fails to show— *a student can read the lecture material.*

Tremendous interest has grown in our sailing heritage and square rigger operation. We added enough information so new sailors also have a foundation in the history of sailing, worldwide weather patterns, plus learning the names of both *Cutty Sark* and *USCG Eagle* sails.

YOU can teach yourself with our materials.

Obtain the workbook, lecture material, *Sailing Illustrated,* and our *Homestudy Guide* to fill in the answers on your own, and at your own speed. You may be able to help start a sail course in your area open to the public.

The *Sailing Illustrated* Course is designed with flexibility to serve varied sailing interests.

dinghy sailing

The *Sailing Illustrated* text and workbook provide a foundation with ample information to sail various one-design dinghies in protected areas.

complex entry-level larger sailboat requirements

The course is just as useful to develop **entry-level sailors** for cabin sailboats, requiring basic information in depth on many subjects besides operation. He needs to know the choice and care of seagoing metals, lightning protection variables, commercial vessel warning signals and lights, etc., and for traditionalists, methods to keep wooden boats healthy with ample information covered in our *Homestudy Guide*.

sailing history and cultures for the curious

The sail course material is equally adaptable to scholars and historians with interest limited to the language and development of sail as half the world's tonnage still roamed the oceans worldwide under sail in 1880, reduced to ¼ by 1900. They can explore the old commercial vessels to modern sailboats seen thru the eyes of a practicing sailor.

the goal is— SELF RELIANCE

The real exam takes place on the ocean. The sail course provides exposure to the mechanics of sail, and the environmental forces of nature for propulsion required to provide the spirited emotional highs of sailing, normal highs seldom found on land.

A short review.......

Lecture One

sail rigs, hulls, keels & rudders thru history

The full lecture should be considered for ALL students... as knowledge of various sail rigs, hulls, keels, and rudders, plus their endless mixtures, will be useful for a lifetime of operation under sail. Numbers are provided on the basic Lightning, workbook page 5, for students to add terms for the hull, rigging, sails, etc.

rigging controls- popular dinghies

Homework— workbook pages 6-8. Students should list all standing and running rigging terms on all the five dinghies ... with answers provided in the reference text.

Lecture Two

how much Admiralty Law?

For inland protected areas, filling the blanks for sailboat regulations on workbook page 11 may be sufficient. Full coverage of Admiralty Law lecture material is needed for coastal and inland areas with a mix of sailboat, powerboat, and commercial traffic.

backing the jib?????

Backing the jib when coming about, is difficult for many students to understand. After filling the blanks on page 19 of the workbook, have students turn to the reference text page 130 to analyze the type of small to large sailing craft requiring backing the jib as normal operation, and others seldom, plus the basic reasons.

the important wind force scale

The **wind force scale** wave patterns are important to recognize so the operator sensing a change, can have the sails reefed the correct amount before a storm moves in. Many students want to change it to miles per hour, losing all touch with natures changing conditions. Their result was summarized by a grinning sailmaker, "They are my best customers for repairs, and new sails to replace damaged ones".

Homework— review workbook pages 12-17 covered in lecture two.

Lecture Three

what is corrosion

Ocean sailors require full knowledge of varied forms of corrosion as seagoing metals are expensive, and must be chosen wisely for their particular purpose.

What is the name of that part?

Marine hardware has its own language. Instructor reads the answers for students to fill blanks on workbook pages 19-23. The owner of a marine hardware store would be an excellent choice as a lecturer providing various hardware parts for the discussion.

Homework— U.S. Buoyage system, color the buoys as indicated, workbook page 9.

Lecture Four

hull stability sail control

Sail raising and lowering sequence follows a similar pattern from a 14' sloop to a 100' schooner to provide hull stability to be peacefully under control at all times.

30 docking situations

The 30 docking patterns workbook pages 26-7 seem complex at first glance. After basic Lido 14 patterns to 12, you soon realize similar patterns are followed on large sailboats with variables. After step 12 for those only interested in inland lake sailing, spend the rest of the lecture on splicing and knot tying.

cabin sailboat rigging controls

Homework— workbook pages 24,28-33. Students should list all running and standing rigging terms on 2, 3, or all the cabin sailboats.

Though some students are only interested in dinghy sailing, owners of cabin sailboats are often looking for new crew members. Dinghy sailors in the snowbelt areas may suddenly become interested in a charter boat sailing vacation in sunbelt areas.

4

Lecture Five

weather patterns, wind force

National weather patterns, wind force scale, displacement hull speed variables, dinghy capsize and recovery.

tides, currents, fogs

River currents and tidal currents workbook page 18; Fog can be predicted with a humidity indicator. Stress time lag variables as a fog moves in... and lifts.

thunderstorms are predictable

Thunderstorms-workbook page 36, are hazards of nature of short duration with sudden strong winds that rapidly change direction, plus downdrafts. Stress the simple, inexpensive AM radio portable static thunderstorm warning.

Homework— review weather information, lightning protection ideas. The positive ion affects everyone when the full moon peaks, and when the *devil winds* move in.

Lecture Six

sailors must know powerboat rules

All sailors need an equal understanding of powerboat rules since a sailboat legally becomes a powerboat when operating with outboard or inboard power. Fill blanks on workbook page 43 if minimum coverage is sufficient.

Admiralty Law— how much?

Our Admiralty Law lecture material is important for areas with mixed traffic so operators can *take appropiate action in time to maneuver out of a misunderstanding.*

Sailing in areas with commercial traffic— discuss workbook page 42, propeller suction and lookout problems on large vessels, special signals and lights, workbook pages 44-5.

worldwide weather

Homework— add terms to sails of *Cutty Sark* and *USCG Eagle*, workbook pages 39,41. Study the 1850 square rig sailing vessel in the text going from New York to San Francisco and return. It provides an exposure to the variables of worldwide weather patterns traditional sailors faced. It is also important background information for anyone reading sea stories in magazines and books.

Lecture Seven

sailing heritage lecture flexibility

The sailing history lecture material is practical for some instructors, while just a foundation for others to build on with a background in American sailing heritage. Instructors will have an easier time if students studied the 1850 square rigger homework, which becomes easy to build upon.

Cutty Sark

The *Cutty Sark* is of major importance, the only clipper to survive the age when commercial sailing technology was at its peak, producing speeds seldom duplicated since then under sail. The text provides six pages of *Cutty Sark* details.

overlapping continuity the Chinese

We provide the sailing continuity of probably 3000 years going back to Chinese luggers and Arab lateeners. We discuss the varied, and sometimes overlapping sail development thru the years to the present with several time presumptions as sailing was so common that records weren't kept. This is particularly important with Chinese sailing craft as only one definitive book has been produced.

the schooner—

Lecture material covers the early colonial schooners of the 1700s, to 1850 when huge fleets started building to roam the Pacific as far as China and Australia. Less is known by Americans of the large fleets of Canadian built schooners beginning roughly around 1850, for British interests in Atlantic commerce.

sailing video

The Last Sailor— is an excellent, outstanding 150 minute video of the tremendous variety of old sailing workboats and their cultures that are slowly disappearing.
Ferde Grofe Films— 3100 Airport Ave., Santa Monica, CA 90405

The brief resume shows adaptability for many uses

Our goal is to help the growth of the sport of sailing... as well as the growth of the sailing industry... thru education.

The *Sailing Illustrated* Course basic lecture sequence on these two pages provide flexibility to cover numerous technical sailing ideas for entry level, oceangoing sailors, to dinghy sailors, as well as background information for the curious... who may soon choose the sport of sailing for their hobby.

the goal is— well-trained sailors

Our approach is to make sailing interesting and filled with fun thru education. Well-trained sailors can then operate dinghies to large sailboats easily and efficiently... to their maximum potentials. This is the kind of enthusiasm that will carry over to neighbors and friends... who may also want to become sailors.

5

Welcome your students. Ask how many have dinghies... sailboats under 20'... over 20' long. How many are interested in leisurely sailing... in active racing.

The new sailor interested in cabin sailboats/ faces a bewildering number of new sailboats/ and adequately maintained used sailboats. The author defines this situation by showing a range of 15 basic types on the cover of *Sailing Illustrated*. Numerous variations are found within each basic type... some longer, and some shorter.

Each of the 15 basic types has a distinctive personality... which will be a happy sailboat IF the owner has a similar personality. It will seldom be a happy combination IF the owner with a cruising personality chooses a high performance racer... or a racing personality chooses a lower performance cruising sailboat.

The most difficult part of sailing is the language/ the oldest international technical language still in daily use. The easiest way to learn the new sailing language/ is to write the following terms starting on page two of your workbook. Afterwards I will return to provide a brief coverage of the rig terminology for the 21 sailing vessels.

first row	Add the following terms to the first row... 1. LUG rig... 2. junk LUG rig... 3. modern LUG rig... 4. LATEEN rig... 5. MALIBU OUTRIGGER... 6. LATEEN rig.
second row	Add terms to second row... 7. SPRIT rig... 8. Thames Barge SPRIT rig... 9. English Pilot CUTTER... 10. Cape Cod CATBOAT... 11. SLIDING gunter.
third row	Terms for the third row...12. Early BERMUDIAN rig... 13. FRACTIONAL sloop... 14. MASTHEAD sloop... 15. HEADSAIL sloop... 16. CUTTER rig.
fourth row	Terms for the fourth row... 17. HOBIE cat... 18. PACIFIC cat... 19. PACIFIC 2/18 cat... 20. and 21. STAYLESS catboat rigs.
sail provides cheap energy	**The purpose of early sailing was to move bulk cargo economically from one port to another. Wind pressure on the sails is transferred thru masts, shrouds, and stays, to push the 21 sailboat hulls thru the water.**
early square rig history	Square rig history goes back over 5000 years with Egyptian traders, and later Greek traders/ sailing the Mediterranean. Phonecians followed/ entering the Atlantic to trade to the north with Vikings/ and with Phonecian hieroglyphs found recently in Texas... they may have been trading with American natives.
Chinese sailing history– the Yangtze delta	Turn to page 281 of your text. Chinese sailing may have started on the huge eastern Yangtze delta/ a protected sailing area with 2000 miles of navigable water/ and 5000 miles of tributories for use by their junks. Their early square sails probably began with reeds and strips of bamboo woven into mats.

6

The lug rig played an important part in upwind sailing history.

Chinese square rig to lug rig	The lug rig may have been invented accidentally by a Chinese pirate in a hot pursuit. He tilted the square sail finding stronger winds aloft/ the difference permitting him to point higher and go faster than the following police vessel.
lug rig uses full-length battens	Efficiency of the new lug rig improved when full-length battens were added. The semi-rigid junk sails the Chinese developed grew in size becoming efficient for downwind AND upwind use. The modern LUG rig on text page 279/ is a semi-rigid sail favored by some American and English cruising sailors.
Arab square rig changes to lug rig	Turn to page 277 of your text. Egyptian merchants found the Nile River useful to float their cargoes downstream to Cairo. Rowing was necessary for the return trip upstream/ as tall hills often blanketed their square sails from the prevailing winds. A merchant may have tilted his mainsail to become a lug rig which was the start of a good idea.
lug rig changes to lateen rig	As experimentation continued/ the yard kept growing longer with the small four sided lug sail developing into a much larger triangular sail called the LATEEN rig used on the Nile today/ the tall rig found on most of their vessels.

the Pacific lateen outrigger	The MALIBU OUTRIGGER is a tiny version of the Polynesian outrigger, canoe hull, and lateen sail.These huge canoes sailed great distances on the Pacific Ocean without compasses/ relying on seamanship and native intelligence.
Polynesian colonization	Polynesian outrigger canoes sailed east from Samoa to colonize the Marquesias 4000 miles distant/ and to New Zealand and Easter Island/ colonizing Hawaii 2000 years ago. The popular Sunfish carries a dinghy LATEEN rig.
Northern Europe ocean sailing square riggers	Turn to text page 283. We go to the Northern Europe, British, and Scandinavian sailing culture which developed later. Stronger, steadier ocean winds favored the square rig beginning with the Viking long boats/ to clippers and huge windjammers still sailing in the 1930s.
British coastal luggers to the gaff rig	*The British tested four variations of the lug rig for protected coastal use/* finding it excellent for customs use to catch smugglers. They next removed the sail area forward of the lugger mast. This started the GAFF RIG to carry an ample supply of sail area on a short mast for coastal and ocean use.
sprit rig	The SPRIT RIG is another version of the British quadrilateral or four-sided mainsail to carry an ample sail area with a short mast/ in the Optimist Dinghy.
Thames Barge— gaff & sprit rig	The Thames Barge with average 85' length and 20' beam/ carries a sprit rig mainsail little changed in 130 years. They operate in the shallow Thames estuary east of London/ sometimes also carrying cargo to France, Holland, Norway, and Ireland. They are often hard aground at low tide with leeboards raised.
loosefooted main, short gaff	The English Pilot CUTTER of the 1860s carried a loosefooted mainsail with a short gaff. These pilot vessels operated twelve months of the year outside their harbor entrances/ carrying pilots to aid large vessels entering their harbors.
American catboat	The Cape Cod CATBOAT is an American idea and term/ appearing around 1830. A catboat was given to the British in 1852 they named UNA... which is still their term for our catboat. The catboat rig shown was used for shallow water fishing and clamming/ with a large storage area and cockpit to take their catch back to market.
sliding gunter— a vertical gaff	A SLIDING GUNTER is another version of the gaff rig with the gaff raised vertically. The British dinghy version shown/ is designed for the sail and all spars being short enough to store in the dinghy when not in use.
Bermudian vs marconi	Around 1850 sailors began removing the mainsail gaff in the Bermudian Islands east of the U.S., called BERMUDIAN rig by the British. Most Americans preferred the term MARCONI rig as it looked vaguely similar to Marconi wireless (radio) tower supports... while others preferred the more formal term JIB-HEADED rig.
fractional sloop rig	While specific sailboats are shown for 13 to 16/ we will instead discuss the four rigs as having identical hulls with the same total sail areas. The FRACTIONAL sloop rig will have the tallest mast and a smaller jib as the JIBSTAY or HEADSTAY doesn't go to the top of the mast. This rig permits mast bending to produce a better mainsail shape for racing.
masthead vs headsail rig	The MASTHEAD sloop rig is a more basic rig with less adjustments for ocean cruising with small crews. The HEADSAIL sloop has a larger jib and a smaller mainsail for better upwind performance.
cutter rig	The CUTTER RIG 16. usually has two jibs. Because of the shorter mast in light winds/ sloops 13. 14. and 15. the same length may have a slight advantage.The cutter rig comes into its own in high winds as it can still move under jib or staysail/ when the sloops are under bare poles drifting downwind or at anchor.
fractional rig dinghy sloops	Most DINGHIES need the FRACTIONAL rig. The mast has to be tall enough to reach better wind flow aloft/ as the first five feet or so above the water surface has disturbed wind flow.

7

full-batten mainsails

The bottom row includes modern usage of the full-batten mainsails, with the HOBIE cat the best known. The second example is the Pacific cat in its 1960 design with its large roach area. The third is the Pacific Cat redesign in 1984/ with both Pacific catamarans the same length.

modern catboats

free-standing masts

Sail rigs 20. and 21. are full-batten modern CATBOAT rigs. All controls go to, and are adjusted in the cockpit for relaxed cruising with single-handed operation. Both use FREE-STANDING masts without shrouds or stays. For several centuries many Chinese junk masts were also free standing/ with the philosophy that a mast should bend in a strong wind like a tree.

revue 8 rigs

workbook— page 3

Turn to page 3 of the reference text. (Provide a brief review of the eight basic sail rigs.)

first row

Turn to page 3 of your workbook to add the following terms.... 23.100% sail 120% power... 24. 85% sail 100% power...25. 50% sail 100% power... 26. STEADYING sails... 27. AFT steadying sail.

second row

Add terms to second row... 28. 29. 30. YAWL rig... 31. a KETCH.

third row

Add terms to third row... 32. Tahiti KETCH... 33. CAT/ KETCH... 34. CAT/ KETCH...35. a LOG CANOE.

fourth row

Terms for the fourth row....36. STANDARD schooner rig...37. TOPSAIL schooner rig... 38. STAYSAIL schooner rig... 39.While British called it a BRIGANTINE, Americans often called it a HERMAPHRODITE brig.

auxiliary sailboat engine power?

The term AUXILIARY sailboat began in the 1930s when larger sailboats had inboard engines installed. Since almost all cabin sailboats today have an inboard engine or outboard power/ the question is how much power.

basic design— 100% sail 100% power

We begin with the basic sailboat design today by its architect wanting it to have ample normal sail area/ and adequate engine power for most use. While 24 hp was designed for sailboat 23 / the owner requested a 32 hp diesel which was installed. When entering Oxnard Harbor with winds recording at 35 to 43 knots/ we still had enough engine power to control the *Minka* / which might have overpowered the 24 hp diesel.

85% sail 100% power

smaller diesels

The 40' Newporter Ketch designed in the 1950s for leisurely cruising/ had a reduced or 85% sail rig. It was designed to operate for longer periods under power than most sailboats of the period. Original specifications were a 37 hp diesel engine/ or a 60 hp gasoline engine... with the diesel engine the largest at the time that could fit the compartment. While talking with the new owner of the first Newporter built/ a 53 hp diesel was installed/ as improved engineering has reduced the size and weight of diesel engines.

powerboat with storm sails?

Vessel 25 is called by some a 50/50 rig or half sail and half power. It is more accurately described as a displacement hull powerboat with 100% engine power used for most operation.Below force 5 the sails provide a smoother ride with less rolling. Above force 5 the sails provide drive.

steadying sails

Large fleets of commercial fishing vessels on the east coast rode comfortably underway in sloppy wave action using steadying sails in the 1940s and 1950s.

aft weathercock sail

Lobstermen may raise to 200 lobster pots on a busy day. Instead of anchoring each time/ the small aft sail weathercocks the bow into the wind long enough to take in a lobster pot. A small sail lashed to a sailboat backstay/ can help hold the bow into the wind and waves at anchor or on a mooring.

8

yawl vs ketch

The RUDDER POST is BETWEEN the masts of YAWLS 28.29. and 30., while the rudder post is AFT of both masts on *Windward Passage* when she was launched in 1968.

yawl jigger

The small aft sail called a JIGGER on a yawl/ was an airfoil trim tab for self steering before the WIND VANE was invented. Joshua Slocum added the jigger in Rio to improve the self-steering ability of *Spray*/ when sailing around the world in the 1890s.

flexible ketch rig

We show the tremendous variables with ketches 32., 33., and 34. More examples are shown on page 269. going back to square rig.

the log canoe

Early Chesapeake Bay colonists used barter to obtain dugout canoes made by local indians/ adding sails as they disliked physical effort. The narrow hulls kept growing longer as the sail rigs kept growing taller. We show the result 400 or more years later with the *Flying Cloud*/ still called a log canoe.

schooners

Both masts are as tall/ or the after mast taller on the SCHOONER rig.

early schooners

tern schooner

The schooner rig is an American contribution developed in the 1700s for coastwise use on a beam reach from Florida to Maine/ see the varied schooner rigs in your text page 271. The British started to build large fleets of schooners in the 1850s for coastwise cargo use/ and trading with eastern Canada where most of the schooners were built. The TERN SCHOONER is a Canadian contribution not shown/ carrying three identical sails, masts, and spars, which were interchangeable.

Pacific schooners

Huge fleets of schooners were built in the San Francisco area after 1850. Little schooners carried logs from the rocky coasts of Washington, Oregon, and Northern California. The logs were transferred in San Francisco to large two, three, four, and five-masted schooners, barkentines, and brigantines, to be carried throughout the Pacific as far as Australia.

Chinese masts

Sixty year old Oregon Pine or fir rapidly became the first choice for Chinese junk masts/ with the masts worth more than their hulls.

communications

The goal of the sailing language... is to communicate. It developed from local slang terms thru the centuries/ into a precise international language for crews to respond instantly to orders/ while in the fo'c's'le below many could barely communicate with each other in their native homeland languages.

Bermudian jib-headed marconi

The sailing language is still evolving/ with the common triangular mainsail called the BERMUDIAN rig by the British. More formal east-coast sailors used the term JIB-HEADED rig in the 1960s/ while less formal sailors rapidly adopted the term MARCONI rig. P.S., Marconi didn't like sailing.

quadrilateral or gaff rig

Our British sailing friends use the term QUADRILATERAL mainsail term for which Americans call the GAFF RIG. These variables are important to know when reading various sailing books and magazine articles.

knockabout?

In the 1950s a sloop had to carry a bowsprit/ without a bowsprit it was called a knockabout... was the *Ranger* (text page 261) a 135' knockabout? The author has called both vessels sloops since 1956/ a change that was needed.

performance—

marconi rig vs gaff rig

Performance of marconi-rigged sloop vs gaff-rigged sloop. The best comparison is with identical hulls and the same total sail area and sail cloth. The marconi-rigged sloop will point higher/ and sail faster to windward. The gaff will sag to leeward/ plus having a shorter mast... will reduce upwind performance.

From a reach to a broad reach downwind/ the gaff rigged sloop also using a working jib/ should sail faster. It will have a more effective sail area with a lower Center of Effort in the mainsail.

Sailing rigs found worldwide seem to have little in common until exploring their evolution beginning with Chinese, Arab, Polynesian, and Northern European sailing cultures... with the merging of ideas seen today on workbook pages 2 and 3.

9

— Workbook pg. 4 —

Air and water are similar mediums/ with flexible airfoils used above the water/ and rigid symmetrical waterfoils below. The difference between the mediums/ water has 800 times the density of air.

We will now analyze rigid keels and movable underwater boards to resist upset/ while minimizing leeway or drift when sailing upwind... plus rudders to steer a straight course.

hull extremes **short keel**	*We show two hull extremes* in the center of page 4. The 1960 5.5 meter hull is very sensitive to weight and sail trim. The short keel makes it difficult to steer a straight course for long periods/ while turning in its own length.
long keel	The 1960 48' cruising hull with a deep full-length keel/ will steer a straight course by itself for long periods. It is very insensitive to weight and sail trim upwind/ with the only way to check sail trim is using the speedometer as the long hull overpowers sail trim. The long keel makes it very difficult to maneuver in tight harbors under sail/ or one engine.
rudder terms	*Add rudder terms* upper left— tiller... pintle... gudgeon... transom... skeg. A rudder lock is needed to lock pintles and gudgeons when underway.
4 basic rudders	*We show four basic types of rudders.* Add terms— 2. TRANSOM mounted rudder... 3. BARN DOOR rudder... 4. KEEL mounted rudder... and 5. aft SPADE rudder with FIN keel.
4 basic cabin hulls	*We examine four basic types of cabin sailboat hulls—* 6. a walk AROUND deck... 7. a STANDARD hull sheer... 8. STRAIGHT hull sheer... 9. REVERSE hull sheer... 10. RAISED deck... 11. walk OVER deck which is the full width of the hull. Three hulls have walk-around decks/ the last has the walk-over deck.
daggerboard	Snipe hull 12 uses a vertically raised DAGGERBOARD. Add terms below Snipe... upwind LEVERAGE stability which minimizes LEEWAY... sailing downwind to reduce DRAG.
bilgeboards **leeboards**	Hull 14 is a SCOW using twin centerboards or daggerboards called BILGEBOARDS. Hull 16 uses LEEBOARDS which are RAISED out of the water on large sailing vessels to protect the leeboards if the hull is hard aground.
weighted centerboard or swing keel?	Hulls 13. and 15. use WEIGHTED centerboards/ also called SWING KEELS. In a knockdown the risk exists that the centerboard may pivot up into the well... changing to a 180 degree capsize. The risk can be minimized when underway/ with the centerboard locked when down with a strong shock cord.
keel/centerboard **Tahiti ketch**	Hull 17 has a combination centerboard and keel for SHALLOW coastal waters. Hull 18 has a long keel to hold course for LONG periods underway.
easy maneuvering	Hull 19. has a short keel with a cutaway FOREFOOT to maneuver in tight moorings... with hull 4. similar but with a little longer keel.
Cal 40	Hull 20. is the Cal 40 which introduced the SPADE rudder and FIN keel combination/ winning many ocean races in a 25 year period.
spade-rudder skeg	Hull 21 has a spade rudder mounted on a SKEG. The skeg protects the rudder in a grounding/ and from driftwood and porpoises when underway.

10

Turn to text page 104. We show a variety of FIN KEEL and SPADE RUDDER waterfoil combinations. Water flowing between keel and rudder sailing upwind/ provides lift to the spade rudder. For a comparison/ we see the air flow wind funnel from the jib across the aft side of the mainsail/ also providing upwind lift. The keel mounted rudder on hull 19 may be compared with the catboat... without the extra lift.

first large ULDB

Hull 22 shows the high performance underwater lines *of* the first large ULDB (Ultra Light Displacement Boat) the 73' *Windward Passage.*

12 meter hulls

Hull 23 is a 1984 12 meter / with a horizontal WINGLET KEEL attached to the bottom of the vertical keel. As the keel weight is concentrated lower/ the hull will be stiffer with less tendency to heel/ than one without the winglet keel/ though the total weight is the same for both. Another example is the Star designed in 1911 on page 19/ with a BULB keel. The adjustable SKEG on the keel is used to reduce weather helm heeling drag.

the mud duck

Hull 24. is the British MUD DUCK three-point hull. When the tide goes out/ the hull will stay upright in mud flats. It will be resting on twin BILGE keels forward/ with a long SKEG aft, which also protects the rudder.

Students turn to reference text page 7. They should fill in all numbers 1 thru 28 on workbook page 5... the terms can be added at home if time is tight.

Homework— add standing and rigging terms to at least 3 of the 5 dinghies detailed on workbook pages 6 thru 8, with referen ce page numbers listed on these pages.

Start with a brief 15 minute review of terms used in the previous lecture. page 1—

sailboat OR powerboat?

A sailboat with its sails up underway is on a port tack or a starboard SECOND lecture tack upwind and downwind. If the sails are up and the vessel is operating an engine also/ the vessel must follow powerboat rules covered on page 43 of this workbook.

port tack
starboard tack

Port tack/ starboard tack. **Add following terms to** page 10-1, port tack... 2. starboard tack... 3. port tack... 4. starboard tack... 5. port tack.

When wind comes over the starboard bow, stern, or quarter/ a sailboat is on a starboard tack. When wind comes over the port bow, stern, or quarter/ a sailboat is on a port tack.

11

running downwind

The boom can be carried on either side when running downwind. The vessel will be sailing WING and WING with jib and main carried on opposite sides of the vessel. When sailing wing and wing... the tack is opposite to the side the boom is carried. If the boom is carried to port/ the sailboat is on a starboard tack.

We will return to 6. 7. and 16. later.

closehauled course

Upwind and downwind sail courses. A vessel is sailing CLOSE HAULED at 8. near the bottom of the page... when it is sailing CLOSE to the wind as efficiency permits... with the sails HAULED tight as efficiency permits.

pinching & luffing
in irons

At course 10. the sailboat is PINCHING... the sails want to LIFT and BREAK... changing from propulsion to AIR BRAKES called IN IRONS. as it has entered 9. the WIND WALL.

course terms

Add terms to sailboat courses—8. close hauled...10. pinching...11. close reach... 12. and 13. reaching on opposite tacks..14. and 15. beam reach on opposite tacks... 17 and 18. broad reach on opposite tacks...19 running wing and wing on port tack.

the awkward
downwind area

Sailboat course 20 is a narrow area with jib undecided to stay on the same side as the boom/ or opposite to the boom/ the confusion reducing speed. Sail a little higher...or lower going wing and wing for self-steering balance.

preventer

We return to 6. which is a PREVENTER to prevent an accidental jibe... and 7. WHISKER pole to keep jib full and pulling sailing downwind.

boom vang

The BOOM VANG number 16. shown on several sailboats/ is used to pull down the boom and stabilize the main for more efficient sailing. The boom vang is shown for all courses from beam reach, to broad reach, or running.

Repeat the various tack and course terms for familiarization.

the sailboat rules

Turn to reference text page 240. Read the rules on workbook page 11 so students can fill the blanks. Briefly discuss these rules an instructor can find listed on pages 26 and 28 of the *USCG NAVIGATIONAL RULES*.

bare-bone definitions

Every instructor should have a copy of this pamphlet, reviewing each rule on workbook page 11 before delivering the sailboat Right-of-Way lecture... which defines the standards in basic terms.

court decisions have depth

It is equally important to study court decisions going into depth of variables involved, with basics little changed in 50 years. Our recommend reference— *The Rules of the Nautical Road* by Captain Farwell, revised by Alfred Prunski, Aug. 1957.

no white lines?

New sailors and powerboat operators in heavy harbor traffic/ find little to compare with auto operation, even the white lines are missing. While powerboats normally tend to stay in main channels, sailboats may be taking long tacks going into, and coming out of the moorings to cross the channels at varied angles.

Sailboats normally have the right-of-way over powerboats under 65' long/ except for Rule (13 (a)... when a sailboat is overtaking a powerboat. **These are strict regulations which must be understood and followed to avoid collisions... and the POTENTIALS of collisions.**

How much Admiralty Law exposure to be provided for your sailing students depends on the sailing area. Will they be limited to exposure to sailboat and powerboat traffic, or will they also face commercial traffic. A local lawyer enjoying sailing can be a good Admiralty Law lecturer and adviser.

civil laws are applied on land

We are a nation governed by civil laws on the city, county, state, and federal level. A person caught driving thru a red light without stopping though no collision results, faces a stiff fine under civil law in a local court.

12 Admiralty Law thinks considerably different!

Sailboat and powerboat operators face a considerably different set of regulations called *Admiralty Law*. It sets up strict standards to follow *to prevent collisions... and the potentials of collisions.* If unusual situations develop in which the only way to prevent a collision is to break most or all of the regulations called *special circumstances Rule 2 (a),(b),* you begin to understand the strict reasoning of Admiralty Law... as compared to driving thru a red light in an auto.

the federal court

When collisions occur, jurisdiction is placed by our Constitution in the hands of U.S. federal courts sitting in as courts of admiralty.

port tack keep clear

Sailors are dealing with one of the oldest forms of law, developed to provide safe passage for cargo-carrying vessels leaving one port, until entering another with minimum hinderances when underway beginning with pirates.

International and Inland regulations

You are dealing with INTERNATIONAL REGULATIONS applied worldwide. You are also dealing with INLAND REGULATIONS applied to public navigable waters capable of interstate commerce including navigable rivers flowing into the sea, or an inlet to the sea.

the rules...and their variables

Present regulations are defined in the publication USCG Navigational Rules finalized June 1983. *This pamphlet covers just the basic rules, many little changed in a century*. The rule variables require considerable coverage and study by professionals of well-defined court case interpretations involving collisions .

port tack KEEP CLEAR goes back a few centuries

Half the world tonnage in 1880 was under sail, which was reduced to ¼ by 1900. Most were clumsy commercial sailing vessels operating under the same rules used today. Earlier recognition of developing collision potentials was required to take appropiate action early for the same reason used today with easily maneuverable sailing craft... to avoid collisions and their potentials.

Admiralty Laws must be observed!

These regulations are strict and must be followed. A good example of this reasoning was an 1870 Supreme Court decision, the result of a collision in an 1865 crossing case... *the obligation of a privileged vessel to hold course... as long as it is still possible for the burdened vessel to carry her own obligation and give way.*

But I thought...	The privileged vessel was the steamship *Corsica,* instead of holding course and speed, swung left, colliding with the side-wheeler *America.* The excuse was the fear the *America* might not give way. The steamship *Corsica* lost the decision.
Good guy in HEAP big trouble!	Suppose your sailboat is on starboard tack, and you want to be a good guy giving the right-of-way to a port tack sailboat. If a collision results with expensive damage... the good guy has a burden almost impossible to defend in court.
any action....	*Rule 8 (a). Any action taken to avoid collision shall, if the circumstances of the case permit, be positive, made in ample time and with due regard to the observance of good seamanship. Rules 8 (b) (c) (d) and (e) elaborated in the regulation.*
court decisions elaborate further	Admiralty law sets mandatory standards that must be obeyed which are amply defined in court decisions. Action must be taken in ample time to prevent collisions... to prevent serious and imminent risk of collision.
take PROMPT ACTION!	ACTION must be taken early in time to be corrected IF misunderstood... in time the maneuver out of a misunderstanding.
	We continually taught students in on the water sailing lessons to initiated the action early in a confusing situation! If you are waiting for the other operator to initiate action... and he is waiting for you to initiate action, you see the basic reason for many unnecessary present-day collisions.
seamanship	*Rule 2 (a) Nothing in these Rules shall exonerate any vessel, or the owner, master or crew thereof, from the consequences of any neglect to comply with these Rules or of the neglect of any precaution which may be required by the ordinary practice of seamen, or by the special circumstances of the case.*
special circumstances	*Rule 2 (b) In construing and complying with these Rules due regard shall be had to all dangers of navigation and collisions and to any special circumstances, including the limitations of the vessels involved,* which may make a departure from these Rules necessary to avoid immediate danger.
IF all rules fail—	To summarize- in rare instances when MOST or ALL the regulations fail, operators are ordered to break most, or all the rules... IF that is the only method to prevent that collision.
bare rules vs court decisions	While the *USCG Navigation Rules* pamphlet defines the regulations sailboat and powerboat operators must follow... it is equally important for the lecturer to review court decisions with the basics changed little in 50 years, to know more of the variables involved with these regulations.
sail trim	(**Sail trim**— workbook page 12. Briefly discuss closehauled sail trim and weight for 1. closehauled light wind, then with closehauled medium wind for comparison. Discuss reaching 3. with sheets eased, plus the need for the vang to stabilize the boom and mainsail. The last is running wing and wing at 4.
closehauled sailing	(Follow with a brief discussion page 13... closehauled sail trim, and the variables of pinching, stalled airfoils, and luffing... and jib telltales.)
coming about	Turn to workbook page 17— Coming about. ....wind direction OVER the BOW of a sailboat...Preparatory order READY ABOUT. Command HELMS ALEE is given. Order CUT is given....
backing the jib	Turn to text page 170. Backing the jib is very important for light, wide beam sailboats such as the 24' *Pink Cloud* and the Catalina 30... as well as the Lido 14 dinghy.
an overcorrection	It becomes an overcorrection on heavier, narrow sailboats in most instances plus the Coronado 15. (Discuss the various sailboats shown).

13

the mainsheet— self tending?	While the mainsheet is self tending on most monohulls when coming about/ the mainsheet should be released on MULTIHULLS when coming about to change tack easily.
jibing	JIBING is the term used for changing the direction of the wind over the stern of a sailboat when changing tack going downwind.
kinds of jibing	Four types are the CONTROLLED jibe... North River or FLYING jibe... wearing or the CHICKEN jibe... and last the ACCIDENTAL jibe to be avoided.
jibing exposure	Turn to text page 111. Discuss your jibing experiences. While jibing is as normal a method to change from one tack to the other as coming about/ a new sailor should gain sufficient practice in light winds to develop his coordination/ before trying to jibe in stronger winds.
will boom hit backstay?	Will the boom hit the backstay when coming about in a strong wind... this may cause damage. On some sailboats if the main halyard isn't up sufficiently/ the boom has a bigger tendency to hit the backstay/ which wouldn't happen normally if the main halyard is hardened correctly.

How much heel angle should be considered sailing upwind?

nine examples	Workbook page 13 shows nine examples of a 24' sailboat (Read the examples on workbook page 13..."The first example is a very light wind..." discussing sail trim and crew weight... also referring to Wind Force, workbook page 35.)
homework	*Homework— review workbook pages 10 thru 17 discussed in this lecture.*

Marine hardware has its own language.

14

corrosion forms	(Read the corrosion statements for students to fill in the missing answers on page 19 of the workbook, with your answers on the facing page.)
seagoing metals	Seagoing metals must be chosen wisely for specific purposes. Stainless rigging is excellent to support a mast after owners learn to understand/ and eliminate potentials of crevice corrosion. Avoid stainless in below the water installations as it is subject to random corrosion.
marine sources only	Obtain seagoing metals only from marine sources to avoid the rapid corrosion and metal failure of carbon steel/ and the brass mixture of zinc and copper sold in home improvement stores for land use.
cost?	Seagoing metals are expensive, The reasons— they require highly complex manufacturing methods... usually produced in small units at a time.
quality	After you understand the various metal families and their varied protection methods for your use... you may soon find they are well worth their cost.
hardware terms	(Instructor turns to *Homestudy Guide* pages 16 thru 19. Read these answers for students to fill in the blanks on workbook pages 20 to 23. This will make it easier for students to return to workbook pages 6 thru 8 to analyze the various dinghy hardware and rigging methods).

Homework— the U.S. Buoyage System, workbook page 9. Use felt tipped coloring pens to color the buoys, with colors indicated on the buoys. It will become easy to pencil in the boundary limits of the various channels.

Remember your first jibe? *Your world would have been very dull if you didn't have that first jibe. Sink, swim, and jibe, is all part of the sport called sailing which has no equal.*

Are you helping your friends and the future generation learn to sail... **don't keep all the fun to yourself.**

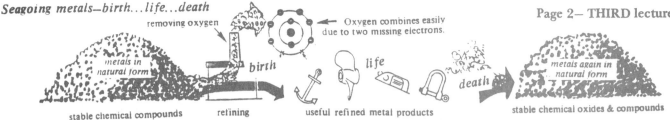

removing oxygen → *birth* → *life* → *death*

← Oxygen combines easily due to two missing electrons.

metals in natural form

metals again in natural form

stable chemical compounds — refining — useful refined metal products — stable chemical oxides & compounds

HEMATITE (red iron-oxide ore) ...becomes pig iron...changes to iron, steel compounds & alloys...corrodes to a brown powder (iron oxide)

BAUXITE is refined to Alumina (aluminum oxide)..to become aluminum compounds and alloys...corrodes to a white powder (aluminum oxide)

Birth, life, and destruction of seagoing metals.

Most seagoing metals exist temporarily in their refined condition. They begin as stable compounds of nature. The oxygen is removed or "cooked out" at the refinery so that the raw products can be refined into compounds and alloys for our seagoing use. Our responsibility is to choose stable metals, then apply a wide variety of corrosion prevention methods to extend their useful life *before they return to more stable oxides* which we can no longer use.

BASIC ELEMENTS only—the electromotive series

protected end-cathodic TAKERS	
flourine	+2.85
chlorine, gold	+1.36
platinum	+0.92
silver	+0.80
copper	+0.34
hydrogen	0.00
lead	-0.12
tin	-0.14
nickel	-0.23
iron	-0.44
chromium	-0.557
zinc	-0.76
manganese	-1.10
aluminum	-1.70
magnesium	-1.86
corroding end-anodic GIVERS	

GALVANIC SERIES— compounds and alloys

protected end— cathodic TAKERS

platinum
gold
graphite

silver

18-8-3 stainless**
18-8 stainless**
chromium-iron**

Inconel**
nickel**

silver solder

Monel
copper-nickel alloys
bronzes
copper
brasses

Inconel*
nickel*

tin
lead
lead-tin solders

18-8-3 stainless*
18-8 stainless*

Ni-Resist

aluminum-iron

cast iron
steel or iron

aluminum 17ST

cadmium

aluminum 2 S

zinc

magnesium alloys
magnesium

corroding end— anodic GIVERS

*active
**passive

Metal destruction can be speeded up by—

- **Oxidation corrosion.** *Salt spray* dries on ocean metals in warm sunshine, the always thirsty ocean salts pulling in moisture at night to produce __brown__ rust on steel, __gray__ rust on aluminum. Wash off ocean salts with fresh water to minimize corrosion action. Wash cameras, etc., with __distilled__ water having all minerals and salts removed.

  Carbon steel — __iron__ with approx. 2% __carbon__, produces excellent nails for houses, and tools for protected land use. Carbon steel corrodes rapidly while expanding in diameter.

- **Oxidation corrosion expansion.** Openings in a shackle shrink, as its bolt diameter expands. Pressures increase against each other until the bolt cannot be removed.

- *The stainless family* is designed to __corrode__ at a programmed rate above the water using chromium ions for turnbuckles, shrouds, etc., requiring a continuous oxygen flow and spray drainage. If taped in a small area, the ions may panic rushing to the area causing __crevice__ corrosion. Avoid stainless underwater fittings due to oxygen variables.

- The marine *bronze family compounds* are excellent for use above the water corroding with a dirty face. Turnbuckles can be __taped__ to seal out oxygen for topside use.

  Choose the bronze family for __underwater__ fittings. The more expensive bronzes have longer lifetime potentials as they go thru more corrosion steps before failure.

- *Brass is a confusing term.* It refers to stable **bronze compounds** in marine stores, while in home-improvement stores it is a shiny gold **mixture** of __copper__ and __zinc__. The unstable **mixture** rapidly dezincs on the ocean leaving a weak copper shell. Even when sealed in a wooden bulkhead, copper/zinc screws rapidly dezinc due to resin electrolytes in the wood.

- **Galvanic corrosion.** *Zinc* is a chemically active underwater __waster__ metal protecting nearby bronzes. When an imbalance occurs starting an underwater ion exchange called galvanic corrosion or action, the zinc flows out to nearby metals to protect them. When a zinc block corrodes rapidly, replace with a same size or smaller block until the **problem** is found, as a larger zinc block may __increase__ the corrosion action. Don't PAINT underwater zinc blocks as it neutralizes and stops their protective action underwater.

- **Electrolysis**— *break the* __circuit__! An hour after turning on a battery charger, the owner returned to his boat finding both outboard motor lower units missing under the water. Shore current flowed to the batteries, thru electrical harnesses to the powerheads, and down the lower units in the water... flowing out to nearby metal parts under the water.

- *Aluminum* uses electrolysis corrosion called anodizing to develop a corrosion __barrier__ for masts, toe rails, etc., with heavy black anodizing preferred. When the surface barrier is broken by chafe, coat with zinc paint to reduce further corrosion action beneath.

- **Intergranular corrosion**— *stress fatigue.* Approximately __100__ parts support the mast of a 30' sloop. A dismasting occurs when one or more parts fail after they lose strength thru aging, with the fatigue process speeded by overstressing. Check all parts periodically for replacement *before* their failure contributes to a dismasting in heavy weather.

Study pages 126-135 of *Sailing Illustrated Homestudy Guide*, pages 180-1 of *Sailing Illustrated*.

15

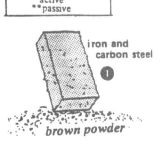

iron and carbon steel

❶

brown powder

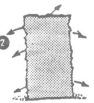

❷

surface damage

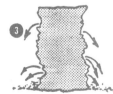

❸

major damage

❹

total damage

basic aluminum

❺

white powder

ROYCE'S **SAILING ILLUSTRATED** *COURSE*

Provide a brief discussion of the buoyage chart. Follow with a short discussion of tacks, courses rules, sail trim, closehauled, reaching, running, and changing tack upwind... and downwind.

weathercock hull raising sails

Turn to your workbook page 25. The same pattern is followed for raising sails on a 14' sloop to a 60' sloop, as well as yawls, ketches, and schooners. *Raise the sail farthest from the wind first. This will weathercock the sail hull upwind for stability/ or weathercock the bow to raise the first sail if a downwind course is desired.*

weathercock hull lowering sails

Whether picking up a mooring to windward...or sailing into a downwind dock/ the sail closest to the wind will be the first down for hull stability.

splice your own snubber line

Splice a snubber line to a dock cleat as shown on page 25 of the workbook. After your sailboat is in its normal slip position/ splice an eye on the other end of the snubber line which will fit snugly over a winch or cleat on your sailboat. The snubber provides an excellent braking action to stop your sailboat in its slip without hitting the end of the dock... if your sailboat is coming in faster than normal.

more complex docking situations

Turn to workbook pages 26 and 27. After providing the basic ideas for raising and lowering sails on page 25 . We next go thru a series of 30 examples for small to large sailboats. This foundation will provide a variety of methods to leave, and return to a wide variety of moorings and slips.

study these patterns

(Instructor lecture material is provided on pages 44 thru 47 of the *Homestudy Guide.* Prior to the lesson, two or three instructors should systematically go thru all 30 situations to understand the basic patterns followed, plus the problems that can develop IF the basic patterns aren't followed.

16

variables?

(Variables are also involved. We found the buckets dropped off the stern of a heavy 40' sailboat provided almost instant braking action with the tremendous forces involved... braking action can be minimal on a light 25' sailboat in a light wind. Braking action is much better in a strong wind on the 25' sailboat.)

begin reading

Begin reading— "When you take the Lido 14....(down to) ..." then tie the boat up to the dock in the desired position".

continue Homestudy Guide page 46... "Tow cutter to cleat W... (down to)... ".. leaving four handles on the dock lines".

(Discuss a few docking situations you've enjoyed as a witness, and some in which you have been a participant in local waters.)

homework

Homework— use red ballpoint pens for terminology.

Homework begins with workbook page 28 analyzing parts of the shroud assembly.

Workbook sailboat details pages 28, 29, 30, 31, and 33.

Add as many standing rigging and running rigging terms to these varied cabin sailboats as student time permits.

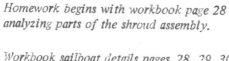

"I won the marconi rig sailboat debate... WHOOPPEEE!"

Every club seems to have a self-appointed non-boat owner expert.We were tied between shad poles on the Hudson River above the George Washington Bridge in 1949.The current was going downstream at 5 knots, and our 20' sailboat was pointed downstream.I began raising sails when our local expert began to loudly tell his friends we were doing everything wrong...while he recounted his last square rigger trip around the horn for the umpteenth time.

I dropped sails,lowered the weighted centerboard,cast off,then drifted 120 or so feet downstream under full control with the water going faster than our boat.As our boat started moving and the speed difference was minimized,we turned to a beam reach,raising the jib. to sail out thru the remaining shad poles.The raucous laughter from the observers was music to our ears.This chapter will help to prepare you for the chance meeting of a self-appointed member of the rocking chair fleet.

centerboard Lido 14

When you take the Lido 14 **1** for a sail your first consideration is the location of the boat.If it is sailed from the present cleat,the Lido will hit the downwind dock on its port before the sails are pulling and the boat is under control.

move to OUTER cleat

backing the jib—pg. C 14

Tow boat to **cleat V 2**,then lower the centerboard for stability. Raise the mainsail to weathercock the bow into the wind,then raise the jib.**BACKWIND the jib,then release bow dockline.**After the bow swings to port and the mainsail fills,the jib sheet is released,then pulled in on the port side.The boat is underway and under control on the port tack *(for backing the jib,see pg. C 14).*

stopping a centerboarder

180 degree water brake with sails up

MINIMUM INERTIA stop. The Lido 14 will be tied up in position **3**.Pull centerboard all the way up on the final downwind leg...then as you enter the slip area, make a **180 degree turn** next to the dock aiming for upper cleat **7** releasing both sheets. The 180 degree turn slams on the water brakes as the hull with the **centerboard up,stalls out.**Turn bow to port,drift to position **3**,drop,stow sails.

the 14' keel Capri

move to outer cleat

MAXIMUM INERTIA stop. You next take a 14' Capri sailboat which has a fixed keel,otherwise it is identical to the Lido 14.Tow the Capri **4** to outer cleat V **5** raise mainsail,then jib. Backwind jib,then release bow dockline.The mainsail fills, the jib sheet is pulled to port with the sails pulling so the boat is under control.

stopping a keel boat
deadstick landing
180 degree water brake with sails down

On the final upwind approach drop mainsail **6**,then turn downwind heading for the slip.When the boat is on course,drop the jib for a dead stick landing to reduce speed and inertia.Make a **180 degree turn** next to the dock to apply the water brakes,the minimum inertia taking the Capri with a keel to the cleat **7**.

17

leave on broad reach

You next take out a 20' keel sloop **8** with the wind on its quarter.Raise jib to sail out under jib only for downwind helm.After the boat has enough inertia and speed, momentarily head up to raise the mainsail,then fall back to the closehauled course until both sails are full and pulling...then enjoy a spirited sail.

upwind docking may be questionable

After a sail the boat is to be left tied to the dock at position **10**.You can make a **beam approach 11** releasing jib sheet,then the main sheet so your boat will drift to a stop in the desired dock position.This approach has a hazard since the boom is beyond the hull,the **mainsheet can snag a dock cleat,with the mainsail filling.**

You are on the same 20' sloop making a **downwind approach** with a dead stick **12** landing,dropping the mainsail just before turning downwind.The jib may,or may not be dropped on the downwind leg depending on the boat characteristics,wind strength,and your reflexes.After boat speed has been considerably reduced,make a 180 degree water brakes turn to stall out the hull,turn bow to starboard,then tie the boat up to the dock in the desired position.

the downwind deadstick landing

Review the situations covered on the facing page for leaving and returning to a dock until the sail raising and lowering sequence becomes automatic...and you understand the inertia differences involved with sloops that are identical except one has a keel while the other uses a centerboard.

After teaching on many centerboard Lido 14's I delivered one of the first Capri keel versions to the Newport Harbor Yacht Club for an adult student.With 60 or more juniors looking on I made a 180° turn to apply the water brakes without dropping the sails.I can still hear the laughter of the juniors who were using our sail course material watching me sail out of the slip without slowing down,on the other tack.

the author goofs

a hand push...
and a foot push

A 747 pilot received a 25' sailboat as a birthday present...the first sail was a disaster. The following day aboard their boat with a hand push one place,a foot push in another,we sailed out without hitting any boats.He grinned,summarizing,"I still can't understand how I bumped seven boats...with only five boats in the slip".

Page references refer to Homestudy Guide.

———————— *The most stimulating part of sailing* ————————

More collision damages occur around docks than elsewhere due to lack of observation.and/or lack of training.

One of the most self-fulfilling parts of sailing is leaving and returning to your dock or slip using wind power only. The sailor with sufficient training should be able to dock most sailboats to 50' long without using engine power which is becoming a lost art for most cabin sailboats.

The exception we found with our boat.was a 20' slip on a port tack beam reach with another boat in the slip to starboard.A 4" clearance existed between the boats.When the mainsheet was released to stop our boat it would snag onto the other boat filling our mainsail...*oops!*

Many of the ideas in our Homestudy Guide were tested in our sailing course evening classes that were open the local public in the sixties.We had excellent cooperation from local racing and cruising sailors,sailmakers, designers, etc., to test various ideas in these lectures, Our common goals were to find the questions,then provide the answers and ideas that the new sailors were seeking.

Our docking charts evolved systematically for the variety of tight docks in our harbor which are even tighter today. Two years of testing were required to find a lecturer who could dock the catboat on the facing page.He grinned, "The answer is easy,I owned a 25' catboat for 2 years".

tow cutter to OUTER cleat	**Tow cutter to cleat W ⑭** .Raise mainsail,inner jib,and outer jib in sequence to weathercock bow into the wind.Slip dockline,then **backwind outer jib** to pull the bow to starboard tack.When mainsail fills,trim outer jib sheet to port side of sailboat.
double mooring— upwind approach	Normal approach to a double mooring is into the wind ⑮ releasing jib sheet, staysail sheet,and mainsail sheet in sequence with the bow next to the tie line using the sails as **air brakes.**Secure boat bow and stern,then stow sails.
double mooring— downwind approach	A secondary approach ⑯ with a very light wind or torn sail,is to ease off all sheets on a beam reach,then head up to **drift into the tieline.**The questionable part of this approach is that the tieline may wrap around the rudder,keel,or prop.
let wind move your yawl	Next you take a **yawl ⑰** for a sail.Let the wind help it drift down to cleat W ⑱ so the boat will swing bow to wind.Raise jigger,mainsail,and jib in sequence to weathercock the bow into the wind.Slip bow dockline,**backwind jib** until the main fills on starboard tack...then sheet jib to port.
head to wind— air brake stop	Traditional approach for the yawl to pick up a mooring ⑲ is to **head up,**release jib sheet,mainsail sheet,and jigger sheet to **weathercock the bow.**The luffing sails will provide air brakes so the boat will drift to a stop at the mooring can.The *close reach* approach ⑳ with the same upwind sheet release sequence is repeated.The advantage, if something unexpected occurs (a diver surfaces,etc.),the sheets can be pulled in, and the sails trimmed with the sailboat soon underway with full steering control.
close reach— air brakes	
the CATBOAT— use a heaving line	You next take a 25' catboat ㉑ for a sail.Walk to upwind dock,then stand next to **cleat X.Heave a light line downwind** to the catboat,tie a heavier line to it then pull end of heavier line to you.Attach other end of heavier line to catboat bow,then pull catboat to cleat X ㉒ .**LOWER centerboard** and raise mainsail.**Back main boom** to starboard so bow swings to port.Release boom after the sail fills and the boat is underway. OOOOPS...did you remember to release the bow slip line????????
the stall out, centerboard up docking	The catboat makes a downwind approach **raising the centerboard ㉓** before docking. Aim bow into the wind so the boat inertia will help the catboat drift sideway ㉔ into dock in its **stalled condition** with the luffing mainsail providing an air brake.
KETCH-leaving downwind	Heavy 40' ketch ㉖ can be sailed downwind from the dock under **jib only ㉗** by jibing the jib.After it gains enough speed and inertia,head upwind to raise the mizzen then the mainsail.Finally fall off to your desired course and enjoy a good sail.
KETCH-leaving upwind	The same heavy 40' ketch ㉘ can cast off after dock line and spring lines so that the bow will *pivot on the heavy bow line* secured to cleat Y.Raise mizzen,mainsail,and jib in sequence to weathercock the bow.*Backwind jib,*slip and take in the bow line, sheet in mizzen and main until they begin to pull,then sheet the jib to port.
downwind steering control MUST be maintained!	We had to dock a heavy 40' ketch in a slip similar to ㉚ .Downwind helm was needed by dropping mizzen,mainsail and jib to reduce the speed,yet maintain minimum steerage to enter the slip as the engine was inoperative.As the bow entered the slip, *five metal buckets* each tied to heavy docklines,*were dropped off the stern* to become water brakes stopping the boat dead in the slip without touching the dock.Total damage was to four buckets which disappeared leaving four handles on the dock lines.
coffin corner water brakes	
summary—	Repeat these docking situations mentally until they become second nature.Then you can begin to consider variables such as short or long keels,keel/centerboard boats.wind funnels,and other vessels underway that may affect your docking operation.

18

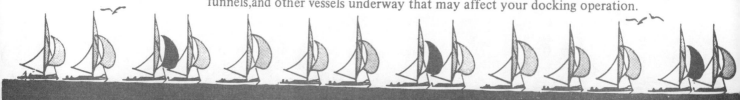

Begin lecture with a brief coverage of raising sails head to wind/ and stern to wind. Then the sequence of a sailboat stopping at a single mooring head to wind/ and to a downwind dock on a broad reach.

"Turn to spinnaker raising procedures, page 32 of the workbook and pages 126-7 of *Sailing Illustrated.*"

spinnaker raising procedures

(Instructor turns to page 40 of the *Homestudy Guide*. Start half way down page 40....) "Begin by stuffing the foot of the spinnaker... (continuing thru page 41 ending with) ...before going into the breaker line, with $800 damage".

AVOID the broach!

" Has any student experienced a spinnaker broach? The broach must be stopped immediately while the rudder forces are still in control of the helmsman. If the wind rapidly increases when the spinnaker is up/ when will it be time to drop the chute to minimize chances of a broach?"

double-ended pole jibe

dip-pole jibe

"Turn to text page 129 for the double-ended spinnaker pole jibing method used on dinghies such as the Lightning page 37/ and many sailboats to 40"".(Describe jibing sequence). "Turn to text page 130 for the single-ended dip pole method with port and starboard outhauls".(while describing method) . Repeat both methods again for student exposure to terminology and jibing sequence).

dinghy upset

"Turn to dinghy upset, workbook page 37, and reference text pages 144-5". (Instructor turns to page 70 of the *Homestudy Guide*. If desired, instructor can read directly from pages 70 and 71 which provides a larger coverage of these ideas than the reference text).

wind pressure

Turn to workbook page 35, and reference text page 137 for the wind pressure scale". (Have students fill in blanks on the right side of the page, repeating the sequence twice to understand the wind force/ wave action forces).

hull and sail must balance INSIDE COVER

"Turn to reference text page 133 for sailboat balance variables". (Discuss pages 132-3 so students can analyze reefing pressure factors following the wind force wave patterns. The sail Center of Effort and the hull Center of Buoyancy must move forward together as the wind increases. This is necessary to protect the rudder from excessive weather helm drag. Pages 74-5 in the *Homestudy Guide*. provides more coverage of this information for those who are interested).

tide, current, tidal current

"Now we turn to tides and currents, workbook page 18, and reference text on page 218". (Briefly go thru ideas for students to fill in the blanks).

fog prediction

"Turn to text page 223 to discuss fog". (This is an excellent method to analyze the cause of fog so it can be predicted. We have had excellent luck with simple humidity indicators in new condition, protected from salt spray and rain. We've found indicators in medical supply stores on the shelves for two or three years that lost their required sensitivity for on the water fog prediction).

Homework

Students should study the sequence of a thunderstorm.. to realize why all sail should be dropped due to strong, rapid wind shifts and downdrafts.

lightning protection

Homestudy Guide pages 64-5 cover lightning potentials... with methods to release the charge as easily and efficiently as possible with minimum damage. Can the bonding system be temporarily unhooked from the mast in a storm?

positive ion

The positive ion, text page 219, is a little understood part of nature. It involves all us, our dogs, cats, and horses, during the 6 to 24 hours required for the mind to recover from the positive ion.

19

Begin lecture with a short review of wind force on sails and wave action. Discuss the reefing sequence to balance the sail Center of Effort with the hull Center of Buoyancy. How do heeling factors differ in a keel sailboat knockdown... and a dinghy capsize.

powerboat vs motorboat

motor vs engine

Questions develop with terms motorboat and powerboat. The term motor is standard for all German and French powerplant installations derived from the French *moteur.* The U.S. Society of Engineers has defined... *Motor as a rotating device with an electrical power source... while an engine converts heat energy by use of a piston into reciprocating mechanical power...* which favors the term powerboat.

boat vs ship

motorship

Our U.S. Navy has defined a *boat* as being up to 70' long that is dependent on/ and capable of being carried aboard a larger vessel or *ship* with a large cruising radius. The *motorship* uses diesel engines to operate electrical motors... that turn the propellers for minimum operating expense.

submarines
ferry boats

Small early submarines were nicknamed *pigboats* which kept growing in size though still called boats or submarines. *Ferry boats* though some are quite large/ are usually called boats due to their short cruising radius.

public usage—

We come to term exceptions of *outboard motor, motor car, and motor oil* which have been long accepted thru public use... in spite of SAE definitions.

powerboat rules

We next discuss powerboat operational rules, workbook page 43, and reference text page 233. (Instructor reads the rules on text page 233 for students to fill in the missing words on workbook page 43).

20

a sailboat becomes a powerboat

During the second lecture we covered the rules sailboats use to avoid collisions with other sailboats... and powerboats. When a sailboat operates with engine power whether the sails are up or down/ the sailboat becomes a powerboat operating under the powerboat rules.

danger zone visibility

Engine operational controls should be installed on the right or starboard side to provide full visibility of the *danger zone* on powerboats AND sailboats to prevent collisions. The exception is a flying bridge powerboat or a high center cockpit on large sailboats with center steering controls having excellent visibility over an arc of 220 degrees or more.

left-hand steering controls are questionable

Can you see the operator of a powerboat or sailboat on a collision course with your vessel? Powerboats with left-hand or port side steering controls/ especially if installed inside the cabin will have blind spots/ with limited visibility of their danger zone. Extra attention may be required to avoid a collision/ if the approaching powerboat has left-hand controls.

LH controls limited to—

Left hand or port side engine controls should be limited to racing powerboats for counterclockwise race courses... and for rescue or police vessels making it easier to pull along side the starboard side of other vessels to talk to operators.

meeting

When powerboats underway are meeting bow to bow/ both vessels are ordered to TURN RIGHT to pass port to port in ample time to avoid collisions. Vessels normally pass starboard to starboard when far enough apart so signals aren't necessary.

overtaking

The overtaken powerboat holds course and speed until the overtaking powerboat has passed and cleared the overtaken vessel using signals shown. If the overtaken powerboat sees a hazard or collision potential/ the overtaken powerboat sounds the danger signal... with the overtaking powerboat holding back until the course is clear.

current variables

We come to the exceptions to these meeting, crossing, and overtaking situations in river and tidal currents. (Discuss these rules covered in the center of the workbook on page 43).

**carry aboard-
rulebook
page 165**

USCG Navigation Rules— Annex V-8805... "The operator of each self propelled vessel 12 meters (39.4') or more in length shall carry on board and maintain for ready reference a copy of the Inland Navigational Rules".

Turn to your reference text page 236. Rule 20 covers these running lights which must be exhibited from sunset to sunrise... and from sunrise to sunset in unusual circumstances. (Read Rule 20 (a) thru (d).)

running lights

Page 236 shows the running lights of a cabin sailboat under sail... plus the additional engine light mounted on the mast indicating it is operating under power.

weak, low lights?

Many existing sailboats and powerboats use low mounted/ weak intensity red and green running lights on the bow/ and a weak stern light. They may be adequate for minimum use in protected smooth water, but...

**lights for
self protection**

If these boats are to be operated in force 4 to 5 wave action at night with considerable water traffic... owners need to install higher, stronger intensity lights AND lenses for rapid identification that can't be momentarily blanketed.

bulbs too strong?

If stronger bulbs are mounted in the previous red and green lenses/ they will overpower the red and green lenses which now show white.

**separate red
and green lights?**

Red and green running lights may legally be combined into one lantern in a sailboat less than 20 meters or 65.6' long. A 24' sailboat can also operate with separate red and green running lights with fresnel or other lenses mounted high on a bow pulpit... to be mistaken at night for a 50' sailing vessel underway. This provides maximum protection for sailboat operating at night with heavy commercial traffic... to avoid the potentials of a collision.

21

**tri-colored
masthead light**

Page 237 shows the single bulb tri-colored masthead running light which can be used under sail only. It must be turned off when the engine is turned on/ with the lower level lights used to show it is operating as a powerboat. Before installing a tri-color light... does it have a flat top pelicans and cormorants want to perch on? Add a cone shape with the top pointing upward so they aren't able to make your mast designer-friendly for our winged friends.

**European strobe
rulebook pg. 122
Rule 36**

Marine use of a strobe light caused confusion in the early 1980s in the U.S. They were used as WARNING lights in European waters with heavy commercial traffic warning... *don't come closer... as our vessels are on a collision course!*

**U.S. strobe
rulebook
page 125**

DISTRESS SIGNAL— Inland Rule 37— *When a vessel is in distress and requires assistance... she may use... (a high intensity white light flashing at regular intervals from 50 to 70 times per minute).*

If you want to test a masthead strobe light at night... test it very briefly when dockside. It should only be turned on *when a vessel is in distress and requires assistance.*

Our sail course is dedicated to my patient bride of 48 years who started this idea, then put up with the project for three decades.

Thanks also go to Frank Butler of Catalina Yachts for his belief in the potentials of our sail course.

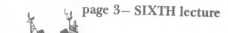

aft bridge lookout

blind spot dead ahead

The next subject is commercial vessels, workbook page 42. (Additional coverage is provided on pages 143-9 of the *Homestudy Guide*. If your students face even a small amount of commercial vessel operation, provide full coverage in this lecture so they will avoid potential problems from tugs to supertankers... which become fun to watch in their varied operations).

large vessel emergency stopping	Your reference text page 241 discusses stopping distances of large vessels from 17,000 ton to 400,000 ton supertankers... and larger ones.
commercial vessel lookouts	If you can't see the lookout on the large vessel/ can the lookout see you?
	The lookout is usually on the bridge after leaving a harbor... they are often peering thru a maze of masts and cargo booms partially blocking their visibility.
the blind spot forward	A blind spot under the bow of some commercial vessels can vary from 50'/ to 1000' on containerships with aft bridges. Supertankers may be lumbering at maximum 12 to 15 knot cruising speeds/ while newer containerships may operate at almost double that speed. If a fully-loaded containership 4 to 5 miles away is headed for your boat... move rapidly at right angles to its course to avoid the huge blind spot directly ahead/ especially if it has an aft bridge.
out of control— at anchor, on a mooring, dockside	Page 241 shows a freighter at anchor, on a mooring, or dockside *not under control*. When the aft ensign/ and the black anchor ball forward are coming down/ stay clear as the vessel is out of control until it has reached steerageway to gain rudder control. Higher speeds are required to gain steerageway in wind conditions for rudder control. The situation is even more critical when a large vessel is said to be *in ballast* without cargo/ riding high in the water with more windage areas to compensate for.
the Union Jack	Vessels under government control from the U.S Navy, the Coast Guard, army transports and supply vessels from tankers to freighters... can be recognized by the *Union Jack* on the bow flown while at anchor, on a mooring, dockside... and high and dry in a shipyard showing the vessel is still in commission.
propeller suction	Propeller suction from freighters to supertankers is tremendous when getting underway. .. and somewhat reduced after reaching cruising speed. Even in deep water when a large vessel is at cruising speed/ smaller vessels should stay their distance from dead ahead to either side/ to avoid the propeller suction pulling them into the larger vessel underway.
large vessel acceleration in deep water	A freighter in deep water near Long Beach/ stopped to pick up a pilot with several small boats nearby watching the operation. When the propellers began turning/ the powerboats were pulled under the stern counter of the large vessel with its engine noise drowning the horns on the small boats.
	An off duty seaman saw the commotion notifying the bridge. The propellers were put in neutral for the small boats to break loose and leave the area... before the large vessel propellers turned again.
large vessel acceleration in in shallow water	In shallow water with the same freighter/ the same volume is required for the propellers which must be pulled in from much greater horizontal distances.
high and dry	A tug pushing barges ahead on a shallow navigable inland river/ may require so much water flowing thru its large propeller /to temporarily pull all the water from a nearby marina... putting sailboats, powerboats, and docks hard aground.
the maelstrom begins	After the tugboat has passed/ the water returns with strong swirling currents to fill the empty marina area causing damage to bucking boats and docks/ breaking docklines and pulling dock cleats loose if not properly anchored.

22

Tugboats with tows have special problems to be recognized.

AVOID—
tugs with tows

Suppose you were operating a tugboat with a string of barges/ with a pleasure boat under sail or power demanding the right-of-way... if you stopped the tug, the barges would come up over your stern sinking or damaging your craft.

This is a problem that must be understood by all recreational boat operators with adequate maneuverability to KEEP CLEAR of tugboats doing their assigned work.

Commercial vessel right-of-way rules.

commercial vessel
right-of-way

Turn to your reference text page 231.We have discussed the operational characteristics of some commercial vessels with limited maneuverability.

submarine light
rulebook pg. 3

Rules 9 (a) thru (d) define the standards to follow to not hinder commercial vessel operation right-of-way... for YOUR protection. Sudden death and/or injuries result when easily maneuverable recreational sailboats and powerboats ignore these rules.

Daytime/ nightime
warning variables

(Read answers to fill blanks on workbook pages 44 and 45, of worldwide commercial vessel daytime and nightime warnings for self protection as they go about their chosen tasks. You can find endless variations of these regulations due to individual vessel configurations... and interest or lack of, by operators).

Homework

Read pages 210 to 214 of your reference text.

Pages 210-211 provide a basic exposure to weather patterns on an 1850 square rigger going from Manhattan to San Francisco, then returning with a considerably different course to make the best use of the varied wind patterns.

Page 214 discusses the westerly wind patterns from 30 degrees North. Coastal wind patterns on the east coast of the U.S. / differ considerably to our west coast, and the west-facing European coast with westerly winds and sea breezes.

Add terms to square riggers page 40, sail terms to *Cutty Sark* and *Eagle*.

23

C.F. Chapman

The year was 1954 when I was fortunate to spend ten days in New York as a guest of C.F. Chapman. While he wanted to publish my sailing book underway, he was hoping to adapt it for the USPS Sail Course a supposedly top secret I wasn't supposed to know about.

Chapman was a very private and reserved person.Our personalities clicked finding the staff quite surprised to find we had many discussions on a wide variety of interests.

I asked why he started the USPS. "I started the United States Power Squadrons to help new motorboat owners, as they have no place to go for help".

"Why shouldn't the Power Squadrons have an equal interest to help new sailors. Probably half the Brooklyn USPS instructors where I attended, had excellent sailing backgrounds?" (My membership Certificate is A 33355 dated April 11, 1951).

"Why should the Power Squadrons help sailors as they are always helping each other?", was the flat reply.

a change has been
long needed!

After 36 years it becomes time to reverse that thinking to help new sailors. The best method is with availability of quality sail courses nationwide open to the public... to help ALL sailors AND the complex high-tech sailing industry.

Today we enjoy instant national TV satellite weather reporting/ plus predictions a few days ahead to anticipate hurricane movement. World weather square rigger sailing predictions in the 1850 trip from New York to San Francisco and return/ were based on a lifetime at sea by the captain. Worldwide weather pattern predictions were in the formative stage... thanks to a stagecoach accident/ with Navy Lt. Matthew Maury no longer able to be a line officer.

early square rigs

The origin of sailing predates recorded history. An educated guess is it began under square rig in various cultures... to replace oars when the wind was aft.

different mix of sailing cultures and time frames

The first lecture began with the early square rig, lug rig, lateen rig, and outrigger. We are dealing with different cultures and religions greatly affecting Arab sailing technology for example, different weather requirements, different wood, rope, and metal sources... developing independently in different time frames. A TV video showing these sailing cultures today is *The Last Sailor* narrated by Orson Wells, 150 minutes*.

Chinese sailing technology

hybrid lorcha

Turn to reference text page 281. Chinese sailing technology remains in its own time capsule with many highly developed ideas 2000 years ago, we use today such as windlasses, daggerboards, centerboards, etc. The only interruption was when the Portugese settled in Macao south of Canton. In the 1850s the Portugese had large fleets of the hybrid *lorcha* built in Macao for commerce and to fight pirates.

farwell lorcha

Arab vs Chinese

When Portugese interest later turned from sail to steam/ the lorcha design rapidly disappeared as Chinese boat builders returned to their ancestrial sailing culture. While Arab traders were reported to be in Chinese ports in 700 A.D./ they had no interest nor influence on the others lateen and lug sailing cultures.

caught between different sailing cultures

Text page 276— Spain merged the Mediterranean lateen sailing culture to the south for upwind sailing/ adding northern square sails also on the same vessel. The *Nina* used by Columbus in 1492/ began with the lateen rig. It had to be rerigged for downwind sailing in the Canary Islands/ adding square sails on all three masts.

24

steering board to stern rudder

worldwide square riggers

Strong westerlies provide the prevailing Northern Europe wind patterns. Long, narrow, double-ended rowing hulls 2000 years ago grew into shallow, extreme long ships of the Vikings/ and smaller, beamier, rounder cargo vessels. As cargo vessels grew in capacity the long "steer-boarde" oar/ moved to the "stern rudder". As masts grew taller, square rig sail technology improved and simplified into smaller sail areas for easier handling and reefing. These are the European vessels that set out to conquer new lands. They established American colonies to the west and spice colonies to the east/to improve their power and commerce.

port to port log records

British were the first to use ships logs to record and analyze sailing conditions, time required, and time of year to sail from one port to another. A major break-thru was the Beaufort wind force scale to record/ and make the best use of wind pressures underway... introduced to the British Navy in 1806.

British Navy wind force scale

Reference text page 137 shows basic *Cutty Sark* reefing pattern that varies for upwind or downwind steering balance/ similar for small clippers to huge iron windjammers. They had to make the most of available wind pressure as engine power was impractical for the tremendous square rig wind resistance.

organized weather predictions

(*Homestudy Guide* pages 66, 78). Line officer USN Lt. Maury suffered a leg injury in a stagecoach accident. His next assignment was to the Depot of Charts and Instruments storing ships logs going back to the birth of the U.S. Navy.

Lt. Maury published the first systematic study of records for weather, wind, and sea conditions for mariners in 1847 from these log records. The purpose was to reduce sailing time around South America... and from port to port on both east and west coasts.

the longer route with less time

The first major contribution was to recommend a route three times as long with steady winds from New York to Rio in 38 days... while the previous record was 55 days following the straight rhumb line fighting prevailing wind patterns.

Ferde Grofe Films– 3100 Airport Ave., Santa Monica, CA 90405

Square riggers sailed long distances on the open ocean using prevailing wind patterns. Problems developed nearing land having to wear about to change tack in a unfavorable wind...or anchor for a better breeze. The major square rigger disadvantage was large crew operational cost.

Turn to *Cutty Sark* in the back of your reference text. It was launched in 1869/ making most of American clipper building technology learned in 20 years of trial and error. She is the exception... the only surviving clipper ship that roamed the ocean world for fifty years. She depended on her speed and ability, with her smaller square rigger crews to make a profit carrying light bulk cargo.

Reference text pages 270-1– our tall-rig schooner development for Atlantic coastal use began after 1700 A.D. Advantages were smaller crew operational costs/ easier maneuverability in shallow harbors/ plus better arrival time predictability from port to port... especially carrying perishable cargo.

westerlies PLUS sea breezes

See reference text page 211. Most of the U.S. is in the westerly pattern above 30 degrees North. Summertime westerly wind strength in the San Francisco Bay/ increases when merging with afternoon sea breezes also flowing from the ocean.

stronger westerlies and sea breezes

The combined westerly and sea breezes are even stronger for Northern Europe coastal sailing farther north. The combination was favorable for square rigs going back 1500 years ago/ to huge windjammers carrying wheat and wool cargoes from Australia to Europe up to 1930s.

conflicitng Atlantic coastal breezes

the colonies answer— schooners

Reference text page 214. Our Atlantic east-coast afternoon sea breezes are weak as coastal onshore sea breezes fight westerlies. Small schooners in the Revolutionary and 1812 wars could point higher and sail faster to windward than pursuing British square riggers. Our weak economy needed schooners costing under half of a similar capacity brig/ with 1/3 the crew. The new colonies had an endless supply of wood for building tall-rig schooners/ that could average a beam reach in the weak afternoon coastal breezes and night land breezes from Maine to Florida.

the largest schooner was an oil tanker

Reference text page 271 illustrates east coast schooners. The largest was the iron hull *Thomas W. Lawson* launched in 1902 as a bulk coal carrier/ later rebuilt with internal tanks. When delivering her first oil cargo to England in the storm of the century, she anchored in heavy weather with all sails torn to shreds. A link broke in her anchor cable/ sinking her on Dec. 13, 1907, south of England on Hellweather Reef.

25

Canadian/ British schooner fleets
Schooners– Basil Greenhill Naval Institute Press Annapolis, MD 21402

Large fleets of Atlantic Canadian schooners were built of spruce on Prince Edward Island in the Gulf of St. Lawrence/ for the British merchant fleet to roam worldwide. Small Nova Scotia schooners fished for cod on the Grand Banks/ with their cargoes transferred to larger schooners sailing to Europe. Note workbook page 38... on a cold foggy beam reach from Halifax to England/ often sailing thru icebergs.

tern schooner

topsail schooner to ketch

Atlantic Canadians built over 800 *tern* (three of a kind) three-masted schooners carrying identical masts, booms, gaffs, and gaff sails. A dismasting was no longer a problem with an extra set of spars and sails aboard. The British preferring topsail schooners with square sails/ eventually changed to the ketch rig for similar capacity hulls costing less/ with the gaff topsail easier to handle than square topsails.

west coast fleets of lumber schooners
Windjammers of the Pacific Rim– Jim Gibbs reference text pg. 270

New England boatbuilders coming west in the 1850 gold rush/ found their real gold endless pine forests. They built little offshore porters to carry lumber from our rocky west coast to San Francisco. It was transferred to larger 3,4,5, and 6 masted schooners plus barkentines and brigantines, mixing gaff and square sails. West Coast Canadians also joined the lumber trade carrying lumber thru the Pacific Islands as far west as Australia and China/ returning with coal, sulfur, phosphorous and other cargoes.

Turn to workbook page 41. The few present day square riggers still operating/ appeared in the New York Harbor OPSAIL— 1986 Tall-Ship Regatta. The *USCG Eagle* is similar to nine barks worldwide used as training vessels by various nations. Others such as the San Diego bark *Star of India* are used as floating museums/ seldom under sail. The complex square sail raising, setting, and furling methods are shown on reference text pages 286-9.

(enjoy the final revue... *Happy Sailing, Patrick M. Royce*).

ventilation?

Caribbean charter?
Christmas

blizzards, gales,
freezing weather

NY Boat
Show

Prepare list of products
to check at boat shows.

other
boat
shows

Dec	
Jan	
Feb	

major
electrical
engine,
hull, and
rigging
maintenance

*preparation
maintenance
time*

RECORDS

The
memory
has
limitations!

brush up on
swimming,
scuba diving

WARNING!!!

Mar

finish the
details to
prepare for
launching

Sun Belt
regatta?

**Time is
running out!**

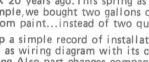
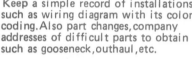

Western U.S.—
long early spring

Eastern U.S.—
what spring?

flooding
begins

Apr

We wish we had started such a record
book 20 years ago. This spring as an
example, we bought two gallons of
bottom paint...instead of two quarts.

Keep a simple record of installations
such as wiring diagram with its color
coding. Also part changes, company
addresses of difficult parts to obtain
such as gooseneck, outhaul, etc.

List parts with periodic maintenance
such as the head joker valve, outboard
motor water pump, inflatable dinghy
parts, lubrication periods for overboard
valves, engine oil changes, etc.

Start a file of articles, new product
announcements, etc., to analyze and
refer to for future use.

heavy spring
storms, flooding

spring showers

launching

yacht clubs
open

Memorial Day

May

**Prolonged lack of use
the greatest destroyer
sailboats...and sailbo
equipment.**

June

4th of July

July

*enjoy ever
moment
of sailing.*

26

hurricane
potentials

Happy Sailing!

add notes to
maintenance
records

Aug

Labor Day

yacht clubs close

Sept

MAINTENANCE

Is your tool kit adequate?
Check periodically to eliminate
unnecessary tool duplication.

Western U.S.—
a very short fall

**MAXIMUM
hurricane risk**

haul out time

**HEADING SOUTH can be the
experience of a lifetime...or
a nightmare, see page F 8.**

Eastern U.S.—
long, lovely fall
an Indian summer
with warm
lovely days until—
storm tracks move
south with arctic
air behind the
northers as they
head south.

prepare work
list

Sun Belt
regatta?

Oct

outboard motor
maintenance?

*decommiss
boat asho*

*Time to tell almost-true
sea stories.*

off-season
sail repair
discount?

Nov

Thanksgiving

inflatable
repairs?

*Dry martini sailing begins...
as the almost true sea stories
of the exciting spring to fall
grow with each fond retelling.*

Finalize maintenance
list in most efficient
sequence.

Good seamanship begins with normal periodic maintenance practices.

Buy a quality sailboat, install quality equipment, then stay within the operating limits of
your equipment. *If your boat is maintained normally it will protect and treat you right.*
If maintenance is below par, any airplane, auto, or sailboat will become dangerous.

We wish we could assign 200 pages to sailboat maintenance...yet we were limited to
19 pages. We have tried to choose the most important and most basic answers facing the
new sailor. We begin with corrosion which has so many twists, turns, and variables it is
little reported since smarter writers often stick to easier, more popular subjects

Any sailor with a small, medium, or large cabin sailboat can handle a variety of basic
maintenance chores turning the rest to the boatyard or to the mechanic of your choice.
Ask endless questions while expanding your maintenance knowledge by observation and
collecting magazine articles. Have a buttermilk, beer, or martini handy when you have the
opportunity to exchange ideas (bribery?) with a good marine mechanic. You may soon
find many other applications for the basic ideas covered in our maintenance chapter.

Prolonged lack of use is the greatest destroyer of sailboats and equipment.

SAIL COURSE
Registration Record

name _____

        last   first   initial   phone   date

address _____

         city   state   ZIP

circle age group—   under 15   under 20   over 20   man   woman

circle sailing exposure— none   crew   owner— 1 year   2 years   3 years   5 or more years

sailboats owned

The following information will help instructors determine subjects to stress... and to minimize—
What type of sailing and in what area or areas are you interested?

How did you learn about the sail course?

Please answer the following questions at the beginning of the last lecture. This information will
help us determine the subjects for the next sail course.

Please circle lectures you were able to attend—   1   2   3   4   5   6   7

What subjects were easiest to understand.   What subjects were the most difficult to understand

1   1

2   2

3   3

4   4

What subjects would you like added... or more thoroughly covered in the next lecture series.

*A variety of people with varied backgrounds are needed to work as a team to maintain future
sailing courses. If you'd like to participate in future courses, what speciality would you
like to contribute?*

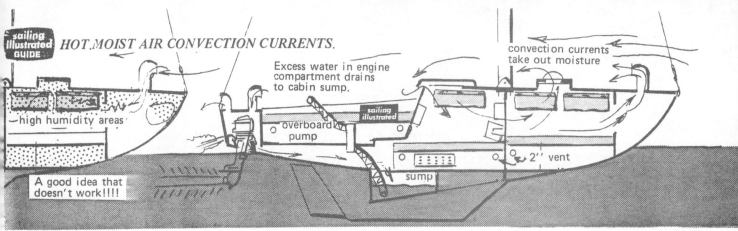

convection currents take out moisture

Excess water in engine compartment drains to cabin sump.

overboard pump

high humidity areas

2″ vent

sump

A good idea that doesn't work!!!!

---

human engineering factors continue—

hot air rises

Get rid of the nasty guys!

suction air flow

28   suction air rising

360 degree Suction Vent is vastly superior to the traditional vents.

NW to W normal westerlies

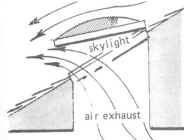

skylight

air exhaust

Skylight updraft ceases when S to SSE winds arrive with high humidity and warm temperature after crossing thousands of miles of tropical ocean.

bulkhead bag

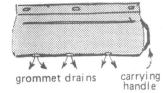

grommet drains   carrying handle

Release moisture...don't bottle it up!

Black mildew will grow on every organic and synthetic surface when the desired heat humidity and oxygen potentials are reached. A new fiberglass hull may look smooth though it has *small microscopic pores* that enlarge with time to provide a surface for mildew to attach to and grow...the major reason for waxing fiberglass hulls and topsides.

Mildew and fungi awaken and grow below in dark enclosed areas where humidity can rapidly build up. If a wooden or fiberglass boat has any mildew potentials below, open all cabinets and doors below, then turn seat cushions up to improve the air flow before leaving. Give your boat a good airing after a storm to remove any mildew potentials.

Our liberal education with mildew began in mid-July 1964 when our fiberglass boat had been in the water only two weeks. Mildew started growing under cushions, in cabinets, on bulkheads, and the overhead. We drilled 22 two inch vents plus a 4″ dia. air scoop to start an air flow to reduce our humidity potentials.

The following year headers were introduced installed on sailboat cabin overheads. They proved an excellent idea to stabilize humidity by absorbing excess moisture... then providing a controlled moisture air release as the humidity goes down.

A storm was moving into our area so we pointed the forward air scoop into the prevailing westerlies to improve the air flow thru our boat. After three days of heavy rain followed by a hot summer day, we returned to find a healthy mildew farm below requiring hours of scrubbing to remove and a lot of ventilation to dry out.

A month or so later when leaving Catalina we turned the forward air scoop aft to prevent spray going below in a sloppy seaway. We forgot to turn the vent into the westerlies after returning to our dock as we were soaked and tired. After two days of heavy rain and two hot summer days we expected to find another mildew farm... finding only a few traces of mildew.

The friendly, helpful convection currents.

The forward air scoop facing away from the prevailing westerlies began a suction flow coming from the aft part of our boat with the moist humid air being pulled up and exhausted out the forward air vents. The idea proved so practical that we decided to use the same idea in our home which was rather warm in the summer. Westerlies can now flow thru our home with the hot moist air convection currents rising and going out the new skylight facing east which dropped the humidity and heat considerably.

The humidity fight continues—when the overpowering 1982-1983 *El Nino*, pg. G 10, gave us the second heaviest rain in local recorded history, all boat owners we contacted had mildew problems. That spring we installed a *suction vent* which provided an immediate improvement in the forward cabin exhaust air flow. Mildew problems disappeared that fall and early 1984, yet results were inconclusive with very little rain.

12/20/84. We returned to our boat after three days of heavy rain and strong winds. 145 pumps by hand were required to empty our large sump, which if the water started to come over the floorboards, would require 270 pumps to empty (IOR sumps, pg. J 17). We found light moisture below with no mildew of consequence.

A sailboat on a single mooring has excellent air flow potentials while slip-berthed boats often have less than ideal ventilation conditions requiring more care to avoid mildew formation below decks. The wooden boat in its cradle laid up for the winter requires special attention for ventilation to reduce humidity as the normal protective wind patterns are seldom observed.

We've had excellent luck with our bulkhead storage bags after grommet drains were added. While they protected organic clothing from mildew, foul weather togs stored wet in the bags for a few days didn't develop any mildew...while mildew growth would have been rapid without the drains. *P.S.*—mildew grows rapidly on the outer surface of the plastic clothing or storage bags.

Page references refer to Homestudy Guide.

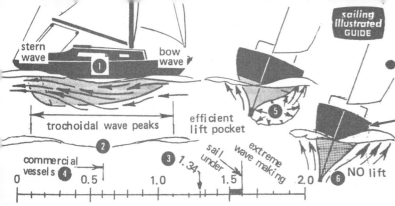

stern wave

bow wave

trochoidal wave peaks

efficient lift pocket

2

commercial vessels **4**

3 1.34

sail under

extreme wave making

5

6 NO lift

0   0.5   1.0   1.34   1.5   2.0

● Displacement HULL SPEED Theory.

The HULL SPEED RATIO of large heavy displacement hulls is based on the *dynamic moving* WATERLINE LENGTH distance **1** between bow and stern wave peaks. These coincide with SPEED of the length **2** between equal peaks of ocean TROCHOIDAL WAVES.

Trochoidal theoretical wave peak speeds coinciding with the 1.34 $\sqrt{WL}$ heavy displacement hull speed—

20.0 feet—6 knots	45.0 feet—9 knots
27.2 feet—7 knots	55.6 feet—10 knots
35.6 feet—8 knots	67.3 feet—11 knots

The MAXIMUM efficient speed a heavy hull can push itself effortlessly and efficiently thru the water with a **3** 1.34 $\sqrt{WL}$ SPEED-LENGTH ratio.

It can go a little faster up to 1.5 $\sqrt{WL}$ at which the hull can't go faster. If the wind still increases, it will blow a spinnaker, or the mast, sails, and rigging will go faster than the hull...called dismasting.

The large square rigger wanted to maintain the 1.34 $\sqrt{WL}$ speed with bow and stern wave trap. It will begin to sink at 1.5 $\sqrt{WL}$ as the wave peaks spread, while at 1.6 $\sqrt{WL}$ it may be sailed under if sail can't be reduced to slow the vessel.

● FRICTIONAL RESISTANCE is the other side of the

story. Water hardens as a vessel goes faster, the reason supertankers, page L 2, travel under 15 knots, 0.6 $\sqrt{WL}$ with minimum resistance **4** to save fuel. A small planing powerboat starts to rise bodily after 2.5 $\sqrt{WL}$ climbing onto a full plane due to lift provided by the water hardening from 3.5 $\sqrt{WL}$ to 4.0 $\sqrt{WL}$.

The MEDIUM displacement Cal 40, page J 14, introduced downwind surfing for short periods on the Hawaiian Transpac due to good bottom lifting action to reduce water friction which increased surfing speed. Sailors began to extend these surfing periods and speeds with experience.

ULDB's may not point quite as high as IOR boats, pg. J 15, but with light, lean, long-waterline hulls they can turn to a reach or run in a force 5 and above to surf or lift for long periods, pg. J 14, as they are designed to make the most of water resistance/lift.

Light dinghies, pg. B 3, have hulls narrowing forward for weatherliness, broadening aft of the chain plates to a wide stable bottom with a sharp transom chine for planing lift. They are light, rising easily as the water hardens for a speed increase, text pgs. 140-143.

There are considerable variables with LIGHT and MEDIUM displacement hulls. My experience is with the Cal 25, page J 13, which surfs easily, page G 9, with good bottom designed for lift, plus the trapped pressure pocket **5** shown above.

7 4.0

all-out planing

water lb. pressure 14 times that of 1.0

3.5

3.0

surfing begins

2.5

frictional resistance—lbs. per ton of disp.

3 1.34

heavy wave making

1.6
1.5

water resistance doubles

30-40 lbs.

1.0

10-15 lbs.

4 0.5

speed/length ratio

frictional 3-4 lbs. resistance

0

the heavy displacement hull

● SMALL heavy displacement SAILBOATS—MAYBE group.

We report on page G 10, our heavy 24 footer surfing for 14 miles with speedometer hard on the 10 knot peg while reaching due to a **5** trapped water lift pocket. A heavy narrow-beam hull without this lift nor speed increase may have had torn sails or a dismasting.

On the same page we report the heavy MINKA peaking up to 10 knots on a run with the stern wave cresting way aft of the stern while the bow was almost sailed under.

The most critical situation was a 30' wooden gaff rigger sailing downwind being caught on an all-out plane with stresses that can never be computed which could have exploded the hull if it had maintained that speed.

Analyze the variables in the MAYBE group so you have an educated guess when to REEF...or when to let it ROMP on a reach to a broad reach. It is easier to shake out an unneeded reef than to make one too late.

PATTY CAT I   **WIND POWER vs HULL SPEED**

Smaller day catamarans gain their speed from hull/water lift to reduce friction...plus twin hull leverage.

7 . WATER PRESSURE RELEASE ...4.0 $\sqrt{WL}$?

The Rudy Choy designed big cats have long, slim displacement hulls designed to RELEASE pressure from under the hulls...also eliminating the monohull bow and stern **1** wave trap.

The big cats depend on beam length-ratio LEVERAGE stability, permitting weight reduction. The twin hulls float higher on the water with minimum displacement, minimum water pressure, minimal frontal area, and less parasitic drag.

The SOFT WATER SUPPORT produces a comfortable ride under ocean conditions. Handling is easy at upper speeds to 20 knots with minimum wake...except the 65' SEASMOKE had a roostertail at 24 knots.

Patty Cat I below, came to an untimely end at 20 knots or so when port tacked by a submerged coral reef about a month after the JFK episode, page H 18.

29

44' PATTY CAT II is detailed, text page 83.

Powerboating Illustrated pages 29-35 cover in detail the speed/length/pressure ratios.

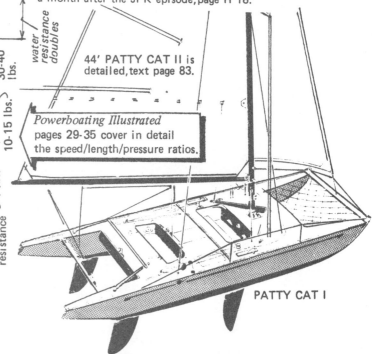

PATTY CAT I

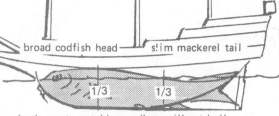
broad codfish head — slim mackerel tail

1/3   1/3

EVOLUTION of the SAILBOAT HULL

Santa Maria

A 3 to 1 length to width hull ratio was common in the 1700's...increasing to 5.7 to 1 with the extreme 1850 early clippers.

*Admiralty and other precious historical model information—

National Maritime Museum—London
SE10 9NF 01-858 4422

Our favorite—*Ships of the Western Tradition to 1815,by A.H.Waite*

Sovereign of the Seas

30

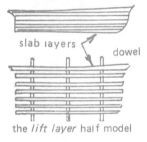

slab layers   dowel

the *lift layer* half model

Chinese junk lug rig

modern lug rig

lateener

Ship of the Desert

Our friends the ducks,seagulls,and pelicans, have displacement hull bodies designed by nature.Their waterlines or *waterplanes* are similar to sailboat monohull waterplanes.

For four decades I've enjoyed exploring boatyards on both coasts,watching endless sailboat hull designs supported by tired blocks of wood,and partially corroded nails Where did each design idea begin,how did it grow to reach the present state of the art, and how can it be improved.

Present day sailing designs started and grew with the practical idea that goods *or cannons may be moved in volume with more cost effectiveness than horse,mule,oxcart...or camel*.

Traditional European hull design had a *bluff codfish bow entry* and maximum beam well forward,narrowing to slim *mackerel stern lines.* Typical vessels were the *Santa Maria* and the *Mayflower* that were cranky downwind with a maximum 6 knot speed,while the flexible hemp rigging reduced practical windward performance,see page E 1.

Admiralty models* began to be submitted for important proposed naval and merchant vessels in the 1600's,often taking 3 to 5 years to build.They were made scale size plank by plank with frames,bulkheads,and interiors below which could be taken apart for analysis...with masts,sails, and rigging functional topside for critical evaluation.The investment was well spent for the winning shipyard which could support it for a few years.The choice was made by European Admiralty naval officers long on practical experience who had worked their way thru the ranks,

Though naval architects began making line plan drawings by the 1700's Admiralty officers still short on hull design theory,preferred making their choice with these beautiful models.

The Revolutionary War was a disaster for our small,novice sailing fleet.The next century was to be the testing ground for faster,more efficient,and more seaworthy sailing vessels such as the **Pride of Baltimore** we can use as a benchmark as it is alive and sailing today.

A middle ground communications method was needed to analyze the strong opinions developed by naval architects short on sea duty,and captains and mates without academic backgrounds but with tremendous practical experience.The seamen,while often on long voyages,built *lift-layer half models* with alternate slab layers of dark and light wood.After the slabs were doweled together the side view,top view,and maximum width were carved on the slab layer assembly.

The final whittling began until it was down to the desired lines.The dowels were then removed, with hull measurements made of the slab layer waterlines...which were enlarged to full size on the shipyard loft floor to which full sections,diagonals,and buttocks were added.

The evolving *duck waterplane theory* began.The wide,bluff codfish bow above developed a distur- bance and **lift action.The reaction** on the other end of the hull tetter totter,text pg.115,was for the slim mackerel tail to begin sinking,dragging its tail without aft hull support.

The bow entry was slimmed down,and the beam increased from midship to the stern to provide an aft waterplane to resist tail dragging.The new concept worked well but required improvement for the bow entry to reduce lift tendencies as the wind increased.The *Baltimore Clippers* then could sail on their fore and aft lines carrying tremendous canvas loads to break all speed records.

Our naval architects adopted the new waterplane theory around 1870 developing new math formulas to take the lead with accurate,precise hull line drawings.This technology has been fine-tuned thru the century with the 1938 **Iris** lines shown at right,page J 22.

The line plans show regularly spaced sections defining the accurate hull section in three dimensions. It shows a hull form from the side,bottom,bow and stern,with each view detailing three sets of lines,two being straight,the third,curved.

The *North Sea double-ender design* developed from Viking long boats to Norwegian rescue lifeboats designed to row out from...and return to the beach thru heavy surf,with sail used only as auxiliary power.Double enders today have reduced hull capacity,with more rolling tendencies downwind,and are more active at anchor than wide transom sailboats.

Chinese sailing history which has been a way of life for 2000 years has been ignored by their historians.It required Marco Polo in 1298 while in a Chinese prison to make a report of fleets of 4 masted junks used by merchants.The large ones had 13 watertight compartments and a single deck with 60 cabins,more or less,for merchants plus pepper,cloth,etc.The larger vessels required crews of up to 300 for handling under sail with four to handle a sweep or oar.

Chinese hull design theory...*it should ride the water like a duck with a wider beam aft,becoming narrower at the bow.* If you ordered a traditionally-built junk,the length would be governed by how many compartments were desired...without any line drawings.The bottom would be built first,the watertight bulkheads added,planking is added to the sides,followed by adding the decking and masts.The Chinese introduced the daggerboard,centerboard,and stern rudders.The balanced lug sail operation is covered on page J 23,introduced by Blondie Hasler to the western world.

Only two books we feel have recorded the great sailing days of the Arab lateener which have gone forever.One is the *Periplus* in Arabic...the other,the **Sons of Sinbad,**was written by Alan Villers,published by Charles Scribner's Sons.

Villiers spent a year sailing Arab lateeners starting in late 1938.He reported the darndest combi- nation of boatbuilding,operation,and sailing procedures governed by religion and tradition. Their hulls also used the *duck waterplane theory.* This is one of the most outstanding sailing books ever published which should be placed on your must read list.

*Islam used the oxcart to the 5th century requiring straighter,wider streets with gentle grades. The sure-footed camel able to carry ¼ ton,replaced the wheeled oxcart.Streets using camel and donkey delivery became narrow and winding,with steep,changing angles.Gulf oil fortunes after 1965 sent camels to the stew pot,to be replaced by new cities,cadillacs...and the 747.

Present hull score—mackerel tail 1...duck 3.Tomorrow...????

Ship Models to 1815,A.H.Waite—Bookshop,National Maritime Museum,Greenwich,London,SE10 9NF
Page references refer to Homestudy Guide.

The LINES DRAWING *shows a hull shape from three views—profile, plan, and sections.*

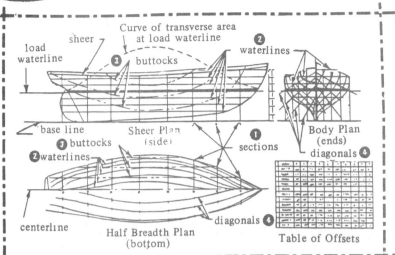

load waterline · sheer · Curve of transverse area at load waterline · buttocks · waterlines · base line · Sheer Plan (side) · buttocks · waterlines · sections · Body Plan (ends) · diagonals · centerline · diagonals · Half Breadth Plan (bottom) · Table of Offsets

The **SHEER PLAN** details the *side view* of a hull, will it be graceful, pudgy, or long and lean. It also shows deck height above the water called the *freeboard* in relation to its length, the gentle *sheer* of its deck line...and the *rake* of its bow and stern.

The **HALF BREADTH PLAN** shows the *beam*, how wide it is, and how the hull width is distributed along its length.

The **BODY PLAN** *(end views)* provide exact shape with accurate offset measurements on the hull shape at each station...or at each point of its width.

After the hull line plans have been approved, the line plans are laid out full size on the mold loft floor using measurements provided in the **TABLE of OFFSETS**.

The drawings at left and the line plans on the mold loft floor should be identical, except the lines on the floor are *full size*...hopefully *within an 1/8'' of measurements in offset table.*

① **Sections**, cross sections, or stations, are athwartship (beam) sections of the hull.

② **Waterlines** are horizontal planes parallel to the load waterline in feet and inches.

③ *Buttock* lines are vertical planes at regular intervals parallel to the keel.

④ Diagonals are lines crossing frames close to right angles to develop hull lines.

⑤ A *rabbet* is a groove cut into a keel, etc., to receive edges or ends of planking.

The naval architect *lines drawing* above...and our perspective interpretations of them at right are of the lovely *Iris*, a 1938 design pg. J 22, text pages 71, 72.

31

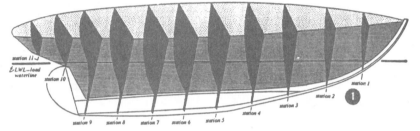

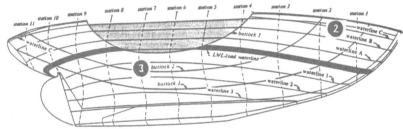

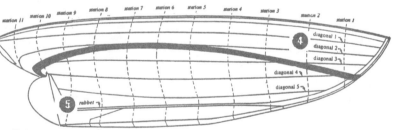

We hope to work with a lines drawing when we detail a new sailboat. It becomes an easy though time-consuming task to translate these plans into perspective which you see in our Homestudy Guide.

We are often limited to a side view and a top view. We have to mark stations on the boat, then draw sections with much measuring. The Pacific Cat was molded by hand without plans nor measurements. We had to mark stations on a hull, then cut cardboard templates to develop the lines in perspective.

The lines of an 83 foot IOR maxi.

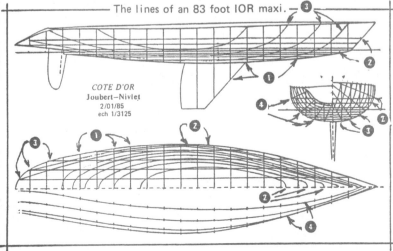

COTE D'OR
Joubert-Nivlet
2/01/85
ech 1/3125

After you understand the lines of the 1938 cruiser above...take an exam to apply this knowledge to the 1985 maxi lines shown at left.

Our responsibility in this *Guide* was to show a full and balanced story of sailing. This posed many interesting problems especially when we wanted to show the latest state-of-the-art set of IOR maxi lines for comparison with *Iris.*

Just before press time we received permission from Joubert-Nivelt* to show the lines of their 1985 maxi. It is a highly qualified team of designers for which we give thanks for helping our readers.

*Michel Joubert-L. Aubrecay-St.-Xandre, 17138 Puilboreau, France

*Bernard Nivelt-15 Main St., Stonington, CT 06378 USA

Page references refer to Homestudy Guide.

New American colonists seeing an endless forest on our eastern seaboard, often began building boats soon after arrival. Since most early settlements were isolated with the best transportation by water, they found a good way to make a profit.

After many centuries of boatbuilding in England and Europe, quality wood was becoming scarce. At the time of the Revolutionary War, a 3rd of the tonnage under the British Flag was made in the colonies. The cost was less, the wood and quality excellent.

During that war the British captured the rest of our vessels they hadn't purchased except a few Baltimore clippers they couldn't catch. This started a new century of boatbuilding in the colonies.

Outward bound American vessels from 1850 to 1900 delivered endless cargoes of wood to European ports

For the homeward passage they added makeshift arrangements to carry immigrants to America bringing along their ideas, skills, and heritage. This new cargo was to soon turn the U.S. into the most diversified and productive nation in the history of the world.

She has been a double-topsail bark since the 1880s, though launched as a full-rigged ship.

Whaler crow's nests high in the rigging, had metal hoops to encircle and protect their lookouts.

LOA— 113' 11"
beam— 27' 8"
draft— 17' 6"
350 tons burthen

cost and outfitting $52,000
1841 to 1921—
37 voyages
27 masters
total earnings—
$1,400,000

main royal
main topgallant
gaff tops'l
main upper tops'l
main lower tops'l
spanker
course or mainsail
fore royal
fore topgallant
fore tops'l
foresail
flying jib
inner jib
outer jib

Her earlier fake gun ports have been painted over.

The **three-masted bark** is a plodding workhorse with tremendous carrying capacity. The bark rig was the mainstay of the wooden whaling fleets in the 1800s, with one surviving. Several cargo-carrying barks survived from the last century in the U.S. such as the *Star of India* in San Diego. She is a floating museum that sometimes operates under full sail Several operational steel barks such as the *USCG Eagle* are found worldwide as training vessels under various flags.

Charles W. Morgan. She was launched in 1841 as a full-rigged ship. Three years later she returned to her New Bedford home port after her first voyage paying her building and outfitting costs, plus a $4000 profit. She is a wooden whaling vessel, broad-beamed, with a wide stern and a blunt bow. She was a working ship with 36 consective voyages, slowly roaming the seven seas searching for whales, knowing every whaling port in the world.

In 1867 she was rerigged and remeasured as a bark, dropping from 351 to 314 tons under new rules. Her single topsails were changed to smaller double topsails for easier handling in rough weather. From 1886 and the next 18 years she sailed out of San Francisco for one to two year voyages, as oil could be shipped east by railroad with less cost and less risk than returning to her home port around Cape Horn. After almost 80 consecutive years at sea under sail, she returned to New Bedford for her last voyage in 1921. She had more active service than any surviving working vessel with more miles under her keel... under 27 masters, making well over $1,400,000.

100 years after her launching, she was towed to Mystic Seaport in Connecticut. She arrived Nov. 8th, with Dec. 7th Pearl Harbor bombing taking place within a month. After being underway almost continuously from 1841 to 1921 you can walk the decks of the *Charles W. Morgan* at Mystic Seaport where she still floats on her own bottom in sea water.

Half the world's tonnage was still under sail by 1880, dropping to a quarter by 1900, as steam slowly, then rapidly took over the cargo delivery business from sail. Sailing officers and seamen, well trained to the exposure of wind and wave action on the ocean, changed to steam-powered vessels. The following generation of seamen without a sailing exposure limited to training on steam vessels underway, had a minimum understanding of heavy weather wind and wave action.

To fill this void— the 395' *USCG Eagle* is just one of several steel hull training barks owned by several nations worldwide are used to provide an exposure to ocean wind and wave action as cadets develop alertness team work and leadership. Russia has several sailing training vessels to teach naval cadets, and seamen in their fishing fleet roaming worldwide.

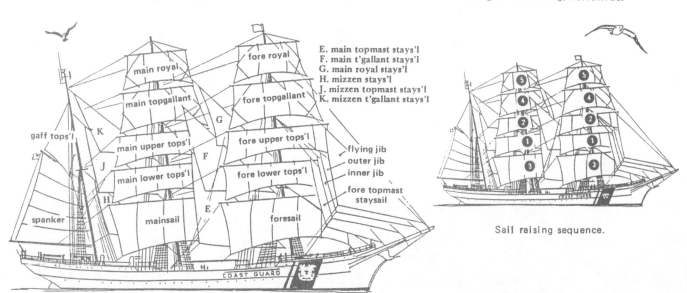

E. main topmast stays'l
F. main t'gallant stays'l
G. main royal stays'l
H. mizzen stays'l
J. mizzen topmast stays'l
K. mizzen t'gallant stays'l

fore royal
main royal
main topgallant
fore topgallant
gaff tops'l
main upper tops'l
fore upper tops'l
main lower tops'l
fore lower tops'l
spanker
mainsail
foresail
flying jib
outer jib
inner jib
fore topmast staysail

Sail raising sequence.

Cutty Sark figurehead witch "Nannie" in a short chemise graced her bow.

Cutty Sark — hard on the wind, force 5, 17½ knots, starb'd tack, all plain sails.

Take ample time to study these square rig pages with reference text pages 210-1.. the square rigger sailing from Manhattan to San Francisco and return.

The outbound course to Rio is difficult, with tremendous flexibility thru islands of the Pacific.

1848-1858 saw the new first generation of American clippers. They were rather small with minimum cargo area, to make profit by their speed in the tea (slavery?) trade. They were high-performance racers with hard-driving captains pushing them to new limits never seen on the ocean.

1869— the second generation clipper *Cutty Sark* was launched. She was composite-built of wood using iron frames, beams, stringers, and diagonal plates added to stress areas. While outbound clippers had to sail around the tip of Africa to sail to China, the Suez Canal opened the same year reducing steamship distance from the British Isles to China by 4000 miles. Steam was just beginning to prove itself, and new coaling stations had to be opened before steamships slowly took over the tea trade.

Cutty Sark made good voyages. but not the tea trade records she was designed for. Her masts and yards were shortened, the skysail and stuns'ls were removed for better performance in the southern *roaring forties.* When outward bound she carried coal sailing down to the tip of Africa, heading east to Australia. She arrived during wool shearing from Sept., thru Oct. She loaded wool for the homeward passage to London for the Jan. to March textile market delivery avoiding expensive warehouse charges. She sailed east below New Zealand with the wind on her stern to round Cape Horn, turning NE for the channel. For ten years Captain Woodget who was a hard driver of men and ships made consistent records of 68, 69, and 70 days from Sydney to the English Channel.

After 26 years under the British flag she was sold to a Portugese owner. Her coal cargo shifted in heavy seas. While on beams end her masts were cut away for survival. She was towed to Capetown to be rerigged as a barkentine. After 53 years service she returned to the Red Ensign in 1922. She was restored to her original state as a full-rigged clipper ship, with her last sea passage in 1938.

We thank *THE "CUTTY SARK" MARITIME TRUST* for permission to detail her. Since records of her reefing sequence were missing, we contacted model sailboat builder Eric Christian. Over 2½ hours discussion was required to show beam reach steering stability to minimize rudder pressure, losing her rudder twice. She carried more sails forward and less sails aft to sail downwind. Detailing the *Cutty Sark* has been the dream of this artist from Wyoming who was drawing square riggers in grade school.

33

1918-1922— her barkentine rig.

(map of the world showing square rigger worldwide freeways, wind patterns, trade routes)

longitude · latitude · Bering Sea · Gulf of Alaska · Newfoundland · Hamburg · London · WESTERLIES · Seattle · New York · Halifax · San Francisco · Long Beach · Bermuda · Azores · Greenwich Meridian · New Orleans · Canaries · Tangier · See page F 5 for worldwide wind patterns · Yellow Sea · Yokahama · Shanghai · descending wind · Midway · Hawaii · Caribbean · Cape Verde Is. · Arabian Sea · Bay of Bengal · Singapore · Wake · Johnston I. · NE TRADES · Christmas Is. · doldrums rising wind · Belem · Philippines · Marianas · Carolines · Marshalls · Sumatra · Java · Solomons · Marquesas · Society Is. · Galapagos · Callao · SE TRADES · Timor Sea · Coral Sea · Samoa · Fiji Is. · Tahiti · Paumotus · Valparaiso · Rio · Adelaide · Melbourne · Sydney · Tonga · Cook Is. · Pitcairn · Buenos Aires · Indian Ocean · Tasman Sea · Tasmania · New Zealand · WESTERLIES the ROARING FORTIES · descending wind · Juan Fernando · Cape of Good Hope · square rigger worldwide freeways · Cape Horn · Falklands · east longitude · west longitude · west longitude · east longitude

The clipper ship era was less than a decade old when one of the first true clipper ships, the *Soverign of the Seas,* afloat for less than a year, left Honolulu.

She was deep in the South Pacific heavily laden with oil heading for Cape Horn, then NE to New York City. She was facing continuous rain squalls since midnight charging thru mountainous cresting seas...while still carrying her royals.

The next morning March 18,1853 at 1000 the mate reported, "Nineteen knots again, sir". The captain replied, 'Now you can take the royals off her mister"

This released some of the pressure, yet at 1100 she was still making 18 knots. The skipper and mate looked at each other. Though they still had an hour to go...this was the first time in history a vessel had sailed more than 400 sea miles in 24 hours, averaging 16.6 knots— *excerpt reprinted by permission of G.P. Putnam's Sons from* **Clipper Ships and Their Makers** ©1966 by professor Alexander Laing, deceased.

Another hundred years were required for the first big catamarans to easily hold 20 knots...with *Aikane* in 1959 covering 178 sea miles in 12 hours, while in 1966 *Pattycat II* covered 316 miles in 24 hours.

royals

34

Sovereign of the Seas

The lieutenant who did his homework.

Basic weather pattern boundaries above have short-time variations due to seasonal changes...plus local conditions such as world-wide **Feons,** *page F 13.*

Monsoons are massive seasonal tropical disturbances, while—

El Niño causes complex normal weather patterns to fall apart with unpredictable time patterns.

The Pacific high, F 12, weakens, with ocean temperatures soaring in the eastern Pacific doldrums. As the trade winds diminish *the child* grows to an unpredictable, all-powerful monster. It caused considerable local damage in 1982-3 in our buffer zone, F 6.

is a new generation of sailing cargo and fishing wind machines practical...

A passenger on his first ocean trip that was trying to impress his square rigger's captain reported a high moving in. The reply, "Give me a low to blow my ship home in record time", was in a tone that could remove 18 layers of varnish. He remembered a square rigger becalmed for two months in a South Sea high with the same island staying on the distant horizon. The vessel was floating in a carpet of that captain's empty, clanking wine bottles surrounding what would be his last command.

Lt. Matthew Maury, page F 8, produced the first Wind and Current Charts in 1847, available to any skippers desiring such information. Square rigger captains who gained their authority by proven performance didn't take kindly to the ideas of a landbound naval officer with less than a decade of sea duty, who gained his expertise from a study of ships logs which eventually began to indicate basic weather patterns.

The shortest route to Rio was 55 days with vessels facing long doldrum periods. Maury suggested sailing east to mid-Atlantic before turning SSW to Rio which was 3 times the distance. Captain Jackson on the *W.H.D.C. Wright* tested the new idea reaching Rio in 38 days...he then returned in 37 days.

The hard-nose captains took another look at Maury's predictions, turning in their reports to update his charts which eventually covered all the world's oceans. Timing was ideal helping **clippers** with their flax sails, wooden hulls, masts, and yards with hemp rigging producing sailing records that still haven't been equalled.

They were followed by much larger **windjammers** using flax sails with tremendous bulk-cargo carrying capacity. The hulls, masts, yards, and standing rigging were made of steel. The steel running rigging however had organic rope tails for easier handling.

The Laeisz Line of Hamburg, Germany, operated their Cape Horn windjammers for a century, taking weather reporting to a new plateau that reduced time underway from port to port. Every master received a thorough briefing month by month of the weather he would face. After he returned he would have to submit a detailed accounting of his records and any ideas to improve the performance of their vessels.

After sailing efficiency peaked, it was replaced by steam. A new generation of deep-sea cargo and fishing wind machines may evolve following traditional square rig sailing routes around the world. The first oil tankers and bulk carriers for several decades were sailing vessels starting with the iron-hull *Atlantic,* launched in 1863. The seven-masted schooner *Thomas W. Lawson,* text page 269, converted to carry bulk oil in tank compartments, was lost on her first trip to the English Channel on her new assignment.

Page references refer to Homestudy Guide.

_____ Mutiny insurance—the officers only protection. _____

Man has roamed the restless oceans under square and lug rig long before recorded history.Crews had ample time and opportunity to take command of these vessels except for the officers only protection...which was to keep all of their navigational secrets to themselves.

Their officers realized that the oceans had predictable pathways which could take vessels for thousands of miles from a beam reach to a run...with a completely different return course.They had to wait for a Lt.Maury who changed their guesstimates to predictability.

Lt. Maury,
wind and current
charts-----1847

PILOT CHARTS
of the ocean

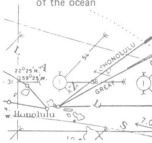

downhill romp
to Hawaii
14-25 days

NE trade wind trap
20-25 day return.

Pilot Chart source—

Admiral Beaufort's Wind Scale started a new idea in eliminating blindfold navigation by recording wind direction and strength on the ocean voyages of English naval vessels.Another 50 years passed until an obscure stagecoach accident started a chain of events which made worldwide ocean weather predictions practical.

The accident broke the leg of line officer Lt.Matthew Maury which never fully healed. His new assignment in 1842 was to the Depot of Charts and Instruments,storing thousands of ship logs going back to the birth of our navy.He and his staff began a systematic study of weather,sea,and wind conditions published as Wind and Current Charts in 1847.The purpose...reduce sailing time around South America from one port to another,and from our east coast to the west coast.

The resulting _Pilot Charts_ were produced monthly for many generations,now issued every four months.While they were simplified beginning in 1983,we show their older concept for a typical July at the start of the L.A.Transpac Race to Hawaii.

The _wind rose,_ shown at left,which is located north of Honolulu indicates the prevailing winds predicted for that area of the ocean.

The _arrows_ indicate the _wind direction,_ while their _length_ indicates the _percentage of time it blows from that direction._ The influence of the northeast trades becomes obvious with over 95% of the winds coming from a 90° easterly arc...without any westerly winds anticipated.

The number of _feathers_ indicate the _average Beaufort Wind Scale_ predicted.A force 4 is expected from the northeast 54% of the time,with a force 3 from the east 38% of the time.The 1% in the wind rose center indicates the _percentage of recorded calms,_ light airs,and variables...with probably one day in three months.

Daily current drift and endless other details are included.At right you can see a couple of days after the L.A.Transpac Race begins the wind moves abeam,to a broad reach, then to a downhill sleigh ride romp with the NE Trades on the stern.You now learn the reason that the long waterline **ULDB** surfing grayhounds are in their home element to come in first.Since ULDB's are not designed by traditionalist's rules they make the Transpac Race Committee members job an uncomfortable one.

You will face another sailing world when returning to the mainland as it is necessary to sail over 1000 miles closehauled due north...to break out of the NE Trades wind trap.After that it is easy to sail to Alaska as it is to Victoria,the Puget Sound,San Francisco,Los Angeles,Long Beach,San Diego,or Acapulco.

Poor performing _sailboats not able to break out of this trap_ drift back to Hawaii, then to downwind islands such as Tahiti where the questionable bargains are for sale. A heavy-displacement 43' ketch didn't quite break out of the return trap when it turned east running into 5 hurricanes with the boat,sails,and rigging deteriorating daily. The boat was lifted to the deck level of a rescuing freighter so the crew could jump aboard.It was abandoned 100 miles off Mazatlan,all sails gone,a helpless derelict with no water and little food.I was stunned to find the owner next bought a 40' ULDB.

Pilot Charts of the **North Atlantic Ocean,** and **Pilot Charts** of the **Northern Pacific Ocean** are published three times a year.Pilot Chart Atlases are available for the South Pacific and Indian Oceans,and the South Atlantic and Central American Waters.Order charts of foreign waters,and the Pilot Charts desired from the— **DMAHC Topographic Center,Washington,D.C. 20315.**

35

_____ Fogs ARE predictable. _____

"Hello,foggy isn't it!"

Fog potentials can be predicted when the humidity increases to the dew point.The questions are...will the fog be light or a peasouper.and when will it arrive and when will it leave.Study text pages 218-219 to analyze fog predictability.

Eighteen months of continuous testing were required to understand the time-lag patterns to predict an approaching fog.Finally if we were on the ocean with students aboard as a peasoup fog moved in,we were there of my choice.

The pattern proved so successful it required seven years for a fog to move in so rapidly it wasn t anticipated on the indicator.The humidity needle rose so rapidly in the next minute it broke the indicator.A humidity/fog indicator is needed which is specifically designed for the sailboat and powerboat environment.

sailing illustrated GUIDE

mycelium

hypha

"Now there is a tasty morsel".

Mildew—black surface spots inside boats;also decaying sawdust,leaves, on wood in storage..is it surface discoloration?

Dry rot—powdery and dry, white to light tan.

Wet rot—light brown to dark brown,moist and crumbling.

Surface rot- decay on outer wood layers becoming soft in tropics under very wet conditions.

Pocket rot—local pocket decay surrounded by apparently healthy wood.

Metal poisoning- black wood stains around keel bolts,chain plates, and hull fastenings that crush surrounding wood—*not* wood rot,page K 11.

Fungi are microscopic plant life with a large and varied menu,plus an enormous appetite.How many contributions can your boat offer to this hungry horde?

spore factory

There are many kinds of fungi with appetites for one or more of the products above. All species have the same basic needs...*1.food,2.oxygen,3.fresh water,and 4.favorable temperature* to survive,grow,and reproduce.Remove any of these items and the fungi's growth will become dormant and go into hibernation...or be killed.

Tap every inch of a wooden boat with a hammer to check for rot.While healthy wood sounds may vary from a sharp to a softer deeper *ping*,use chalk to mark every area that has a *mushy sound*. During an inspection use protective goggles and gloves, also protect your mouth and lungs as fungi spores may produce allergies.

Healthy wood fibers separated by a dull ice pick while probing will soon go back together.

Is splinter long and flexible or short and brittle?

1 End grain infection begins.

36

Soft, punky splinters— probe for soft spots.
...surface discoloration?

2

Wood barely able to hold shape and support its weight.

3

Rot spreads along wood grain.

highly contagious to nearby wood

4

Earth to earth...dust to dust...

Is paint beneficial..or a hazard?

Did paint cause this damage?

Was wood dry and well seasoned before painting?

permeable paint

enamel paint

After wood is seasoned or cured with it's moisture down to 15% of its weight, the natural resistance depends on protective natural oils and resins,how water-tight the wood is,plus fungacidal protection chemicals added to retard decay. Hopefully nature has well plugged the pores of the wood,but—

The spores that seed a culture are everywhere in the air remaining inactive until the wood moisture content reaches 20% of its weight.A baby spore lands on damp,warm wood to enter the end grain where it starts an invisible invasion making itself at home.The *mycelium* sends out tiny *hypa threads* producing *that sweet smell* while eating the cellulose,their voracious appetite changing it to sugar.The splinter may be too flexible **1** if the wood isn't fully seasoned.

The *hypa threads* are becoming so numerous **2** that the *mycelium plant* causing the action and damage has become a visible mass.*Most damage begins at the ends of planks...then follows a damp wet path thru the wood grain.*The mycelium produces more hungry growing spores as the hypa threads push thru the wood to continually branch out.The fungi is now hard at work eating the cellulose and possibly other organic chemicals.The timber is an empty shape or shell **3** barely able to support its own weight at rest without movement.

After the cellulose has been eaten away,comprising 2/3 of the wood content,it will crumble **4** into small chunks with the least pressure or movement,the stage at which early sailors discovered *dry rot*. Fungi scavengers have completed natures routine by returning the organic chemicals to what it thought was food for the next generation of forest vegetation...that can help your local garden.

Pocket rot can occur inside of what seems to be healthy wood.If the PING doesn't sound right...use a hand drill with an 1/8" bitt.When the normal wood resistant eases.this indicates you have reached the damaged area.Keep drilling until the normal wood resistance returns...indicating the depth of the rot area.Slowly remove the bitt to check sawdust,smell,color,and moisture.The next step is to find how large the pocket is,then treat the part...or have it replaced.

Light color *permeable paints* have small holes to aid breathing action,plus ventilation and drainage that maintain better temperature control,low moisture content,and better immunity to the ever-present contagious spores in the air.

Enamel produces a hard,glossy,waterproof coating reducing wood breathing to inside the boat.*A thick outer paint layer* increases the problem...especially if a *dark,heat-absorption enamel* was used.The heat expansion squeezes caulking out from between the planks,increasing humidity/moisture content inside the planks. If the wood was painted when damp,or before it was seasoned sealing moisture and oxygen inside the planks...the fungi will awaken after a long,cold. winter's hibernation with a ravenous appetite for a spring cellulose feast.'

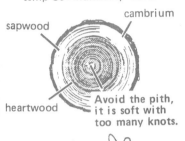

temp 80° humidity 100%

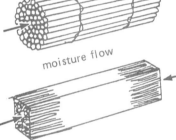

Avoid the pith,
it is soft with
too many knots.

sapwood · cambrium · heartwood

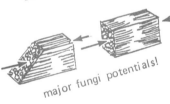

moisture flow

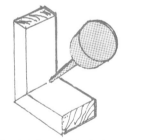

major fungi potentials!

Squirt fungacide twice
yearly into all end joints.

Protecting metals or
irrigating fungi?????

Do you desire a year
or two sailing vacation?

CULTIVATING YOUR OWN FUNGI FARM...

_____ Moisture and heat variables. _____

Wood moisture content—is the major factor.Fungi begins to awaken above 18% water content by weight with maximum growth potentials occurring between 20% and 35%.Above that fungi growth decreases,then becomes dormant at 75% due to insufficient oxygen.When wood is submerged or waterlogged with moisture content up to 150% of its weight,the lack of oxygen kills the fungi while marine borers move in for a gourmet underwater feast.

Heat sensitivity—growth ceases below 40° F as the fungi becomes dormant.Maximum fungi growth potentials are between temperatures of 70° to 90°...while decreasing above 100°.If sufficient temperature time above 150° is involved but below the ignition point,it can kill the fungi . though the wood can be reinfected later.

Wood must breathe continuously to keep the moisture content below 18% to 20% that requires continuous ventilation.If enamel is used on the hull outside,wood on the inside should remain bare,or permeable paint used to release the heat and moisture especially if darker colors are used.After fungacide protection has been added to wood in the bilges it is often left unpainted to aid its continuous breathing.

Choose *heartwood* for boatbuilding with it's low moisture and sap content.The only part of a tree alive and growing is the thin *cambrium layer* of cells beneath the bark, about 1% of a tree's bulk.This outer layer begins at the root tips,comes up the trunk, then goes out the branches to the leaves and buds.This layer has a high moisture and sap content called *sapwood,a major cause of rot*,which must be avoided.

Consider wood a tightly-bound bundle of drinking straws.Condensation and fresh water can enter these pores running with the grain developed by nature...however minimum moisture absorption goes thru the sides of a plank against the grain.

Short timbers or joints with end-cut angles have the greatest rot potentials.These are the areas in wooden boats that require continuous checking,especially with fresh water sailing due to the large areas of end grain exposed to humidity and rain.

Pickling—wooden fishing boats use *rock salt in the bilges* and areas above the water prone to rot that are difficult to check.Since melting ice to protect the fish is continuously present,fresh water drains into the bilge,changing to salt water which retards fungi growth in the wood...with mixed blessings.This increased the metal corrosion rate since the least corrosion resistant metals for ocean use are often found on wooden fishing vessels.Older wooden cargo vessels used tons of *salt packing* for critical areas such as between inner and outer planking.

Marine plywood has it's inner voids filled to provide maximum fungi resistance for exterior use which makes it quite expensive.Quality exterior grade plywood will have many boatbuilding uses as it is also temporarily sterilized by heat lamination bonding.Since it has voids the cost is considerably less.

Cold-molded,laminated veneer strips glued together are considerably lighter than planked wooden hulls.Laminated hulls have weight and structural strength equal to fiberglass and aluminum hulls.Hidden wood defects are prevented as veneers are not thick enough to hide a wood fault...and underwater borers don't like the epoxy glue.

Epoxy glues create a water-vapor absorption barrier by penetrating 1/16" into the veneer surfaces isolating the inner plies.This stabilizes the wood's dimensional and mechanical characteristics,eliminating moisture absorption and rot potentials called the *Wood Epoxy Saturation Technique...or WEST*.The method is also excellent to build hot tubs,furniture,etc.Contact the Gougeon Brothers,Bay City,MI 48706.

We were washing a teak deck on a 40' sailboat with ocean water.Little did we realize that the owner of a new 34' production powerboat was watching to follow our procedure without protecting his metals (1958).His rapidly corroding topside metals had to be rechromed two years later.

When we pulled into our slip we saw him washing his wooden boat with fresh water to protect his metals...his *sweet smelling* powerboat now facing a new problem.We wanted to warn him,yet his authoritative barking commands to his wife and three children changed our mind...also the wind was blowing his spores away from us. How would you have responded in this situation?

37

_____ Does a wooden sailboat meet your requirements? _____

The long line of wooden cruising sailboats in Papeete,page J 22,provides better recommendations for this type of craft than endless advertising.The wooden sailboat may be ideal for a year or two cruise after being subjected to a thorough survey by a wooden boat expert.Your initial investment is often returned when the boat is sold after the cruise.

If a dismasting occurs in the backwaters of nowhere a craftsman may often be found to chop down a tree to build your new mast,oops—*AVOID Iceland*. An aluminum mast by air freight may be prohibitively expensive.Also how long would it take to reach your sailboat when the last 87 miles is by dugout canoe thru hippos and crocodiles?

Royce's *POWERBOATING
ILLUSTRATED*

The portable powerplant—
How many sailboats
use outboard motors?

sailboat and powerboat
owner hostility?

A well-maintained
sailboat engine provides
the best of both worlds.
38

To sailing purists—
live honestly by
removing your engine.

Study your engine
basic operation.

Analyze your sailboat
powerplant thru the
questioning eyes of your
engine mechanic.

Sailboat simplicity?

Planing hull operation
and maintenance is
similar to that of a
light airplane.

Should sailing purists learn engine operation?

After our new sailing book was on the market slowly gaining acceptance, I was operating a new 40' Newporter ketch, an excellent 1932 40' wooden ketch, and a 32 foot twin-screw powerboat. It was heady stuff until buying our 14' ski boat that could easily reach 33 mph. While the big ones seemed easy to operate, *my 40 hp outboard motor hated me, operating only when it so desired... we named it* **Blunder**. A better answer was needed.

After three years research and four outboard rigs later, we published our *Trailerboating Illustrated.* The present 1992 edition of our 416 page powerboating revision required 8 years to produce, engineered to help the future generation of marine mechanics.

It was a warm, lazy day at the South Shore Corinthian Yacht Club in Marina del Rey, of which I am a honorary member. To liven the discussion I asked, "How many of you enjoy outboard motors?" A motion was soon underway to banish me forever to Cape Horn.

"Would anyone like to stop at any local marina dock, and without moving, count the number of outboard motors on sailboats?"

The volunteer returned twenty minutes later. "I still can't believe I counted 28 sailboats with outboard motors on their sterns, and on the sailboat dinghies. Do sailboats rely more on outboard motors than inboard engines?" he asked. It was time to change the subject.

Few sailors know my sailing and powerboating background, in the friendly rivalry (hostility?) that sometimes surfaces between the two with boat owners only knowing one side of the story. One weekend I invited planing powerboat owners to go sailing, and the following weekend, the sailors operated their powerboats, learning from each other. Neither side were short handed for crew members during the following months.

Tom Kelly was my diesel engine adviser for two decades, see facing page. His crew serviced large local 'diamond plater' powerboats and sailboats. Tom also distributed GM diesels thru the Pacific. When in his shop one afternoon, orders came for engines from Mazatlan and Tahiti, plus a mid-Pacific call for help for a broken down engine on a large powerboat. I provided answers to professional skippers with embarrassing questions thru Tom, for the dinghy outboard motor monsters they hated... by a sailor without professional credentials.

Cruising sailor purists with inboard engines, are problems looking for a place to happen. I have enjoyed asking, "Why don't you remove your engine?" with interesting, confused answers. Tom could quote endless South Sea sinkings on reefs, etc., *".. due to sudden unexpected engine failure",* especially if he was involved in the installations or repairs on their engines. He continued, *"An engine with maintenance ignored and not operated for long periods, will seldom function normally in emergency conditions".* If you are a sailing purist, remove the engine, and add a wine cellar. You can follow the pattern of Lin and Larry Pardee as they sailed engineless around the world on their *Seraffyn.*

If your sailboat has an outboard motor, inboard gasoline or diesel engine, keep it well maintained and operated often. Obtain your engine operational manual and parts catalog from the engine manufacturer. If new to marine engines, paint names on engine parts, tag electrical leads, and add directional arrows to fuel and water hoses. Potential engine failure becomes easy to predict and correct as most sailboat engines are basic.

Periodically study our powerboating book written from the viewpoint of the marine mechanic looking for answers to his problems. The simple outboard motor has tremendous complexity due to its wide variety of applications... NOT covered in an operational manual. When problems develop, it will help to properly evaluate and diagnose them to your mechanic in his own terms, that may help to considerably reduce repair bills.

It is easy to buy a fully-engineered 30' sailboat. Choose your sailmaker, and add your choice of navigation and other instrumentation. Except for a few loose ends it is ready to sail.

The planing powerboat under 30' may seem simple, but... it is similar to a light airplane with an annoying complexity of mechanical maintenance details that must be anticipated so only a minor inconvenience can be expected. For those with little interest in engine operation it is fun to ask, "Will you land on a nearby cloud bank the next time you have to change spark plugs?"

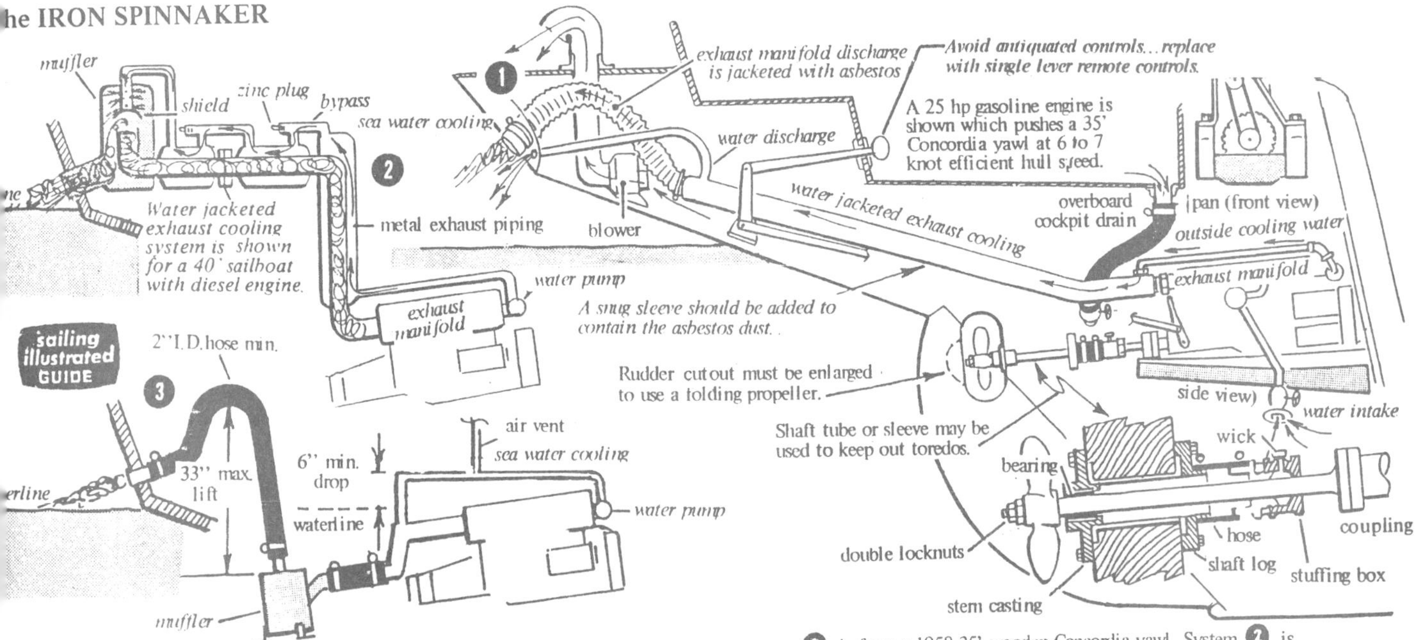
muffler
shield
zinc plug
bypass
sea water cooling
Water jacketed exhaust cooling system is shown for a 40' sailboat with diesel engine.
metal exhaust piping
exhaust manifold
water pump
blower
exhaust manifold discharge is jacketed with asbestos
water discharge
water jacketed exhaust cooling
A snug sleeve should be added to contain the asbestos dust.
Avoid antiquated controls...replace with single lever remote controls.
A 25 hp gasoline engine is shown which pushes a 35' Concordia yawl at 6 to 7 knot efficient hull speed.
overboard cockpit drain
pan (front view)
outside cooling water
exhaust manifold
Rudder cutout must be enlarged to use a folding propeller.
side view)
water intake
Shaft tube or sleeve may be used to keep out toredos.
wick
bearing
coupling
hose
double locknuts
shaft log
stuffing box
stem casting
sailing illustrated GUIDE
2" I.D. hose min.
33" max. lift
6" min. drop
waterline
air vent
sea water cooling
water pump
muffler

*The iron engine block develops a considerable heat buildup—the reason it should be idled before being put under load, then idled afterwards to release its heat before turning off the engine if it uses outside cooling water**

Exhaust system 1 is from a 1958 35' wooden Concordia yawl. System 2 is from a 1960 Newporter using a heavy, corrosion-prone metal piping exhaust system. System 3 reduces weight and corrosion problems with its weight concentrated low in the hull. A warning—if you keep cranking the engine with this system when the engine won't start, engine cooling water flowing into the muffler without exhaust pressure may back up the engine exhaust and into the cylinders requiring a major engine overhaul to repair the compression/corrosion damages.

Are you able to hand crank a sailboat gasoline or diesel engine?

The ignored, overlooked engine has its final chance to fight back.

"Most sailboat sinkings in the Pacific occur after reaching a protected area... due to a sudden unexpected engine failure", said local GM diesel distributor Tom Kelly, deceased, a close friend and adviser for 20 years.

most engine failures follow predictable patterns

The number of engine failures I've witnessed while teaching or crewing on sailboats seems average with many more occurring on powerboats. The factors involved— ***thoroughly know how all of your engine components operate....keep your equipment adequately maintained...then OPERATE the engine often.*** If any of these factors are overlooked it won't be a matter IF...but WHEN engine failure will occur.

operational manual and parts catalog

Whether it is a new or used sailboat obtain the *operational manual* and *parts catalog* of your engine from it's manufacturer, then become familiar with the names and functions of all it's components. Periodically check intake, manifold, and exhaust systems, the hoses and clamps of all exhaust systems which ***must go upward***...with an outer water jacket to cool the hot exhaust. This check is especially important with gasoline engines to ***avoid the danger of carbon monoxide leaks.*** *IF you smell any engine exhaust you are also smelling carbon monoxide gas.*

If you smell exhaust fumes— **you are ALSO smelling dangerous carbon monoxide fumes.**

problems of lower engine operating temperatures

Engine heat is important. Sulfur from incomplete combustion plus ***water*** from condensation collecting in the lubricating oil produces weak but ***corrosive sulfuric acid.*** High auto engine temperatures help to boil out a large percentage of these contaminants.

**Water temperature must stay below 150° in a continuous flow system.*

The reason is for the ocean water to keep flowing thru without the minerals and salts falling out of suspension.

Above this temperature the minerals and salts fall out of suspension to form *boiler scale* **which will plug the cooling system passages.**

Most gasoline sailboat engines use *a continuous flow of outside cooling water* . They operate in a maximum heat range with a 150° cooling system thermostat so minerals and salts flowing thru the cooling system stay in suspension to be exhausted overboard.

An owner had his sportscar mechanic check his sailboat engine, replacing the 120° thermostat with a 180° thermostat plus some snide remarks. I helped sail the boat with its new owner soon afterwards to Long Beach Terminal Island. I turned on the engine while dropping the sails when entering the harbor due to heavy traffic. Engine temperature skyrocketed with the salts and minerals falling out of suspension. They had plugged the cooling system with ***boiler scale***, causing an expensive engine repair bill and a difficult sail for a heavy 40 footer in tight channels to its awkward dock.

Warm operating captive cooling systems **provide a long life yet add considerable to the system's compl**

Marine engines used in water-taxi service normally have *captive cooling systems* with 180° or higher cooling system thermostats. With normal maintenance they operate many more hours than auto engines before a major overhaul. The reason— marine inboard engine carburetors don't have to digest *abrasive concrete and asphalt dust particles* from pounding tires, a major destroyer of auto and truck engines.

The story behind the lecture material.

Our *Sailing Illustrated* was published in 1956, and we published our *Trailerboating Illustrated* in 1960 covering the portable powerboat planing hull. It was also the year our new California boating department demanded boat operator licensing. Industry members feeling it was just a method to raise taxes to gain power, asked for my ideas.

A positive approach is necessary with sailing and trailerboating courses open to the public, the problem, to develop instructors. The next few months were spent developing large charts and lecture material. This was followed by week-long seminars of 40 to 44 hours, and weekend 16 hour seminars in sailing OR trailerboating.

It was fortunate to be involved in both fields as sailing ideas are useful in powerboating, and powerboating ideas, in sailing, especially engine operation.

These seminars helped test and improve the lecture sequence and ideas. I occasionally had a few hostile students, who by the second day usually became my best students. My secret was a list of traps to avoid with ideas to follow you may also find useful.

- Sailing education covers many fields of basic knowledge. LOCATE and DEFINE usable facts in simple terms, and give practical APPLICATIONS. In the beginning it will be difficult to separate usable FACTS... from unnecessary or secondary details.

  Stick to— theory vs application... theory vs facts... simple usable facts.

- Keep it SIMPLE... good analytical thought PATTERNS... test 180 degree thinking. Don't talk when you should be thinking.   Our job is to HELP, not criticize.

- DEPENDABILITY isn't accidental in sailing, powerboating, flying, or driving.

- Avoid product PARTIALITY... as most problems are caused by owners. Most can be eliminated when quality public sailing courses are available nationwide.

A

- speaking—
words are precious,
  don't waste them
think POSITIVE
THINK first, talk later
don't FUMBLE
breathe DEEPLY
SMILE & RELAX
talk DEEP & LOUD

- organized thinking
SHOW first
WORD explanation
  comes second
build a FOUNDATION o
  basic knowledge others
  can DEVELOP on

- DO—
be SPECIFIC,
  stick to FACTS
be CLEAR and BRIEF
sound easy going, gracious
  use HUMOR

- DON'T—
WANDER
WASTE words
FUMBLE
fall for TRAPS
sound OPINIONATED
don't ask for opinions
give reasons, don't ALIBI
avoid CONTROVERSY

- 5 minute REST
every hour lecture!

- when PROBLEMS develop—
answer- I don't know
further study is needed
is it IMPORTANT?
is it a secondary DETAIL?
I'm coming to that...

- an IDEA—
it is generally ACCEPTED
it is generally MISUNDERSTOOD
it is my belief
it is my observation
  our RESEARCH indicates
  there are VARIABLES

DEFENSIVE THINKING is
dangerous--don't get hooked

- accident PREVENTION
  isn't accidental
statistics are past history often
hiding the real cause of accident
FAILURE- personal or mechanical?
COMMON SENSE is a naive term
  as it can't be legislated
SAFETY is often overworked,
  a negative attitude that should
  be avoided
- *EFFICIENCY is positive and useful*
  for a boat owner WANTING to learn
at what time was the accident
  CAUSED or STARTED
define FACTS so students can see
  the potentials developing so damage
  can be stopped or minimized

P.S.— enjoy your lectures!

The list of positive ideas and sticky pitfalls to be avoided, proved very useful in 16 to 44 hour seminars... and to a lesser degree, evening lectures. Many lecturers asked for copies, the reason it is included.

The rest of the Sail Course manual discusses various ideas involved with starting sail courses in your organization and in your area.

You will find repetition of some ideas falling into various areas.

We cover variables to avoid unexpected surprises beginning with the facing page of ideas for sticky situations... and how to avoid traps.

Our first evening sail course was to be held in a meeting hall with a limit of 30 people. We found a mob waiting outside, requiring us to go to the Sea Scout Base with over 115 registering.

The lecturer had barely studied the notes and charts. Our photographer was arrested by the FBI two days later for an armed robbery bank holdup in Florida. He left a problem behind... what to do with his full grown pet lion in his bungalow he raised from a tiny cub.

Several students came forward to volunteer their services, with a different instructor for every lecture.

Each covered the assigned material adding their own experiences that were often hilarious. They all did excellent lectures with students seeing sailing in they eyes of a variety of sailors.

For the weekend seminars we found it best to have one, or two lecturers at the most to cover bare-bones basic information.

We invited a USPS or CGA instructor for a lecture in every series as they explored our materials and methods, adding some of their own ideas to the following pages.

A second sail course?

If you live in an active sailing community, consider a second sail course in a year or so. Many skilled specialists are available, each having excellent information from sailmakers, to brokers, to designers, sailboat builders, marine surveyors, etc. Their limitations, a five minute break for every hour of lecture. Their objectivity was quite a surprise with no show of product partiality.

This provides an excellent method for students to know local industry leaders and their ideas. Most were nervous before their first lecture. After they started they relaxed as their ideas flowed.

Your unexpected warehouse of sailing expertise.

We had sailmakers who stressed ideas to consider for racing sails, plus a British sailmaker producing a different viewpoint.

Naval Architect Bill Crealock provided the best lecture we've heard on cruising hull designs, plus his world cruising background.

Designer builder Rudy Choy was available for lectures on design, building, and operation of his ocean catamarans... with many of his ideas to soon enter monohull construction.

A USCG judge, his specialty being involved in collisions of professional operators, provided surprises. While radar was becoming a method to reduce collisions in low visibility, he provided cases where collisions resulted when vessels changed courses sufficiently to collide using radar, that would normally have missed each other.

Many excellent communicators—

You will find many people involved in both the recreational and industry side of sailing will be good lecturers, with vast storehouses of experience and information. Much more expertise may be waiting in your corner just for the asking than you realize.

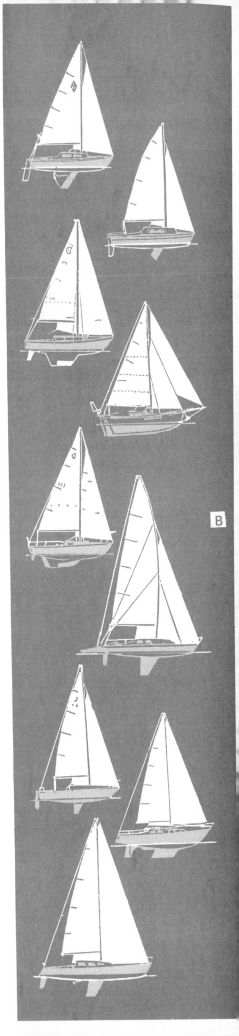

B

New sailors need a few good men... to help new sailors help themselves.

Sailing has advanced technologically in all fields more than any other sport in the past 30 years. During this period the needs of new sailboat owners have been ignored with few sail courses open to the public, and most of their concepts are little advanced from 1960 sailing technology. Let us go back 30 years to define the various steps in this growing problem.

wooden sailboats and canvas sails
Wooden sailboats of the 1950s and earlier with canvas sails, can best be describe with 6 hours of maintenance for 2 hours of sailing.

the start of a new sailing world
1960 saw the new emerging technology of fiberglass hulls, Dacron sails, stainless rigging,aand aluminum masts. If your boat has minimum varnish trim... you can return to your sailboat the next weekend, hose it off to remove   dust, and go sailing.

expanding sailboat technology
Sailboat technology kept expanding thru the next 30 years to produce more efficient and comfortable hulls for large cruising and racing sailboats... while all kinds of one-design classes kept multiplying nationwide.

THEN—
While sailing technology is at an all time peak... then what happened?

the problem becomes obvious
The sailboat market now accounts for less than 5% of the new boat market. That is, auxiliary and non-powered sailboats— Sailing Scene 6/89. Source is Jeff Napier, president, National Marine Manufacturing Association.

our local harbor
The problem is obvious in our local harbor filled with sailboats on moorings and in slips that rarely move... then mostly under engine power.

lack of training
Many sailboats seldom leave their slip as their owners don't have enough training, experience, or confidence to operate their sailboat under sail.

sailboats looking for new owners

new owner training?
Many good fiberglass sailboats have served the needs of a growing family... that are now looking for new owners. How will the potential owner be able to know which sailboat fits his personality? How will he be able to sail his boat with confidence and efficiency in heavy local powerboat and sailboat traffic? And how well is the cabin layout designed to be enjoyed as a floating bungalow with ever changing scenery for special lazy weekends?

C

sail course availability?
The problem goes to the lack of availability of adult sailing training courses. They are limited to a few areas of the U.S. Then what is their quality?

Most offer little more than the limited basics of 1960 technology as they serve a secondary purpose. Their primary purpose little changed in 30 years, is to obtain new members for their organizations.

Why can't members of the sailing industry help start this sailing course nationwide?

industry members can help the industry and their customers
Industry members face considerable competition daily. At the end of the day they want to return home to enjoy the evenings and weekends with family and friends. Sailing education as a result was left to organizations holding a few sail courses in limited areas .

boat brokers have the local pulse of sailboat economy
Since no organization has shown interest to expand quality sail courses open to the public, it is time for industry to analyze to find how their members can become involved to help start this sail course nationwide. Boat brokers have the continual pulse on the local market of new sailboat and powerboat owners... to those with boats for sale. Most have many industry contacts plus high exposure to help start such sail courses.

starting courses to impartial advisers
A broker has an excellent background to be impartial to help instructors understand the variables in the local sailing environment which differs considerably even in Southern California ports. His first choice to start such sail courses is to contact local yacht clubs, and his yacht club friends.

a growing problem
The need for quality sail courses has been growing steadily for 25 years.

one interested person?
If you want this trend reversed... it takes just one interested person wanting to become involved with ways to start regular sail courses in your area taught by local sailors... to help the next generation of sailors.

Basic ideas to consider for your new sail course.

the format— for rapid identification

> This reading format was developed so instructors can glance thru ideas listed at the left of the page for instant reference.

The sail course method... is to teach the answers.

THE GOAL—
exposure, not
memorization

The instructor provides the answers for students to write down without any interruptions, using workbook page 2 for the first 21 sailboats. He then returns to repeat each sailboat term with a brief discussion of the sailboat rig. This teaching method covers a variety of important technical terms in a short period of time. He can add to it with types of cabin sailboats found in your area or nearby areas.

Concentration span limitations are important.

a 5 minute break is required for a 55 minute lecture

A five minute break is needed for every hour of lecture, the maximum time limit to teach the new sailing language and theories. Let students relax in the rest period, walk around, or.. A problem facing instructors is a student who wants to test his technical ideas with you in the rest period. AVOID it, as the short rest period is the best time to plan the next 55 minute lecture.

All sail course lectures should be limited to 6 or 7 lectures.

most efficient lecture series with few dropouts

We experienced few dropouts with seven lectures, with an extra one added for a review, or questions and answers. Testing lecture patterns with other organizations found class size dwindling to 70% after the eight lecture... and 50% by the ninth or tenth lecture. If more lectures are required, consider 12 to 13 lectures broken into two series, with a week break between.

Starting time 7:00 p.m. on Tuesday or Wednesday.

D

time and weekday

Most businessmen had time to go home, have a short break and a quick meal to reach class promptly. Tuesday had minimum conflicts. Monday had several conflicts... while Friday had many conflicts with other meetings.

A 2 hour lecture is practical... the 2½ hour lecture is much better.

stay on course

Instructor should follow lecture material closely to cover as much information as practical for 55 minutes. After a 5 minute break, the second hour begins, followed with another 5 minute break.

last half hour for discussion, review answers/questions

The last half hour is relaxed with discussions on items in the evening lecture. Instructors usually have endless humorous examples they've seen around docks when they have been witnesses... and often, participants. Other times it may be more practical to provide a question and answer period to test terms and theories covered in the lecture.

instructor flexibility

Flexibility is important to make the best use of instructor personalities so students can make the best use of the information under discussion. Workbook pages 11 & 43 were often handled by lawyers who were ex students. They enjoyed analyzing considerably different legal concepts... for which they were excellent communicators.

The goal.... sailing competency and self reliance thru education.

the real exam— is on the water

Lecturers have been preparing students for the real exam... on the water, hardly a written exam. If your lecture team has done its job and students their homework, the ocean challenge will be spirited and interesting... not a statistic.

fill as many empty spaces—

If students want an eighth lecture, it could be a review of terms and theories covered, while as many workbook page blanks should be filled that answer the needs of your students and sailing area.

Additional sail course ideas... plus avoiding reference to 'boating safety'

**the important
first lecture
exposure**

The first lecture sets the pattern for following lectures. It is important for new lecturers, feeling uncomfortable with imaginary hecklers due to variables in term use, to keep a potentially critical student busy... to become a very cooperative student in following lectures as the course isn't a debating society.

**note taking keeps
students awake-
video puts them
to sleep**

Students are kept too busy with the first lecture pattern making notes, to fall asleep. We cannot emphasize the importance of having them write down the new terms to inscribe the new sound in the mind... then repeat the term later that evening, and in the following lecture. Students using videos showing similar technical information without organized note taking become sleepy as concentration disappears... and some may fall asleep.

**15 minute revue
for all following
lectures**

Start all following lectures with a 15 minute revue. A rapid speaking talker with clear pronounciation, can provide the third exposure to the new sailing terms... lawyers did an excellent job.He then introduces the next lecturer with a brief coverage of his sailing background.

For 30 years I've tried to find a practical answer to the term 'boating safety'... who goes boating to be safe?

**negative bureaucratic
boating 'one-liners'
are negative...
accomplishing little
besides confusion**

We want to enjoy a lively, spirited sail using the best, most efficient equipment for dinghies to large cabin sailboats. By showing the positive approach to sailing, new sailors spend more time and attention to better sailing products... *instead of minimal 'safety' requirements acceptable by law.* If boating safety were the real issue instead of printing endless reams of questionable 'one liners... *National Safe Boating Week* would be rapidly replaced with a *Safe Bathing in the Bathtub Week* which is the real major   killer   and crippler we all face daily.

**marlinspike
requirements?**

Rope, knots, and splicing requirements vary considerably to fill local needs of lakes, reservoirs, river, coastal areas, and the open ocean. We favor the USPS system. At the end of a lecture, six students were assigned to a member for 15 minutes per lecture to fill knot and splicing requirements.

eye splice-a must

A three-strand splice is required before completion with endless uses on the boat and dock, around the home or farm, and for decorative work.

Your most important asset is an ample supply of interested, relaxed, and prepared instructors.

**your best basic
sail instructors**

The best basic sail course instructors we've had sailed for less than three years. They still remembered painful mistakes which may be repeated by students they are facing in the audience tonight. Expert sailors especially with a racing background who have long forgotten these basic traps, can deliver excellent impressive lectures. The important communication with new sailors may be minimum, or missing in most cases. But keep looking for the exceptions as they are excellent racing lecturers.

**helping the
new lecturer**

To avoid overcompensation, new lecturers should only have a week with their lecture material. They should read instructor material aloud at least three times for familiarity and pronounciation, and check all text references.

**regular instructor
notification**

To avoid overcompensation, regular instructors were seldom notified to handle the next lecture... until two days before the lecture.

**your BEST
lecturers will
have jitters**

Last minute jitters are common, with phone calls from probably half the evening before the lecture. Your confidence in them in your voice provides their needed answer... with most of them becoming your best, most qualified instructors.

**If an instructor
doesn't have
an answer—**

If a question develops for which the instructor doesn't have an answer... he says we will have that special answer at the beginning of the next lecture.The confidence that idea provided gave new lecturers confidence for endless situations.

**IF everything fails...
don't congressmen
also read their
testimony**

If the instructor doesn't show... a student can read the lecture material word by word. I had to give a lecture when the instructor didn't show at the first sail course in 1956 held by the Santa Monica Power Squadron... using loosejointed material. That early exposure is the reason for the lecture material which has been provided.

ROYCE'S **SAILING ILLUSTRATED** COURSE

Yacht clubs should teach at least two adult sail courses yearly.

new members?

Most yacht clubs are in a continuous search for new members, some more than others... for the self perpetuation of their future.

yacht club familiarity

Few potential sailors have an understanding of the functions of a yacht club. And in our local Newport Beach, a second problem develops with six yacht clubs ranging from one with the most expensive initiation fee in the U.S., while on the other extreme is a family oriented yacht club. The highlight after racing, is weekly summer hamburger barbercues, with juniors as chefs.

2 courses yearly?

A sail course should be offered starting mid-September, and the second beginning in February, both being open to the public.

advantages of two-way screening

Potential sailors become familiar   with the yacht club and their members holding the lectures. Meanwhile yacht club members are monitoring students who might become potential members for their yacht club.

let students crew for exposure with club members

As students learn more about sailing, and the kinds of sailboats students are interested in, members can take them out for an afternoon sailing exposure... as the majority of cabin sailboat owners are always looking for new crew members.

everyone loses with an untrained sailor

If one of the items involved with club membership is the sail course, it will help the person buying a sailboat, and the yacht club integrity as I've seen too many new members with sailboats that want to race...but how will they learn first to sail... then second to race. The horror stories are endless.

racing courses?

Yacht clubs should also hold two evening racing courses yearly, also open to the public for those with sailing experience wanting to fine-tune the highly complex racing rules.

racing courses have their own complexity

We held racing evening classes locally for I believe 5 years. While a basic pattern was used, personalities of racing instructors, and the wide variety of protests, etc., were considerably different for each lecture. When looking back, the courses were all successful with learning never stopping.

The successful racer must grow upward thru THREE plateaus.

racing is not for everyone

Page 152 of our *Homestudy Guide* covers these three plateaus in depth. Potential racers would do well to study that page so they can analyze how much racing and in what depth, fits each skipper personality.

F

racing crews?

For a permanent berth crewing on ocean racers— he should still analyze his racing personality on page 152, then page 114.

Don't overlook the Sea Scouts.

Sea Scouts

We probably have the largest Sea Scout base in the U.S., with a large fleet of dinghies to the 67' *Argus, Sailing Illustrated* page 269.

the ship

Girls and boys at age 14 can join the Sea Scouts. They are assigned to a group called a SHIP, with an adult leader. Most learning is done while performing a task on a sailboat. .. with a stress to learn teamwork as a crew member.

present training

The leaders are volunteers for their Sea Scout crew from ages 14 to 20. Major responsibility for the quality of their education is left to the leader.

Sea Scout dry-land sail course

This sail course was also designed with the hope that it might eventually be adoped for Sea Scout use. Lecture material could follow the same process to add terms to the workbook...though at a slower pace. It could give new life to the Sea Scouts locally and nationwide. The lectures could be held in the evening, and winter evenings in the snowbelt areas so most of the warm summer days can be devoted to on the water operation.

Sea Scout future?

An investment in Sea Scout sail course training may be an efficient way to help the future of recreational sailing...and the sailboat industry.

Ideas to develop and expand your instructor staff.

personal exposure before a lecture
The sail course charts were developed in 1960 for our local Newport Beach evening sail course, and for the first Long Beach CGA sail course. I was able to spend ample time a day or so before the lecture with the next instructor to discuss the basics, plus strong and weak points such as language variables.

weekend seminar lectures
For places farther away such as Redondo, Santa Monica, and Santa Barbara, a weekend was chosen with a meeting room. Potential instructors came for the two day 7 to 8 hour sessions, to go thru seven lectures.

exposure to the full six lectures
The first three lectures were covered on Saturday, and the rest, on Sunday. A timekeeper was assigned to provide a 5 minute break for every 55 minutes of lecture. This provided covering a tremendous amount of information, which was assimilated and well understood in the following week.

limit to potential instructors
For a yacht club wanting to start a sail course, the weekend seminar limited to potential instructors, is excellent. Members from other yacht clubs can be invited if they want to help, or teach their own sailing course.

Sea Scout lecture exposure
Sea Scout leaders throughout a county, can choose a central meeting location for a seminar. This exposure will help them understand the course methods and potentials. Also to cover the new sailing language and theories following the same adult lecture sequence ... but at a slower pace for Sea Scouts ages 14 to 20.

the first lecture sets the pattern
The first lecture sets the pattern beginning workbook page 2. The sailboat names are written under the illustrations from lugger 1., to stayless catboat 21. The instructor returns to read the short background behind each vessel in simple terms. This pattern exposure method is continually repeated thru all lectures so potential instructors can see how the full sail course pattern pulls together, instead of being exposed to a few parts of the jigsaw puzzle with a lecture at a time.

G

Choosing the lecturer for the weekend seminar.

clear voice with good pronounciation
He should have a good foundation in sailing, spending enough time to understand the lecture material, possibly reading much of it. This provides enough instructor exposure for those attending to choose their desired lecture. It also provides an ample group of instructors to handle any lecture if required on short notice.

Docking variables are important for all slip-berthed sailboats, workbook pages 26 and 27.

what was dreaded became fun!
We had slip shortages even in 1960. Instructors pooled their ideas we see on these pages, to provide almost every kind of variable sailors may face to make docking and undocking spirited and fun for small to large sailing craft.

the fun is missing
Few of the 115 sailboats in our marina regularly leave the dock. Then it is usually under power to the jetty where sails are raised. After returning from the ocean, sails are dropped inside the jetty to power back thru main channels to their slips.

an expensive bungalow luxury?
Slips are expensive. Our 24', 30 year old sailboat operated all year, pays $325 monthly for a 20' slip. Sailboats are an expensive luxury requiring considerable dry-land sail course exposure to be sailed efficiently... otherwise becoming expensive floating bungalows for new sailors not understanding the complexity.

harbor sailing has no equal!
The most stimulating part, is to leave the dock without engine power. Then to sail thru the harbor to the jetty, and return to dock under sail. The longest and most efficient tacks go thru moorings... not just limited to the main channel.

eliminate the mysteries so sailing becomes fun!
Instructor begins discussing sail raising sequence upwind and downwind in workbook page 25. He next covers pages 26 and 27, taking ample time to discuss all 30 docking situations systematically. Lecture material for these 30 variables will instead be found on pages 44 to 47 of our *Homestudy Guide*. Sailors should no longer be on the defensive after they understand the unique sailboat complexity.

If your sail course location is midwest lakes... most sailboats may be dinghies.

The temptation will be to avoid ocean cabin sailboats, to apply as much time to dinghy operation, but...

why not just cover dinghies?

We recommend completing the first lecture with workbook pages 2 thru 5, to gain a firm background in all kinds of sailboats, keels, boards and rudders. This permits students to study and understand a variety of books and magazines where the various terms are commonly used.

inland sailors often want ocean exposure

We've had several private sailing students from inland areas who raised their families, have an ample income and time for leisurely cruising. Some I remember were from Jackass Flats, Nevada; Silver City, New Mexico; Pocatello, Idaho; Denver, Colorado; Amarillo, Texas; ranchers from Northern California and Oregon, and others.

the year vacation under sail... with minimum cost

The doctor and his wife from Silver City are an example. I picked them up at our airport, both were pilots having their own Cessena. After three days sailing, I returned them to their plane. Two months later we received a postcard finding they bought a 30' wooden sailboat in Florida after passing survey.

sailboat was sold a year later at the buying price

For a year they enjoyed a leisurely cruise thru the Bahamas, thru the Panama Canal, up to San Diego where the boat was for sale. They enjoyed the sailing vacation with, after making minor repairs, the sailboat was sold for about the same amount they paid for it in Florida. They had their long dreamed vacation, with the medical doctor anxious to return to his practice he missed.

chartering?

You may have students wanting to charter sailboats in various areas of the U.S., or worldwide. This sail course will provide an excellent foundation to choose a sailing school on the water to develop their potentials for chartering sailboats.

intense, competitive dinghy sailing

A 26 year old woman from Ohio wanted dinghy lessons. She was easy to work with, thorough, and very intense. "You are spoiled with 11 months of local sailing... while we are limited to four months. I want to race my own dinghy as wild and competitive as possible. That seems the only way I can release the excess energy that is stored up during the winter months".

H

snowbelt vs sunbelt

Many inland sailors limited to dinghies develop enough exposure to compete in regional, national, and international dinghy racing, though living in the midwest snow belt. Sun belt regattas are excellent for winter vacations.

race two, NOT just one class

We provide five competitive dinghies for analysis on workbook pages 6 thru 8. Students should add as many terms to them as possible with a RED ballpoint pen for contrast. .. so your students can easily race in more than one dinghy class.

know hardware and rigging systems thoroughly

We recommend competitive dinghy racers also buy our *Homestudy Guide* to develop a good foundation with hardware part names pages 12-21... as well as being able to analyze, and improve rigging methods for dinghies pages 82-99. A meticulous foundation is needed AS improved hardware and minute rigging adjustments, may separate the first sailboat from tenth in a competitive class.

the Baharin Yacht Club?

Our student coming the farthest distance was an American living in Baharin on the Red Sea on one of his two yearly paid vacations. A year later we received a postcard finding he started the Baharin Yacht Club, buying a 28' sailboat.

Timbucktu sailing?

A book order arrived from the British consul in Timbuckto. I sent the book for pouch delivery to the local consulate, no charge for the book asking where in h... he was sailing 1000 miles inland in the middle of the Sahara Desert. "I can't wait to leave in a few months after 3 years here, to be in India next to the ocean to buy another sailboat. Your book will help me meanwhile dream of sailing".

evening snowbelt dinghy classes

Inland snowbelt sail courses should be held in the winter. This will provide more time for thorough lecture coverage if desired by your students.

serendipity?

Many times we found the students accomplishing the most in sailing, seemed to have the least potentials in the beginning. Study their registration ideas, and listen closely... as surprises will occur in almost every sail course series.

Sailing age groups 9, 12, and 15... follow predictable patterns.

During a four year period, instructors in charge of juniors ages 9 thru 15 for the two largest local yacht clubs, helped our sail classes as regular instructors. We in turn helped work out charts, etc., for their students.

minimum age for juniors is nine

Age 9 was the minimum for juniors to learn basic sailing in Sabots with mothers often trying for an earlier start. An 8 year old boy that was accidentally accepted was alone and usually in tears as he was too young to understand the ideas.

age twelve is action oriented

For our private lessons on the water teaching families, the children age limit had to be a minimum of 12. I would explain the page charts to the parents on the sailboat underway as the kids watched with parents doing much talking.

age twelve is too early for word discussion

The watchful kids aren't word oriented so they aren't old enough to ask questions. Parents are stunned to find they are action oriented, able to rapidly pick up the complex tiller movement of a sailboat underway. Their unique, early coordination ability diminishes later as they become talk oriented... which disappears by middle age.

word orientation is adequate by age fifteen

We arrived at a minimum of age 15 for our adult evening sail classes as they were able to take down the terms and ideas in their workbooks. When 12 and 13 year olds showed up with parents, their shorter concentration spans, plus the difficulty to write down the strange words, soon lost interest. The situation grew worse as the parents tried to compensate with the kids causing distraction from boredom.

Yacht club junior sailing programs.

juniors learn by doing

We provide considerable coverage on page 158 of our *Homestudy Guide*. The important factor for ages 9 to 12 is to learn to sail with others in their age group. These are competitive age groups with the goal, to win as many racing trophies as possible. After age 13 or 14 a new testing period begins going in different directions, often taking a priority over dinghy racing.

take them to adult sail classes

At age 15 take the ex juniors into the adult evening sailing courses, even under protest. By the end of that first lecture they often begin to take another look and interest in sailing. They may become good crew members for the family cabin sailboat which they couldn't understand earlier, for which they had no foundation.

Children vs 30' to 50' sailboats and powerboats.

double surprise

Dad announces he bought a sailboat expecting the rest of the family to share his enthusiasm. In our area it is for that first sail to Catalina.

a floating prison

Mom and dad are enjoying the 20 mile sail topside, while below a revolt is underway in the kids floating prison. The revolt comes as a complete surprise to the parents... though I've seen endless kid revolts going back over 30 years.

keep kids physically active in their own sailing world!

The secret is happy, participating, action-oriented kids in their own water world.

burn off excess energy!

After you anchor, does your boat have a sailing dinghy? Kids think a 6' to 8' dinghy their own 'little ship' they enjoy hour after hour after they push off from their big floating prison. Teenagers have a tremendous amount of energy that must be burned off with the sailing surfboard a first choice, easy to carry aboard.

good swimmers a must

The entire family should be good swimmers. Use swim fins to swim easily and effortlessly. When poor swimmers go overboard, they need swim fins and a quality ski belt for positive flotation.

SCUBA training recommended

All family members if practical, should take SCUBA diving lessons to gain honest confidence in the water, though they never use an air tank again. WARNING— the pool needs to be 13' to 15' deep for ample practice to clear your ears continually without tanks below the 10' depth.

coordination extremes

Private sailing lessons provided interesting surprises. Athletes, dancers, choreographers, fighter pilots, etc., often had poor coordination. Their secret— continually practicing routines until becoming flawless, enjoying this kind of challenge.

Happy Sailing,
Pat M. Royce

Seven students had perfect, instant mental and physical coordination. *NONE* knew they had this gift. They seldom owned a sailboat more than three years. They became bored, continually in the search of new challenges and interests.

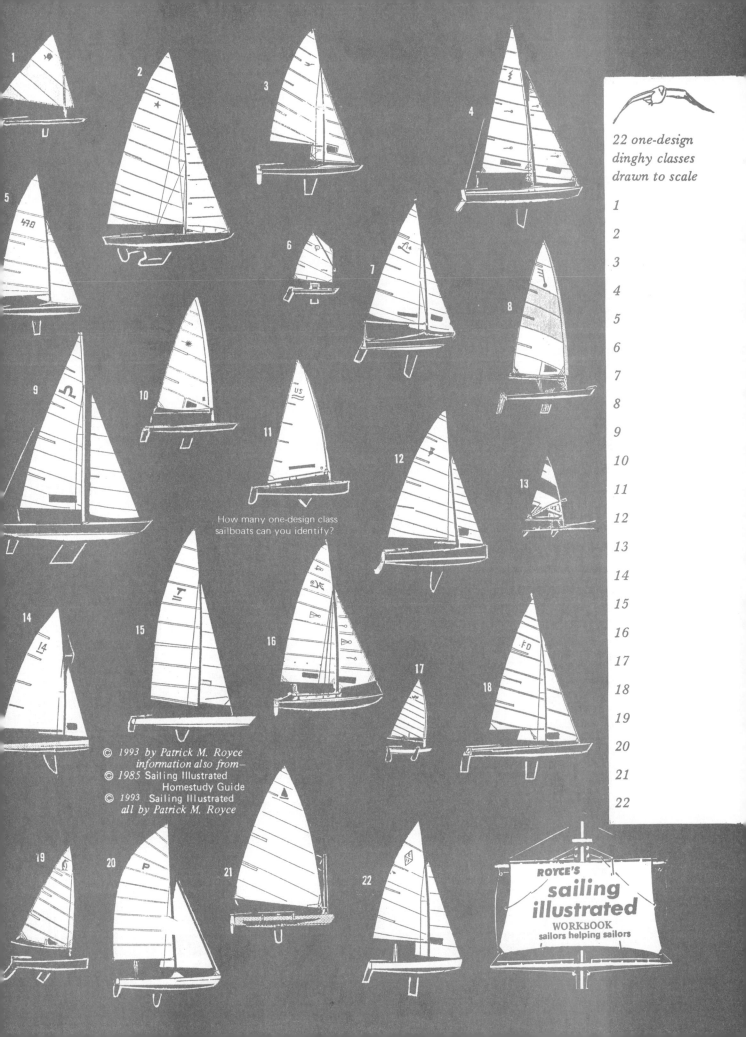

22 one-design
dinghy classes
drawn to scale

1
2
3
4
5
6
7
8
9
10
11
12
13
14
15
16
17
18
19
20
21
22

How many one-design class
sailboats can you identify?

© 1993 by Patrick M. Royce
information also from—
© 1985 Sailing Illustrated
Homestudy Guide
© 1993 Sailing Illustrated
all by Patrick M. Royce

ROYCE'S
sailing
illustrated
WORKBOOK
sailors helping sailors

WIND MACHINES thru the centuries

the lugger
1 *text-281*

2 *text-279*

3

the lateener
4 *text-277*

5 *text-17*

6 *text-26*

1 *the ___ rig* 2 *junk ___ rig* 3 *modern ___ rig* 4 *___ rig* 5 *Malibu ___ rig* 6 *Sunfish ___ rig*

the sprit rig
7 *text-271* *text-23*

8

Revenue Cutter— text-289
9 *text-263*

gaff or quadrilateral rig
10 *text-5*

11 *text-271*

7 *___ rig* 8 *Thames Barge ___ rig* 9 *Pilot ___ rig* 10 *Cape Cod ___* 11 *Gunther*

2 *marconi or bermudian rig*

12 13 *airfoils above* 14 *text-63* 15 *sloop rigs vs cutter rig* 16 *text-263*

waterfoils below

12 *early ___ rig* 13 *___ sloop* 14 *the ___ sloop* 15 *the ___ sloop* 16 *the ___ rig*

the full-batten mainsail
17 *text-48*

18 19 *text-49* 20 21

17 *___* 18 *___ cat* 19 *the ___* 20 *___ catboat rig* 21 *___ catboat rig*

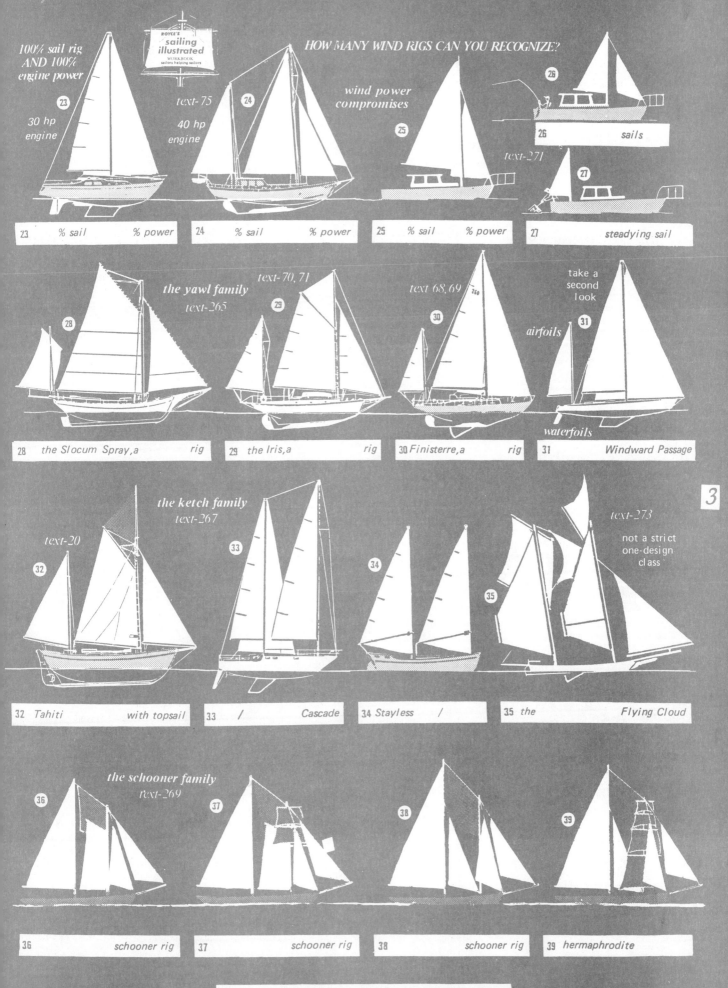

100% sail rig AND 100% engine power

ROYCE'S sailing illustrated WORKBOOK sailors helping sailors

HOW MANY WIND RIGS CAN YOU RECOGNIZE?

23 30 hp engine

text-75

24 40 hp engine

wind power compromises

25

26

26 sails

text-271

27

23	% sail	% power
24	% sail	% power
25	% sail	% power
27	steadying sail

the yawl family
text-265

text-70, 71

29

text 68,69

30

take a second look

airfoils

31

28

waterfoils

28	the Slocum Spray, a	rig
29	the Iris, a	rig
30	Finisterre, a	rig
31	Windward Passage

the ketch family
text-267

text-20

32

33

34

text-273

35

not a strict one-design class

3

32	Tahiti	with topsail
33	/	Cascade
34	Stayless	/
35	the	Flying Cloud

the schooner family
text-269

36

37

38

39

36	schooner rig
37	schooner rig
38	schooner rig
39	hermaphrodite

ROYCE'S SAILING ILLUSTRATED COURSE

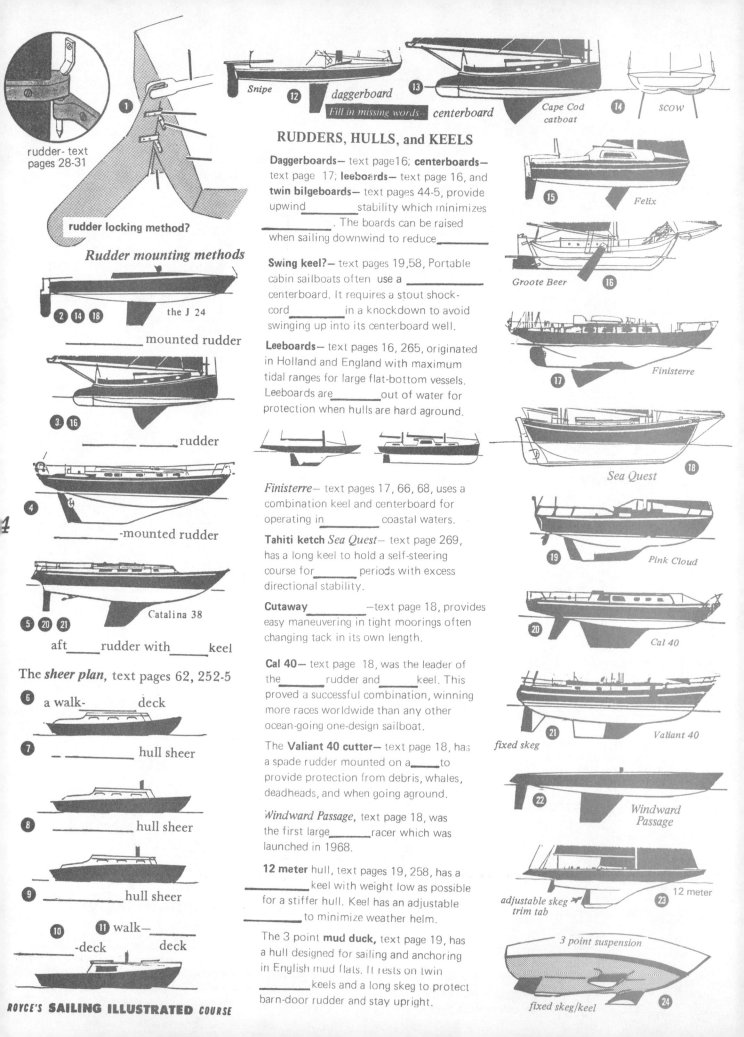

rudder- text
pages 28-31

rudder locking method?

Rudder mounting methods

② ⑭ ⑱   the J 24

_____ mounted rudder

③ ⑯

_____ rudder

④

-mounted rudder

⑤ ⑳ ㉑   Catalina 38

aft_____rudder with_____keel

The *sheer plan*, text pages 62, 252-5

⑥ a walk-_____deck

⑦ _____ hull sheer

⑧ _____ hull sheer

⑨ _____ hull sheer

⑩   ⑪ walk—_____
-deck   deck

Snipe   ⑫   *daggerboard*
Fill in missing words—   *centerboard*   ⑬

Cape Cod
catboat   ⑭   *scow*

RUDDERS, HULLS, and KEELS

Daggerboards— text page16; **centerboards—**
text page 17; **leeboards—** text page 16, and
twin bilgeboards— text pages 44-5, provide
upwind_____stability which minimizes
_____. The boards can be raised
when sailing downwind to reduce_____

Swing keel?— text pages 19,58, Portable
cabin sailboats often use a _____
centerboard. It requires a stout shock-
cord_____in a knockdown to avoid
swinging up into its centerboard well.

Leeboards— text pages 16, 265, originated
in Holland and England with maximum
tidal ranges for large flat-bottom vessels.
Leeboards are_____out of water for
protection when hulls are hard aground.

Finisterre— text pages 17, 66, 68, uses a
combination keel and centerboard for
operating in _____ coastal waters.

Tahiti ketch *Sea Quest—* text page 269,
has a long keel to hold a self-steering
course for_____periods with excess
directional stability.

Cutaway_____—text page 18, provides
easy maneuvering in tight moorings often
changing tack in its own length.

Cal 40— text page 18, was the leader of
the_____rudder and_____keel. This
proved a successful combination, winning
more races worldwide than any other
ocean-going one-design sailboat.

The **Valiant 40 cutter—** text page 18, has
a spade rudder mounted on a_____to
provide protection from debris, whales,
deadheads, and when going aground.

Windward Passage, text page 18, was
the first large_____racer which was
launched in 1968.

12 meter hull, text pages 19, 258, has a
_____keel with weight low as possible
for a stiffer hull. Keel has an adjustable
_____ to minimize weather helm.

The 3 point **mud duck,** text page 19, has
a hull designed for sailing and anchoring
in English mud flats. It rests on twin
_____keels and a long skeg to protect
barn-door rudder and stay upright.

⑮   *Felix*

Groote Beer   ⑯

⑰   *Finisterre*

Sea Quest   ⑱

⑲   *Pink Cloud*

⑳   *Cal 40*

㉑   *Valiant 40*
fixed skeg

㉒   *Windward
Passage*

*adjustable skeg
trim tab*   ㉓   *12 meter*

3 point suspension

fixed skeg/keel   ㉔

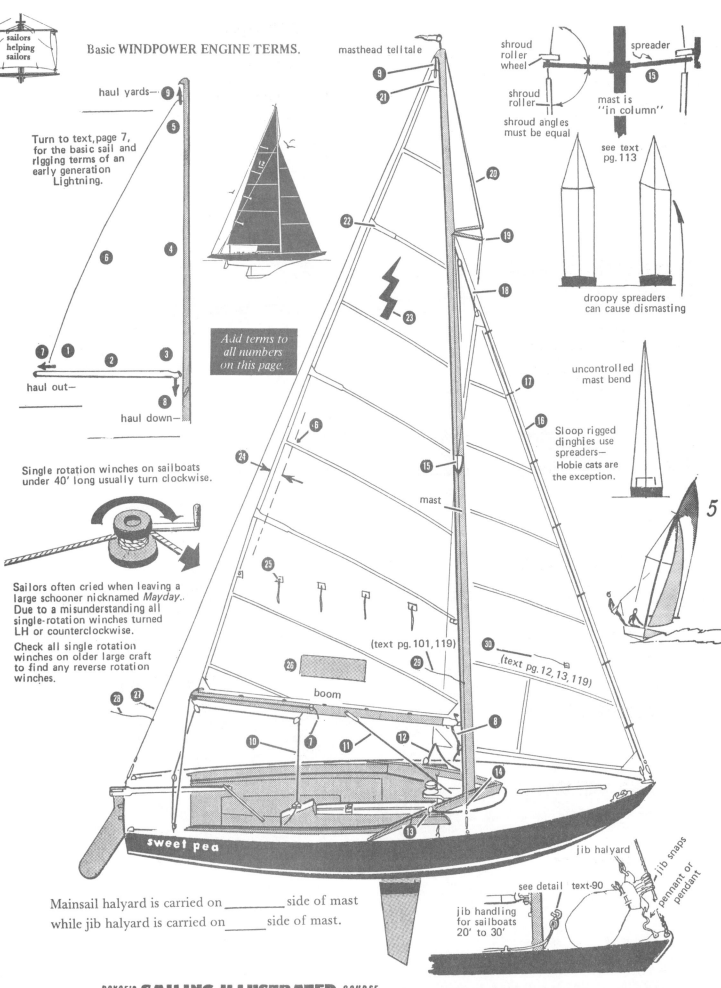

Basic WINDPOWER ENGINE TERMS.

masthead telltale

shroud roller wheel

spreader

shroud roller

mast is "in column"

shroud angles must be equal

see text pg. 113

haul yards—

Turn to text, page 7, for the basic sail and rigging terms of an early generation Lightning.

Add terms to all numbers on this page.

droopy spreaders can cause dismasting

uncontrolled mast bend

Sloop rigged dinghies use spreaders— Hobie cats are the exception.

haul out—

haul down—

Single rotation winches on sailboats under 40' long usually turn clockwise.

Sailors often cried when leaving a large schooner nicknamed Mayday. Due to a misunderstanding all single-rotation winches turned LH or counterclockwise.

Check all single rotation winches on older large craft to find any reverse rotation winches.

mast

(text pg. 101, 119)

(text pg. 12, 13, 119)

boom

sweet pea

5

Mainsail halyard is carried on _____ side of mast while jib halyard is carried on _____ side of mast.

jib halyard

jib snaps

pennant or pendant

see detail text-90

jib handling for sailboats 20' to 30'

ROYCE'S SAILING ILLUSTRATED COURSE

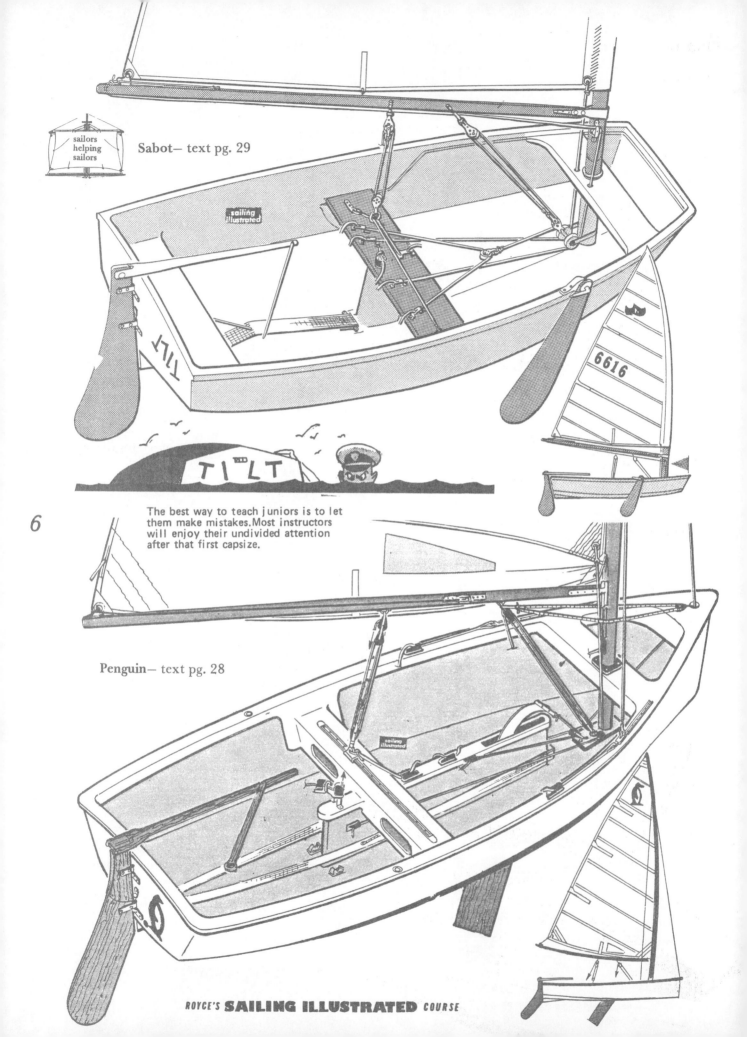

sailors helping sailors

Sabot— text pg. 29

TILT

6616

6

The best way to teach juniors is to let them make mistakes. Most instructors will enjoy their undivided attention after that first capsize.

TILT

Penguin— text pg. 28

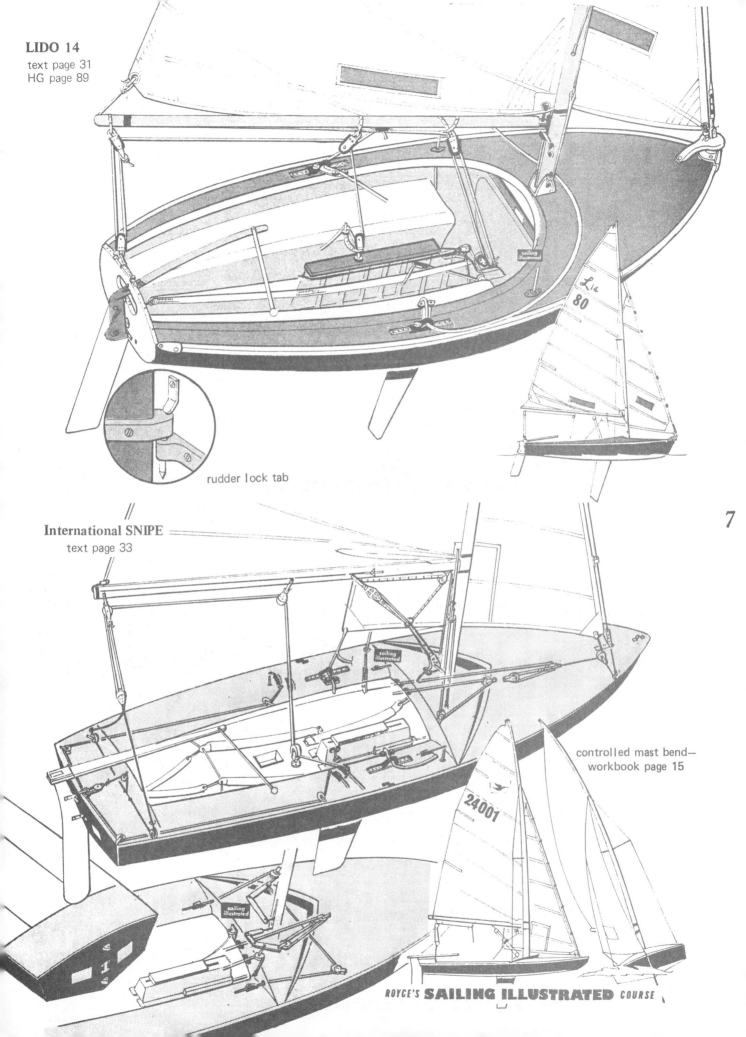

LIDO 14
text page 31
HG page 89

rudder lock tab

International SNIPE
text page 33

controlled mast bend—
workbook page 15

24001

7

ROYCE'S **SAILING ILLUSTRATED** COURSE

Lightning--text pgs.34-37

Lightning-- a small 12 meter?

13191

SEA FEVER

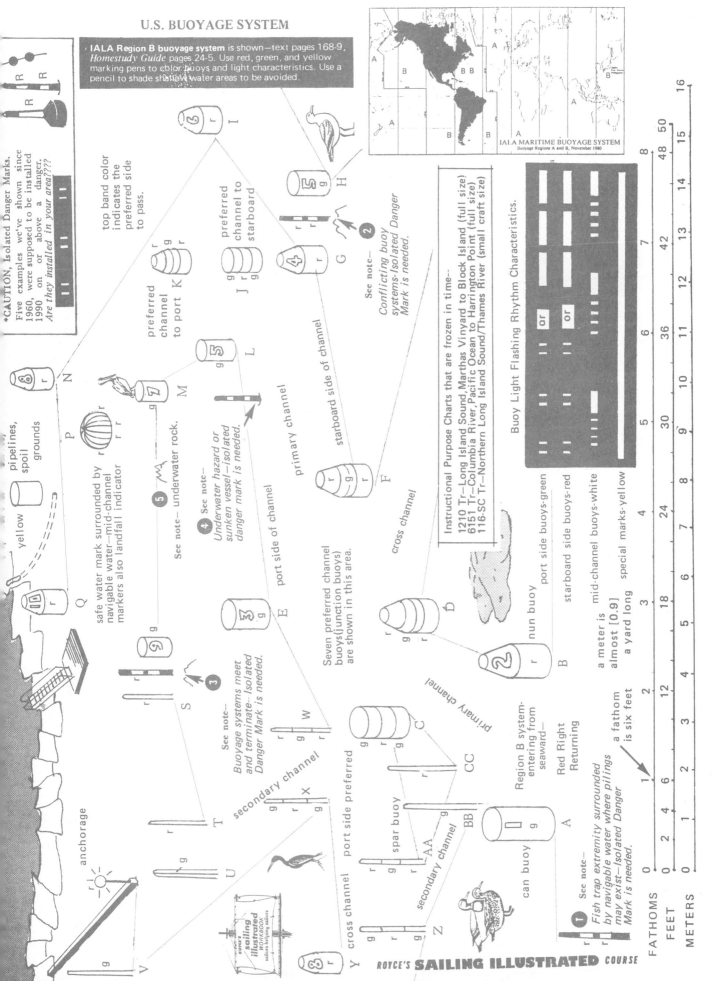

U.S. BUOYAGE SYSTEM

IALA Region B buoyage system is shown—text pages 168-9, *Homestudy Guide* pages 24-5. Use red, green, and yellow marking pens to color buoys and light characteristics. Use a pencil to shade shallow water areas to be avoided.

IALA MARITIME BUOYAGE SYSTEM
Buoyage Regions A and B, November 1980

*CAUTION, Isolated Danger Marks. Five examples we've shown since 1960, were supposed to be installed 1990, on or above a danger. *Are they installed in your area???*

top band color indicates the preferred side to pass.

preferred channel to starboard

preferred channel to port

See note— Conflicting buoy systems-Isolated Danger Mark is needed.

Buoy Light Flashing Rhythm Characteristics.

Instructional Purpose Charts that are frozen in time—
1210 Tr–Long Island Sound, Marthas Vinyard to Block Island (full size)
6151 Tr–Columbia River, Pacific Ocean to Harrington Point (full size)
116-SC Tr–Northern Long Island Sound/Thames River (small craft size)

pipelines, spoil grounds

yellow

safe water mark surrounded by navigable water-mid-channel markers also landfall indicator

See note— underwater rock.

See note— Underwater hazard or sunken vessel—Isolated danger mark is needed.

starboard side of channel

primary channel

port side of channel

cross channel

Seven preferred channel buoys(junction buoys) are shown in this area.

nun buoy

port side buoys-green

starboard side buoys-red

mid-channel buoys-white

special marks-yellow

a meter is almost [0.9] a yard long

a fathom is six feet

See note— Buoyage systems meet and terminate- Isolated Danger Mark is needed.

anchorage

secondary channel

cross channel

port side preferred

spar buoy

secondary channel

can buoy

Region B system- entering from seaward—

Red Right Returning

See note— Fish trap extremity surrounded by navigable water where pilings may exist—Isolated Danger Mark is needed.

See note— Fish trap extremity surrounded by navigable water where pilings may exist—Isolated Danger Mark is needed.

primary channel

ROYCE'S **SAILING ILLUSTRATED** COURSE

sailing illustrated WORKBOOK sailors helping sailors

9

FATHOMS
FEET
METERS

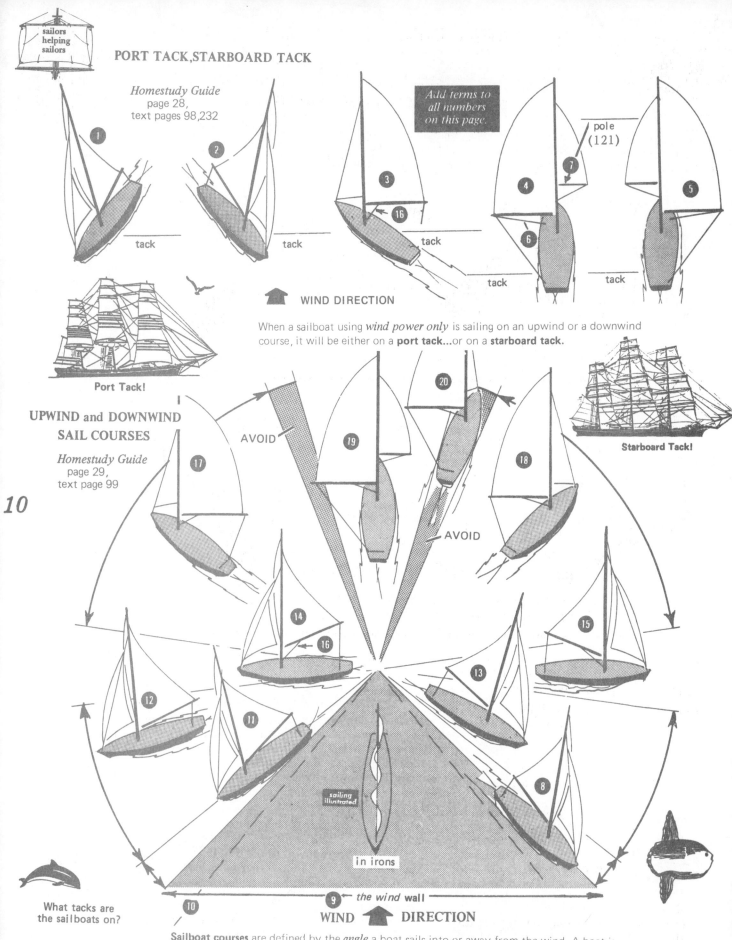

PORT TACK, STARBOARD TACK

Homestudy Guide
page 28,
text pages 98, 232

Add terms to
all numbers
on this page.

pole
(121)

tack

tack

tack

tack

tack

tack

▲ WIND DIRECTION

When a sailboat using *wind power only* is sailing on an upwind or a downwind course, it will be either on a **port tack**...or on a **starboard tack**.

Port Tack!

Starboard Tack!

UPWIND and DOWNWIND SAIL COURSES

Homestudy Guide
page 29,
text page 99

10

AVOID

AVOID

sailing
illustrated

in irons

What tacks are
the sailboats on?

← *the wind* wall →

WIND ▲ DIRECTION

Sailboat courses are defined by the *angle* a boat sails into or away from the wind. A boat is sailing **closehauled** when sailing as **close** to the wind as efficiency permits, and the sheets are **hauled** as tight as efficiency permits... **running downwind**... or **reaching,** comprised between the extremes of running and sailing closehauled.

ROYCE'S **SAILING ILLUSTRATED** *COURSE*

Laminated Right-of-Way Charts in three colors, have been prepared for your use by the author, approx. 8½ x 11 inches, with the sailboat rules on one side, and powerboat rules on the other. This chart is an excellent method to introduce a new helmsman to these complex operational rules.

ROYCE'S **SAILING ILLUSTRATED** COURSE

"I suppose youse gentlemen know the rules regarding my sailboat right-of-way!"

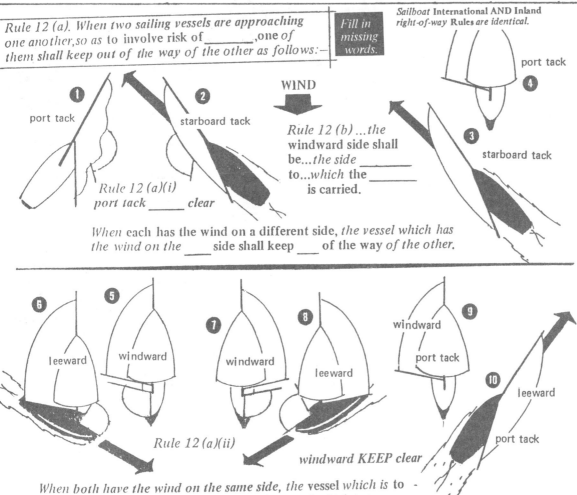

Rule 12 (a). When two sailing vessels are approaching one another, so as to involve risk of _____, one of them shall keep out of the way of the other as follows:—

Fill in missing words.

Sailboat International AND Inland right-of-way **Rules** are identical.

port tack

port tack

starboard tack

WIND

Rule 12 (b) ...the windward side shall be...the side _____ to...which the _____ is carried.

starboard tack

Rule 12 (a)(i) port tack _____ clear

When each has the wind on a different side, the vessel which has the wind on the ___ side shall keep ___ of the way of the other.

leeward

windward

windward

leeward

windward

port tack

leeward

port tack

Rule 12 (a)(ii)

windward KEEP clear

When both have the wind on the same side, the vessel which is to - _____ shall keep ___ of the way of the vessel which is to _____.

11

Rule 2 (a)—Nothing in these rules....shall exonerate any...master or crew... from the consequence of the neglect to comply with these Rules. If your vessel is involved in a collision and you didn't know the rules, ignorance becomes a questionable defense. If your vessel has the right-of-way, and you want to be a nice guy giving the right-of-way to another vessel and a collision results...you are in trouble for breaking Rule 2 (a).

Admiralty law exists for a single purpose—to prevent collisions. You have strict regulations to follow to avoid collisions, yet when a collision is inevitable, you are ordered to break some or all the rules to prevent a collision. You then begin to realize the basic concept in an unclear situation, **is to initiate action so both vessels will have time to maneuver out of a misunderstanding.**

© 1985 by Patrick M. Royce, from *Sailing Illustrated Homestudy Guide*

Responsibilities Between Vessels—Rule 18 (a):
A power-driven vessel underway shall keep out of the way of: *(iv) a sailing vessel. Exceptions are—*
Rule 9—Narrow Channels   Rule 10—Traffic Separation Schemes   Rule 13—Overtaking.

Overtaking, Rule 13 (b). A vessel shall be deemed to be _____ when coming up... from a direction more than 22.5 degrees abaft her beam...to the vessel she is overtaking.
Rule 13 (d)...keeping clear of the overtaken vessel until she is finally ___ and ___.

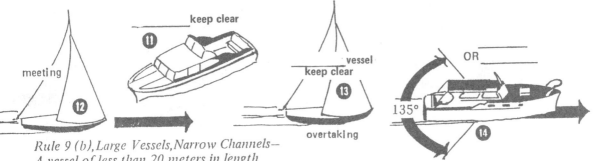

meeting

keep clear

vessel
keep clear

OR _____

135°

Rule 9 (b), Large Vessels, Narrow Channels—A vessel of less than 20 meters in length (65.7 feet) or a sailboat shall ___ impede the passage of a vessel that can safely navigate only within a narrow channel.

overtaking

Overtaking, Rule 13 (a). Nonwithstanding anything contained in the Rules... any vessel _____ ... shall keep ___ of the way of the vessel being _____

Admiralty law is highly complex differing considerably from auto driving regulations.
Homestudy Guide pages 26, 27, 30, 31, 143-9, provide variables of Admiralty law.

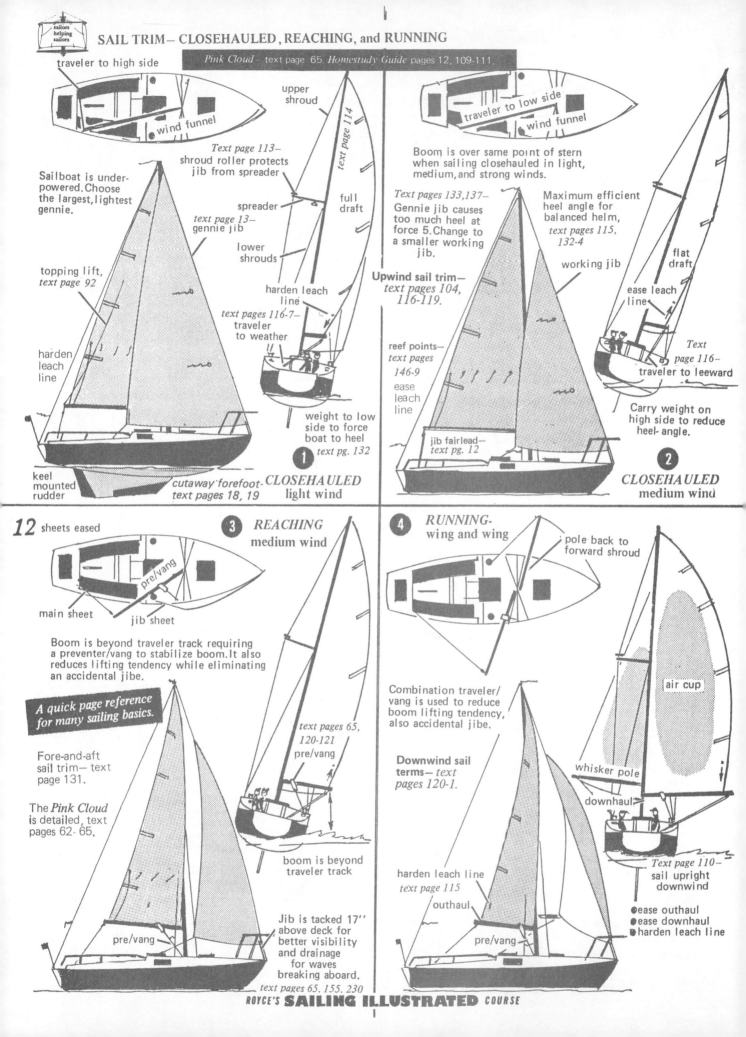

traveler to high side

wind funnel

upper shroud

text page 114

Sailboat is under-powered. Choose the largest, lightest gennie.

Text page 113– shroud roller protects jib from spreader

spreader

text page 13– gennie jib

lower shrouds

full draft

topping lift, *text page 92*

harden leach line

harden leach line

text pages 116-7– traveler to weather

weight to low side to force boat to heel *text pg. 132*

keel mounted rudder

cutaway forefoot- *text pages 18, 19*

① CLOSEHAULED light wind

traveler to low side

wind funnel

Boom is over same point of stern when sailing closehauled in light, medium, and strong winds.

Text pages 133,137– Gennie jib causes too much heel at force 5. Change to a smaller working jib.

Upwind sail trim— *text pages 104, 116-119.*

Maximum efficient heel angle for balanced helm, *text pages 115, 132-4*

working jib

reef points— *text pages 146-9*

ease leach line

jib fairlead— *text pg. 12*

flat draft

ease leach line

Text page 116– traveler to leeward

Carry weight on high side to reduce heel- angle.

② CLOSEHAULED medium wind

12 sheets eased

③ REACHING medium wind

pre/vang

main sheet

jib sheet

Boom is beyond traveler track requiring a preventer/vang to stabilize boom. It also reduces lifting tendency while eliminating an accidental jibe.

A quick page reference for many sailing basics.

Fore-and-aft sail trim— text page 131.

The *Pink Cloud* is detailed, text pages 62- 65.

text pages 65, 120-121 pre/vang

pre/vang

boom is beyond traveler track

Jib is tacked 17" above deck for better visibility and drainage for waves breaking aboard. *text pages 65, 155, 230*

④ RUNNING- wing and wing

pole back to forward shroud

Combination traveler/ vang is used to reduce boom lifting tendency, also accidental jibe.

Downwind sail terms— *text pages 120-1.*

harden leach line *text page 115*

outhaul

pre/vang

air cup

whisker pole

downhaul

Text page 110– sail upright downwind

- ● ease outhaul
- ● ease downhaul
- ● harden leach line

Wind Force— workbook page 35.
Hull Balance— inside back cover.

sailors helping sailors

1 Force 2, sailing closehauled. *Crew weight on low side, use large genoa jib. Full-draft mainsail— harden leach line, traveler car to high side.*

2 Force 3, sailing closehauled. *Crew to low side, traveler car amidship.*

Luff is breaking— is sailboat pointing too high or pinching; should mainsail be hardened?

3 Force 5, sailing closehauled. *Crew to high side, traveler car to low side, flat draft mainsail— release leach line on main. Time to change from genoa jib to working jib.*

4 Force 6, sailing closehauled. *Tremendous weather helm, minimum drive, maximum leeway... too much mainsail area.*

5 Force 6, sailing closehauled. *First mainsail reef... maximum heel, time for 2nd reef?*

6 Force 7, sailing upwind. *Working jib only! Weight on high side, mainsail must be lashed down so it can't break loose underway.*

7 Force 5, beam reach. *Crew on high side.*

Boom end is beyond traveler track. **Boom vang or prevang** *is required to limit boom movement, to flatten mainsail for drive.*

The boom will lift and move considerably disturbing the mainsail airfoil, reducing hull speed if vang or prevang isn't hardened.

8 Force 3 to 5, **running downwind wing and wing.** *Harden leach line to cup mainsail, vang boom, whisker pole stabilizes jib.*

9 Approach mooring closehauled. *Jib is luffing. Mainsail luffs considerably to reduce speed, with upwind stability for the hull to quietly point into the wind.*

13

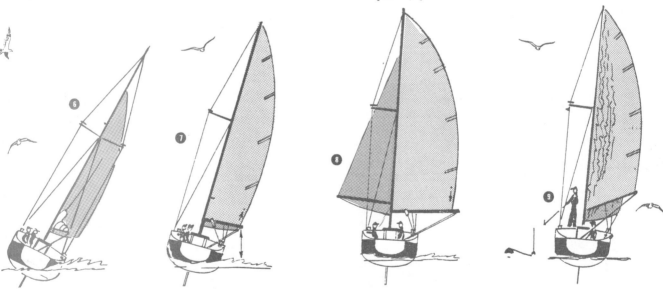

──── **The most difficult ideas we found while teaching on the water...** ────

Backing the jib— is often standard procedure on many light, wide-beam sailboats, while an overcompensation on heavy narrow hulls, except for unusual situations. Much practice is required for the timing. The jib sheet is held until the bow has turned sufficiently for the main to start filling, with the helmsman compensating to come about in the length of the sailboat... and be on course for the next tack.

Wind force to analyze wave pattern wind strength, has no similarity in other fields. Students continually try to change it to *Miles Per Hour* ignoring its purpose— to predict a storm moving in, with sails reefed to the expected wind force beforehand.

Hull balance— workbook, inside back cover. Continual practice and reference to that page is required as the factors involved have no similarity in other fields. Considerable practice is required to pull together the various forces for a balanced hull and rudder... plus ways to compensate for weather helm or lee helm in steady AND/OR changing weather conditions.

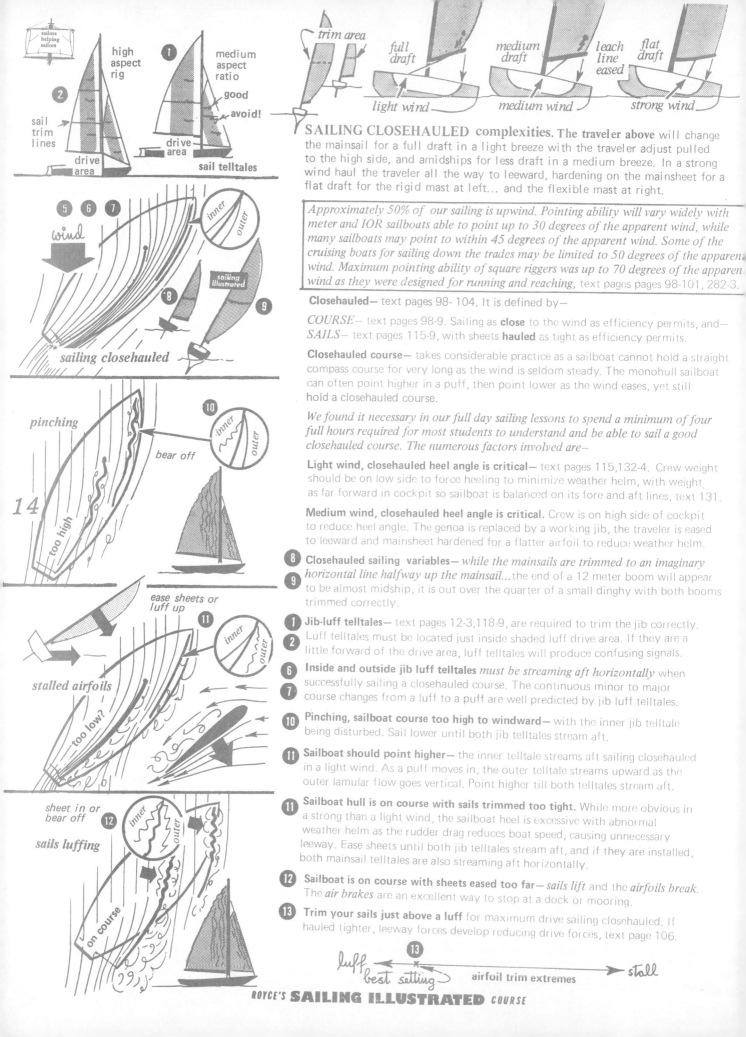

high aspect rig

medium aspect ratio
good
avoid!

sail trim lines

drive area

drive area

sail telltales

trim area
full draft
light wind

medium draft
leach line eased
medium wind

flat draft
strong wind

wind

inner
outer

sailing illustrated

sailing closehauled

pinching

bear off

inner
outer

14

too high

ease sheets or luff up

inner
outer

stalled airfoils

too low?

sheet in or bear off

sails luffing

inner
outer

on course

SAILING CLOSEHAULED complexities.
The traveler above will change the mainsail for a full draft in a light breeze with the traveler adjust pulled to the high side, and amidships for less draft in a medium breeze. In a strong wind haul the traveler all the way to leeward, hardening on the mainsheet for a flat draft for the rigid mast at left... and the flexible mast at right.

Approximately 50% of our sailing is upwind. Pointing ability will vary widely with meter and IOR sailboats able to point up to 30 degrees of the apparent wind, while many sailboats may point to within 45 degrees of the apparent wind. Some of the cruising boats for sailing down the trades may be limited to 50 degrees of the apparent wind. Maximum pointing ability of square riggers was up to 70 degrees of the apparent wind as they were designed for running and reaching, text pages pages 98-101, 282-3.

Closehauled— text pages 98- 104. It is defined by—

COURSE— text pages 98-9. Sailing as **close** to the wind as efficiency permits, and—
SAILS— text pages 115-9, with sheets **hauled** as tight as efficiency permits.

Closehauled course— takes considerable practice as a sailboat cannot hold a straight compass course for very long as the wind is seldom steady. The monohull sailboat can often point higher in a puff, then point lower as the wind eases, yet still hold a closehauled course.

We found it necessary in our full day sailing lessons to spend a minimum of four full hours required for most students to understand and be able to sail a good closehauled course. The numerous factors involved are—

Light wind, closehauled heel angle is critical— text pages 115,132-4. Crew weight should be on low side to force heeling to minimize weather helm, with weight as far forward in cockpit so sailboat is balanced on its fore and aft lines, text 131.

Medium wind, closehauled heel angle is critical. Crew is on high side of cockpit to reduce heel angle. The genoa is replaced by a working jib, the traveler is eased to leeward and mainsheet hardened for a flatter airfoil to reduce weather helm.

(8) (9) Closehauled sailing variables— *while the mainsails are trimmed to an imaginary horizontal line halfway up the mainsail...the end of a 12 meter boom will appear to be almost midship, it is out over the quarter of a small dinghy with both booms trimmed correctly.*

(1) (2) Jib-luff telltales— text pages 12-3,118-9, are required to trim the jib correctly. Luff telltales must be located just inside shaded luff drive area. If they are a little forward of the drive area, luff telltales will produce confusing signals.

(6) (7) Inside and outside jib luff telltales *must be streaming aft horizontally* when successfully sailing a closehauled course. The continuous minor to major course changes from a luff to a puff are well predicted by jib luff telltales.

(10) Pinching, sailboat course too high to windward— with the inner jib telltale being disturbed. Sail lower until both jib telltales stream aft.

(11) Sailboat should point higher— the inner telltale streams aft sailing closehauled in a light wind. As a puff moves in, the outer telltale streams upward as the outer lamular flow goes vertical. Point higher till both telltales stream aft.

(11) Sailboat hull is on course with sails trimmed too tight. While more obvious in a strong than a light wind, the sailboat heel is excessive with abnormal weather helm as the rudder drag reduces boat speed, causing unnecessary leeway. Ease sheets until both jib telltales stream aft, and if they are installed, both mainsail telltales are also streaming aft horizontally.

(12) Sailboat is on course with sheets eased too far— *sails lift* and the *airfoils break*. The *air brakes* are an excellent way to stop at a dock or mooring.

(13) Trim your sails just above a luff for maximum drive sailing closehauled. If hauled tighter, leeway forces develop reducing drive forces, text page 106.

luff
(13)
best sailing   airfoil trim extremes   stall

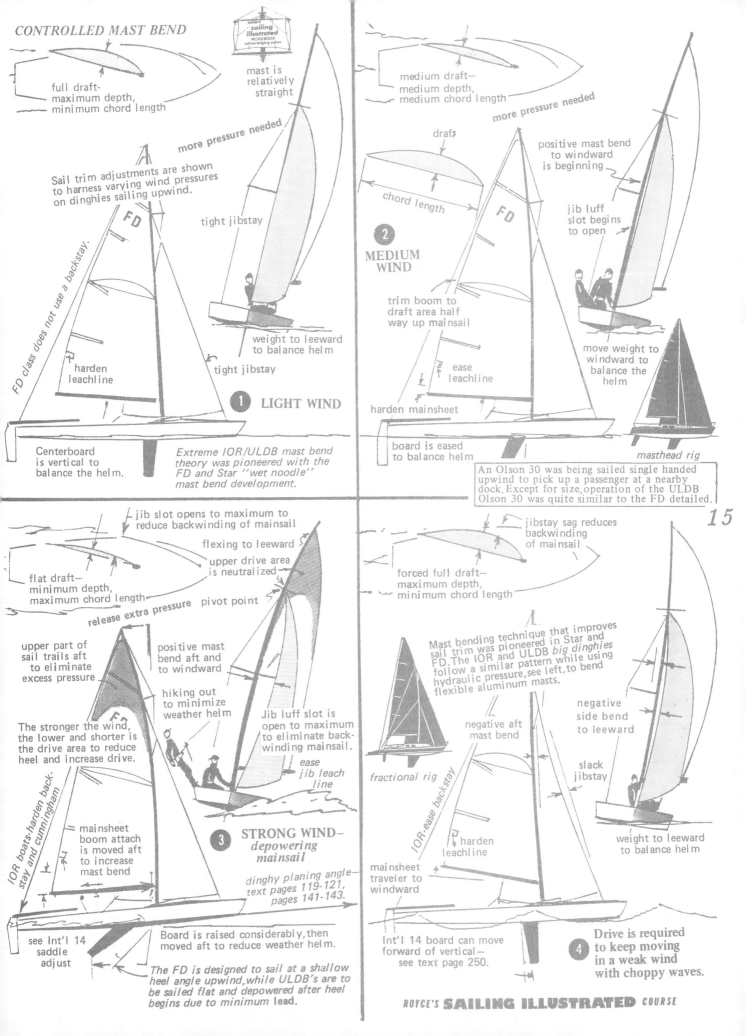

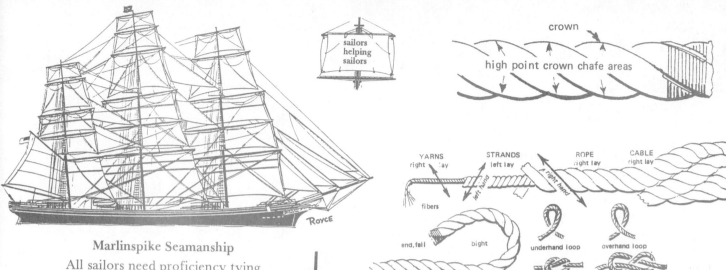

sailors helping sailors

crown

high point crown chafe areas

YARNS right lay · STRANDS left lay · ROPE right lay · CABLE right lay

fibers

end, fall · bight

underhand loop · overhand loop

standing part

overhand knot · figure 8 knot

Marlinspike Seamanship

All sailors need proficiency tying basic knots, splicing, coiling lines, and whipping rope ends.

3- strand eye splice has endless applications on the boat, farm, and warehouse. The method has changed little from an eye splice found in an Egyptian tomb 7000 years old.

Coiling rope is required for storage, coiling halyards, etc. The coil must run freely when released.

Braided heaving line has endless uses from 12' dinghies to large sailboats. *Avoid 3 strand heaving lines* subjected to unexpected snafu's in critical situations... though used by professionals.

16

Permanent whipping requires needle and thread, especially for synthetic rope with slippery surfaces.

Braided eye splice has many uses, pages 195-9. Follow each step in the sequence shown.

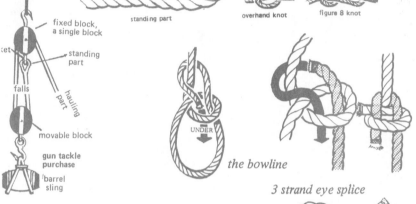

fixed block, a single block

standing part

falls

hauling part

movable block

gun tackle purchase

barrel sling

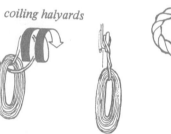

the bowline

3 strand eye splice

coiling halyards

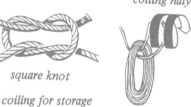

square knot

coiling for storage

① ② ③ ④

the braided heaving line

whipping

McGrew Fid-O ®

spade point · spike · hollow handle

McGrew splicing video and tools—
8120 Rio Linda Blvd., Elverta, CA 95626

ROYCE'S SAILING ILLUSTRATED COURSE

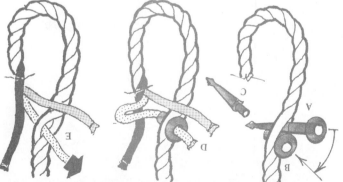

Splicing for right-handed sailors...

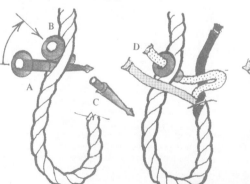

Splicing for left-handed sailors...

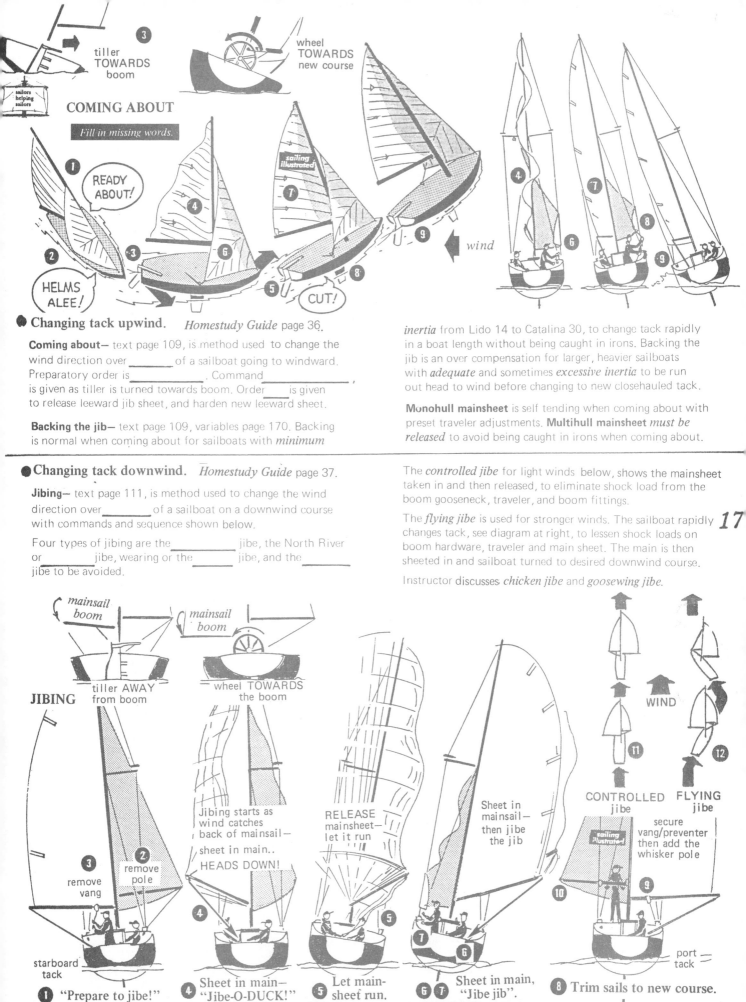

tiller TOWARDS boom

wheel TOWARDS new course

COMING ABOUT

Fill in missing words.

READY ABOUT!

HELMS ALEE!

CUT!

wind

● **Changing tack upwind.** *Homestudy Guide* page 36.

Coming about— text page 109, is method used to change the wind direction over _____ of a sailboat going to windward. Preparatory order is _____. Command _____ is given as tiller is turned towards boom. Order ____ is given to release leeward jib sheet, and harden new leeward sheet.

Backing the jib— text page 109, variables page 170. Backing is normal when coming about for sailboats with *minimum*

inertia from Lido 14 to Catalina 30, to change tack rapidly in a boat length without being caught in irons. Backing the jib is an over compensation for larger, heavier sailboats with *adequate* and sometimes *excessive inertia* to be run out head to wind before changing to new closehauled tack.

Monohull mainsheet is self tending when coming about with preset traveler adjustments. **Multihull mainsheet** *must be released* to avoid being caught in irons when coming about.

● **Changing tack downwind.** *Homestudy Guide* page 37.

Jibing— text page 111, is method used to change the wind direction over _____ of a sailboat on a downwind course with commands and sequence shown below.

Four types of jibing are the _____ jibe, the North River or _____ jibe, wearing or the _____ jibe, and the _____ jibe to be avoided.

The *controlled jibe* for light winds below, shows the mainsheet taken in and then released, to eliminate shock load from the boom gooseneck, traveler, and boom fittings.

The *flying jibe* is used for stronger winds. The sailboat rapidly changes tack, see diagram at right, to lessen shock loads on boom hardware, traveler and main sheet. The main is then sheeted in and sailboat turned to desired downwind course.

Instructor discusses *chicken jibe* and *goosewing jibe*.

17

mainsail boom

mainsail boom

tiller AWAY from boom

wheel TOWARDS the boom

JIBING

3 remove vang

2 remove pole

1 starboard tack
"Prepare to jibe!"

Jibing starts as wind catches back of mainsail—sheet in main.. HEADS DOWN!

4 Sheet in main—"Jibe-O-DUCK!"

RELEASE mainsheet—let it run

5 Let mainsheet run.

Sheet in mainsail—then jibe the jib

6 7 Sheet in main, "Jibe jib".

WIND

11 CONTROLLED jibe

12 FLYING jibe

secure vang/preventer then add the whisker pole

10

9

port tack

8 Trim sails to new course.

TIDE, CURRENT, TIDAL CURRENT, FOG.

text pages 220-1

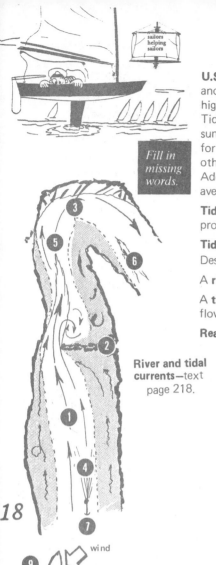

Fill in missing words.

River and tidal currents—text page 218.

U.S. tidal day— requires approx.. 24 hours and 50 minutes, corresponding to two highs, and two lows in a full tidal day. Tide results from gravitational pull of sun and moon alternately pulling together for maximum tides, and against each other producing minimal tide ranges. Add terms at right for maximum, average, and minimal tidal ranges.

Tidal surges caused by hurricanes produce even greater tidal ranges.

Tidal wave or *tsunamis*— text pg. 220. Describe its action on a facing ocean beach...then on a sailboat in mid ocean.

A **river current** has a horizontal one-way flow caused by_____

A **tidal current** results when a tide change also causes a_____ directional current flow such as found on the lower reaches of the Hudson River.

Reading the river current— is required by many sailors across the U.S. at left. Fill in blanks—

Current flow is normally smoother and faster in the_____ , while it is_____ and_____next to the river banks.

The open center of a V pointing downstream indicates_____depth.

The tip of a V pointing upstream indicates a _____ , an underwater _____ , or a mooring; give it maximum upstream clearance.

Deeper water will be on the _____ of a bend next to the higher side of a river bank.

Shallower, more disturbed water will be on the_____of a river bend.

A whirlpool can develop on the _____ stream side of the jetty end.

Leebowing— a sailboat makes better headway towards its destination with the current on its _____ bow.

While river patterns are rather constant, the tidal current will_____direction in the lower reaches of the Hudson and other rivers. To this add a strong wind going with the current, against it, or at an angle to the current flow.

18

wind

current

FOG PREDICTABILITY— text pages 222-3.

Fog has been the enemy of sailors since they first went to sea. It was one of the worst fears facing Vikings until they found the compass. We show a fresh, new temperature/ relative humidity indicator at right.

Moisture particles in suspension.

Air contains water vapor invisible below the saturation or_____point.

Heavy falling moisture particles.

With an inflow of moist air, or a temperature drop, a light fog develops. It provides enough visibility for sailboat displacement speed operation, while not enough visibility for planing powerboat operational speed. It doesn't allow enough visibility at night for sailboat or powerboat operation.

Heavy blanket of moisture particles.

As humidity increases, the light fog may lift with excellent visibility. A peasoup fog can move in, be over a hill, or a couple of miles away.

Time lag. One exists from a half hour to five hours before a fog moves in. Your boat may be in the middle of a peasoup fog while the humidity is down to 50% or 60%. The same time lag also occurs most of the time as the fog wants to move out.

The time lag, puzzling at first, becomes the sailor's best friend after he can anticipate and avoid being caught unexpectedly in an incoming fog. Inexpensive temperature/ humidity indicators we tested developed a 5% humidity error or more in 10 to 12 months requiring replacement.

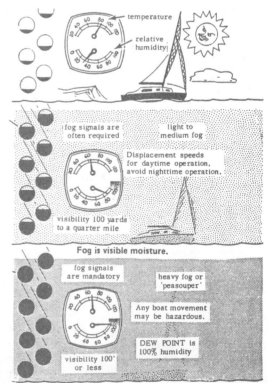

temperature

relative humidity

fog signals are often required

light to medium fog

Displacement speeds for daytime operation, avoid nighttime operation.

visibility 100 yards to a quarter mile

Fog is visible moisture.

fog signals are mandatory

heavy fog or 'peasouper'

Any boat movement may be hazardous.

DEW POINT is 100% humidity

visibility 100' or less

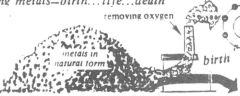 

removing oxygen

birth

life

death

Oxygen combines easily due to two missing electrons.

metals in natural form

metals again in natural form

stable chemical compounds   refining   useful refined metal products   stable chemical oxides & compounds

HEMATITE (red iron-oxide ore) ...becomes pig iron...changes to iron,steel compounds & alloys...corrodes to a brown powder (iron oxide)

BAUXITE is refined to Alumina (aluminum oxide)..to become aluminum compounds and alloys...corrodes to a white powder (aluminum oxide)

Birth, life, and destruction of seagoing metals.

Most seagoing metals exist temporarily in their refined condition. They begin as stable compounds of nature. The oxygen is removed or "cooked out" at the refinery so that the raw products can be refined into compounds and alloys for our seagoing use. Our responsibility is to choose stable metals, then apply a wide variety of corrosion prevention methods to extend their useful life *before they return to more stable oxides* which we can no longer use.

BASIC ELEMENTS only-- the electromotive series	
protected end-cathodic TAKERS	
flourine	+2.85
chlorine,gold	+1.36
platinum	+0.92
silver	+0.80
copper	+0.34
hydrogen	0.00
lead	-0.12
tin	-0.14
nickel	-0.23
iron	-0.44
chromium	-0.557
zinc	-0.76
manganese	-1.10
aluminum	-1.70
magnesium	-1.86
corroding end-anodic GIVERS	

Metal destruction can be speeded up by—

● **Oxidation corrosion.** *Salt spray* dries on ocean metals in warm sunshine, the always thirsty ocean salts pulling in moisture at night to produce _____ rust on steel, _____ rust on aluminum. Wash off ocean salts with fresh water to minimize corrosion action. Wash cameras, etc., with _____ water having all minerals and salts removed.

Carbon steel —_____ with approx. 2% _____, produces excellent nails for houses, and tools for protected land use. Carbon steel corrodes rapidly while expanding in diameter.

● **Oxidation corrosion expansion.** Openings in a shackle shrink, as its bolt diameter expands. Pressures increase against each other until the bolt cannot be removed.

● *The stainless family* is designed to _____ at a programmed rate above the water using chromium ions for turnbuckles, shrouds, etc., requiring a continuous oxygen flow and spray drainage. If taped in a small area, the ions may panic rushing to the area causing _____ corrosion. Avoid stainless underwater fittings due to oxygen variables.

● The marine *bronze family compounds* are excellent for use above the water corroding with a dirty face. Turnbuckles can be _____ to seal out oxygen for topside use.

Choose the bronze family for _____ fittings. The more expensive bronzes have longer lifetime potentials as they go thru more corrosion steps before failure.

19

GALVANIC SERIES— compounds and alloys
protected end— cathodic TAKERS
platinum
gold
graphite
silver
*18-8-3 stainless***
*18-8 stainless***
*chromium-iron***
*Inconel***
*nickel***
silver solder
Monel
copper-nickel alloys
bronzes
copper
brasses
*Inconel**
*nickel**
tin
lead
lead-tin solders
*18-8-3 stainless**
*18-8 stainless**
Ni-Resist
aluminum-iron
cast iron
steel or iron
aluminum 17ST
cadmium
aluminum 2 S
zinc
magnesium alloys
magnesium
corroding end— anodic GIVERS
*active
**passive

● *Brass is a confusing term.* It refers to stable **bronze compounds** in marine stores, while in home-improvement stores it is a shiny gold **mixture of** _____ and _____. The unstable **mixture** rapidly dezincs on the ocean leaving a weak copper shell. Even when sealed in a wooden bulkhead, copper/zinc screws rapidly dezinc due to resin electrolytes in the wood.

● **Galvanic corrosion.** *Zinc* is a chemically active underwater _____ metal protecting nearby bronzes. When an imbalance occurs starting an underwater ion exchange called galvanic corrosion or action, the zinc flows out to nearby metals to protect them. When a zinc block corrodes rapidly, replace with a same size or smaller block until the **problem** is found, as a larger zinc block may _____ the corrosion action. Don't PAINT underwater zinc blocks as it neutralizes and stops their protective action underwater.

● **Electrolysis—** *break the* _____! An hour after turning on a battery charger, the owner returned to his boat finding both outboard motor lower units missing under the water. Shore current flowed to the batteries, thru electrical harnesses to the powerheads, and down the lower units in the water... flowing out to nearby metal parts under the water.

● *Aluminum* uses electrolysis corrosion called anodizing to develop a corrosion _____ for masts, toe rails, etc., with heavy black anodizing preferred. When the surface barrier is broken by chafe, coat with zinc paint to reduce further corrosion action beneath.

● **Intergranular corrosion—** *stress fatigue.* Approximately _____ parts support the mast of a 30' sloop. A dismasting occurs when one or more parts fail after they lose strength thru aging, with the fatigue process speeded by overstressing. Check all parts periodically for replacement *before* their failure contributes to a dismasting in heavy weather.

Study pages 126-135 of *Sailing Illustrated Homestudy Guide*, pages 180-1 of *Sailing Illustrated*.

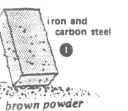

iron and carbon steel

① *brown powder*

② *surface damage*

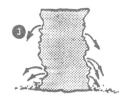

③ *major damage*

④ *total damage*

basic aluminum

⑤ *white powder*

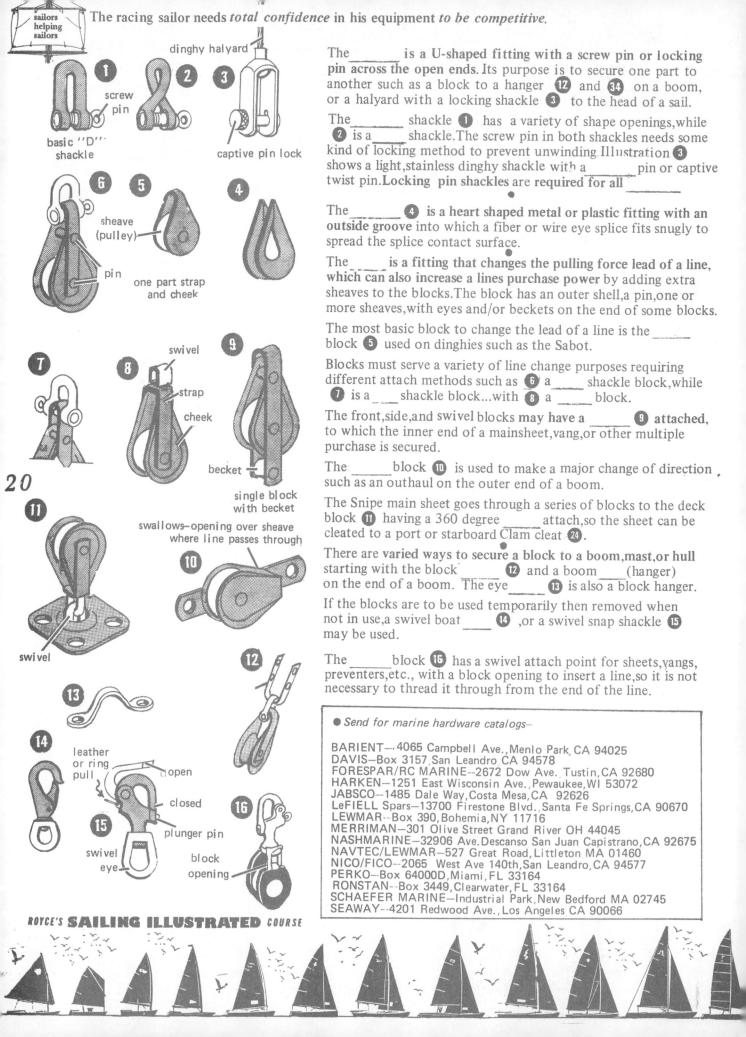

The racing sailor needs *total confidence* in his equipment *to be competitive*.

screw pin

basic "D" shackle

dinghy halyard

captive pin lock

sheave (pulley)

pin

one part strap and cheek

swivel

strap

cheek

becket

single block with becket

swallows–opening over sheave where line passes through

20

swivel

leather or ring pull

open

closed

plunger pin

swivel eye

block opening

The _____ is a U-shaped fitting with a screw pin or locking pin across the open ends. Its purpose is to secure one part to another such as a block to a hanger ⑫ and ㉞ on a boom, or a halyard with a locking shackle ❸ to the head of a sail.

The _____ shackle ❶ has a variety of shape openings, while ❷ is a _____ shackle. The screw pin in both shackles needs some kind of locking method to prevent unwinding. Illustration ❸ shows a light, stainless dinghy shackle with a _____ pin or captive twist pin. Locking pin shackles are **required for all** _____

The _____ ❹ is a heart shaped metal or plastic fitting with an **outside groove** into which a fiber or wire eye splice fits snugly to spread the splice contact surface.

The _____ is a fitting that changes the pulling force lead of a line, **which can also increase a lines purchase power** by adding extra sheaves to the blocks. The block has an outer shell, a pin, one or more sheaves, with eyes and/or beckets on the end of some blocks.

The most basic block to change the lead of a line is the _____ block ❺ used on dinghies such as the Sabot.

Blocks must serve a variety of line change purposes requiring different attach methods such as ❻ a _____ shackle block, while ❼ is a _____ shackle block...with ❽ a _____ block.

The front, side, and swivel blocks **may have a** _____ ❾ **attached**, to which the inner end of a mainsheet, vang, or other multiple purchase is secured.

The _____ block ❿ is used to make a major change of direction such as an outhaul on the outer end of a boom.

The Snipe main sheet goes through a series of blocks to the deck block ⑪ having a 360 degree _____ attach, so the sheet can be cleated to a port or starboard Clam cleat ㉔.

There are **varied ways to secure a block to a boom, mast, or hull** starting with the block _____ ⑫ and a boom _____ (hanger) on the end of a boom. The eye _____ ⑬ is also a block hanger.

If the blocks are to be used temporarily then removed when not in use, a swivel boat _____ ⑭, or a swivel snap shackle ⑮ may be used.

The _____ block ⑯ has a swivel attach point for sheets, vangs, preventers, etc., with a block opening to insert a line, so it is not necessary to thread it through from the end of the line.

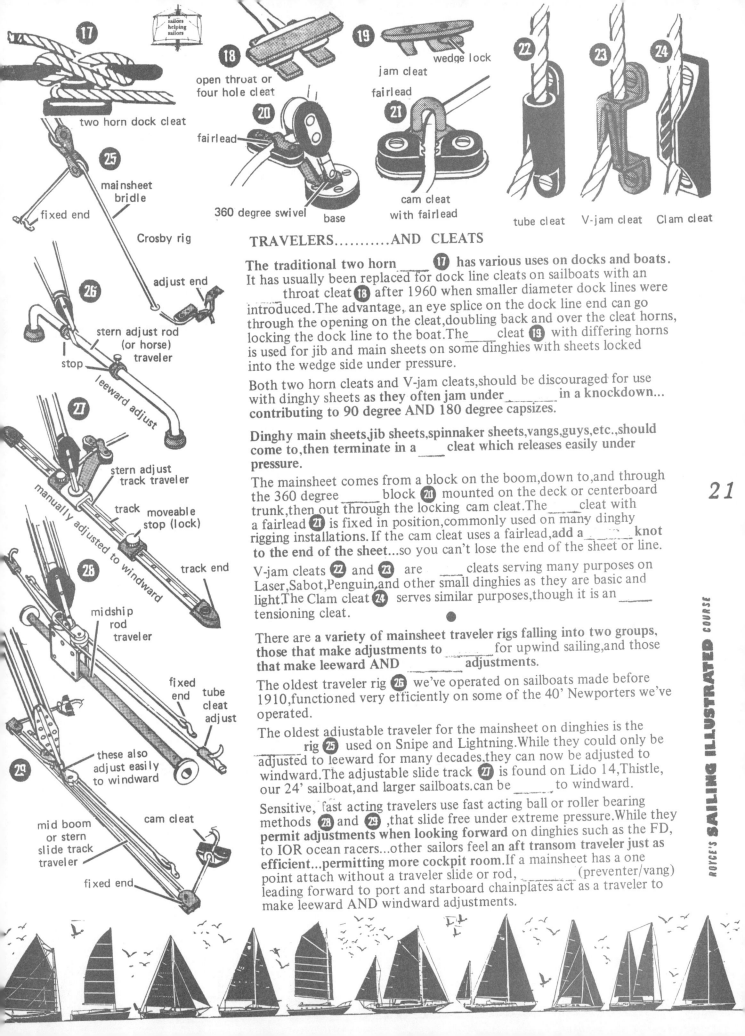

two horn dock cleat ⑰

open throat or four hole cleat ⑱

wedge lock

jam cleat ⑲

fairlead

⑳

fairlead

360 degree swivel base

cam cleat with fairlead ㉑

tube cleat ㉒ V-jam cleat ㉓ Clam cleat ㉔

mainsheet bridle ㉕

fixed end

Crosby rig

adjust end

stern adjust rod (or horse) traveler ㉖

stop

leeward adjust

stern adjust track traveler ㉗

track moveable stop (lock)

manually adjusted to windward

track end

midship rod traveler ㉘

fixed end

tube cleat adjust

these also adjust easily to windward

mid boom or stern slide track traveler ㉙

cam cleat

fixed end

TRAVELERS..........AND CLEATS

The traditional two horn _____ ⑰ **has various uses on docks and boats.**
It has usually been replaced for dock line cleats on sailboats with an
_____ throat cleat ⑱ after 1960 when smaller diameter dock lines were
introduced. The advantage, an eye splice on the dock line end can go
through the opening on the cleat, doubling back and over the cleat horns,
locking the dock line to the boat. The _____ cleat ⑲ with differing horns
is used for jib and main sheets on some dinghies with sheets locked
into the wedge side under pressure.

Both two horn cleats and V-jam cleats, should be discouraged for use
with dinghy sheets **as they often jam under _____ in a knockdown...
contributing to 90 degree AND 180 degree capsizes.**

**Dinghy main sheets, jib sheets, spinnaker sheets, vangs, guys, etc., should
come to, then terminate in a _____ cleat which releases easily under
pressure.**

The mainsheet comes from a block on the boom, down to, and through
the 360 degree _____ block ⑳ mounted on the deck or centerboard
trunk, then out through the locking cam cleat. The _____ cleat with
a fairlead ㉑ is fixed in position, commonly used on many dinghy
rigging installations. If the cam cleat uses a fairlead, **add a _____ knot
to the end of the sheet...so you can't lose the end of the sheet or line.**

V-jam cleats ㉒ and ㉓ are _____ cleats serving many purposes on
Laser, Sabot, Penguin, and other small dinghies as they are basic and
light. The Clam cleat ㉔ serves similar purposes, though it is an _____
tensioning cleat.

There are **a variety of mainsheet traveler rigs falling into two groups,
those that make adjustments to _____ for upwind sailing, and those
that make leeward AND _____ adjustments.**

The oldest traveler rig ㉖ we've operated on sailboats made before
1910, functioned very efficiently on some of the 40' Newporters we've
operated.

The oldest adjustable traveler for the mainsheet on dinghies is the
_____ rig ㉕ used on Snipe and Lightning. While they could only be
adjusted to leeward for many decades, they can now be adjusted to
windward. The adjustable slide track ㉗ is found on Lido 14, Thistle,
our 24' sailboat, and larger sailboats. can be _____ to windward.

Sensitive, fast acting travelers use fast acting ball or roller bearing
methods ㉘ and ㉙, that slide free under extreme pressure. While they
permit adjustments when looking forward on dinghies such as the FD,
to IOR ocean racers...other sailors feel **an aft transom traveler just as
efficient...permitting more cockpit room.** If a mainsheet has a one
point attach without a traveler slide or rod, _____ (preventer/vang)
leading forward to port and starboard chainplates act as a traveler to
make leeward AND windward adjustments.

21

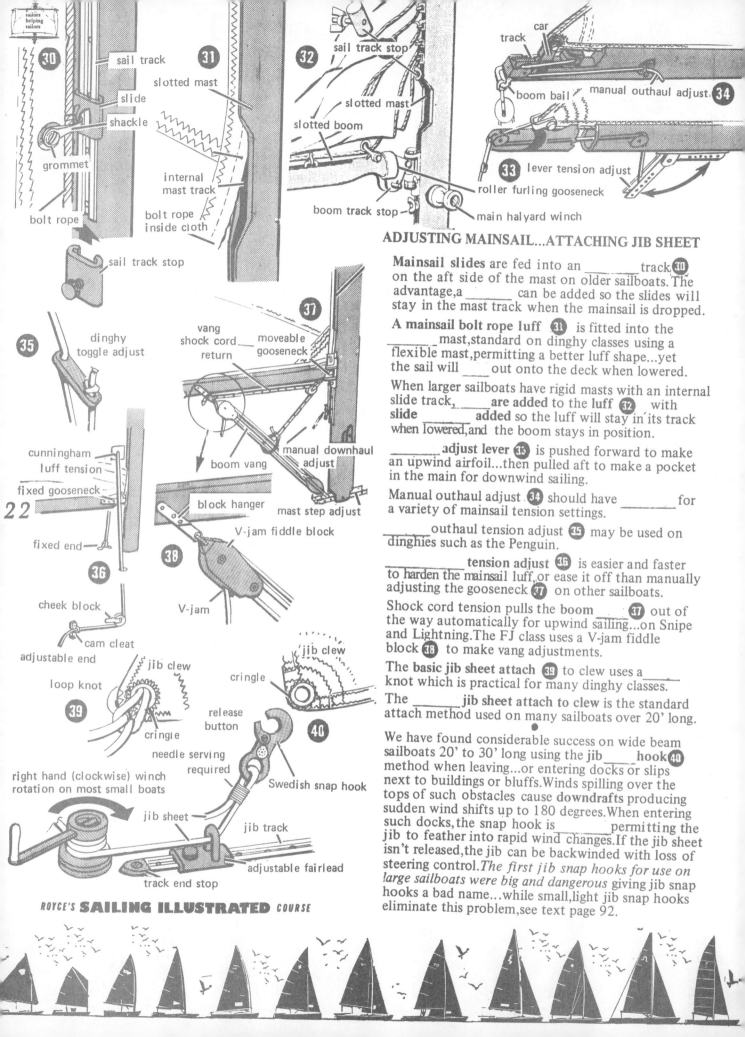

30 sail track
slide
shackle
grommet
bolt rope

31 slotted mast
internal mast track
bolt rope inside cloth

sail track stop

32 sail track stop
slotted mast
slotted boom
boom track stop

car
track
34 manual outhaul adjust.
boom bail
33 lever tension adjust
roller furling gooseneck
main halyard winch

35 dinghy toggle adjust

37 vang shock cord return
moveable gooseneck
boom vang
manual downhaul adjust
block hanger
mast step adjust

cunningham luff tension
fixed gooseneck
22
fixed end
36 cheek block
cam cleat
adjustable end
loop knot
39 jib clew
cringle

38 V-jam fiddle block
V-jam

jib clew
cringle

release button
needle serving required
40 Swedish snap hook

right hand (clockwise) winch rotation on most small boats
jib sheet
jib track
track end stop
adjustable fairlead

ADJUSTING MAINSAIL...ATTACHING JIB SHEET

Mainsail slides are fed into an _____ track **30** on the aft side of the mast on older sailboats. The advantage,a _____ can be added so the slides will stay in the mast track when the mainsail is dropped.

A mainsail bolt rope luff **31** is fitted into the _____ mast,standard on dinghy classes using a flexible mast,permitting a better luff shape...yet the sail will ____ out onto the deck when lowered.

When larger sailboats have rigid masts with an internal slide track, _____ **are added** to the **luff** **32** with **slide** _____ **added** so the luff will stay in its track when lowered,and the boom stays in position.

_____ **adjust lever** **33** is pushed forward to make an upwind airfoil...then pulled aft to make a pocket in the main for downwind sailing.

Manual outhaul adjust **34** should have _____ for a variety of mainsail tension settings.

_____ outhaul tension adjust **35** may be used on dinghies such as the Penguin.

_____ **tension adjust** **36** is easier and faster to harden the mainsail luff,or ease it off than manually adjusting the gooseneck **37** on other sailboats.

Shock cord tension pulls the boom ____ **37** out of the way automatically for upwind sailing...on Snipe and Lightning.The FJ class uses a V-jam fiddle block **38** to make vang adjustments.

The **basic jib sheet attach** **39** to clew uses a _____ knot which is practical for many dinghy classes.

The _____ **jib sheet attach** to clew is the standard attach method used on many sailboats over 20' long.

We have found considerable success on wide beam sailboats 20' to 30' long using the jib ____ hook **40** method when leaving...or entering docks or slips next to buildings or bluffs.Winds spilling over the tops of such obstacles cause **downdrafts** producing sudden wind shifts up to 180 degrees.When entering such docks,the snap hook is _____ permitting the jib to feather into rapid wind changes.If the jib sheet isn't released,the jib can be backwinded with loss of steering control.*The first jib snap hooks for use on large sailboats were big and dangerous* giving jib snap hooks a bad name...while small,light jib snap hooks eliminate this problem,see text page 92.

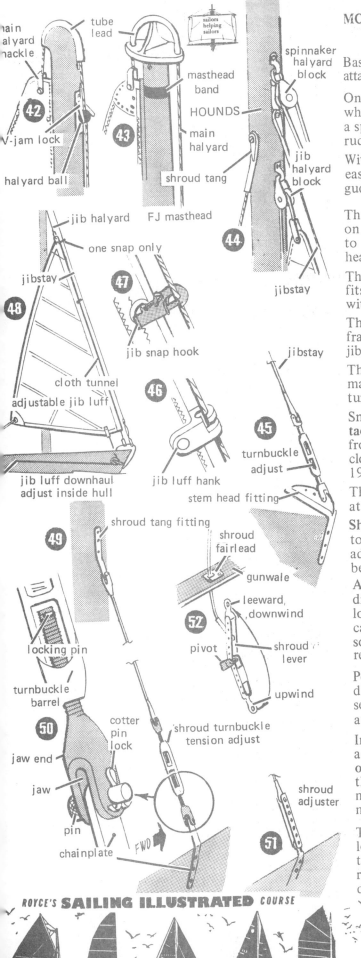

MORE HARDWARE DETAILS

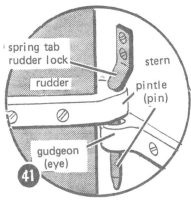

Basic ____ and ____ rudder attachment

One of the first items to consider when buying a dinghy is to add a spring tab or other kind of a rudder ____ as shown at right.

Without a locking method it is easy to lift the rudder out of the gudgeons when underway.

The **external** _____ **halyard** may lead through a tube on top of the mast 42 and 43 on Snipe and FJ classes, to make a 180 degree lead turn. This tube reduces masthead windage and weight.

The **mainsail halyard** ___ is used on Snipe and Star classes, fits into a V-jam lock with mainsail luff tension applied with the cunningham downhaul. 36

The **HOUNDS** (a British term) is the _____ area of a fractional rig **dinghy mast** 44 where the shrouds, jibstay, jib halyard, and spinnaker block are installed.

The **jibstay** is bolted to a ____ fitting on a fractional rig mast, goes to a _____ fitting on the bow 45 with a turnbuckle used to adjust jibstay tension.

Snipe, Lightning, Star, and other classes often use a **jib tack** _____ 48 so jib luff adjustments can be made from the cockpit. The jib wire luff rides inside the sail cloth tunnel. This adjustment was very popular in the 1960's before Dacron cloth had been fully stabilized.

The **upper shroud attach** to the mast, and the lower shroud attach parts are called _____ 49

Shroud tension is adjusted with _____ 50 attached to chainplates bolted to the hull. After shroud and stay adjustments have been completed, _____ pins should be added to eliminate turnbuckles from unwinding, or—

A new 30' sailboat launched in the Chicago area was dismasted two days later. The rigger forgot to add locking pins to the turnbuckles that unwound.. which can also occur to new metals during the first month or so on the ocean before sufficient corrosion begins to retard turnbuckle unwinding potentials.

Positive **locking shroud** _____ 51 are used on some dinghies where weight and windage factors are involved, secured to the chainplates...or below deck adjuster shown at left.

International 14, Thistle, and FD classes have taken shroud adjusting to the ultimate, using a **shroud lever** 52 **to cast off the** _____ **shroud for downwind sailing.** This eliminates the hard line a leeward shroud would put across the middle of the mainsail, dividing it into two air pockets. The mast tension downwind is carried on the windward shroud.

The lever must be pushed down before _____ to let the leeward shroud carry its load again, or changing course to sail upwind. We wonder when the leeward shroud release method will become the latest twelve meter dinghy discovery.

23

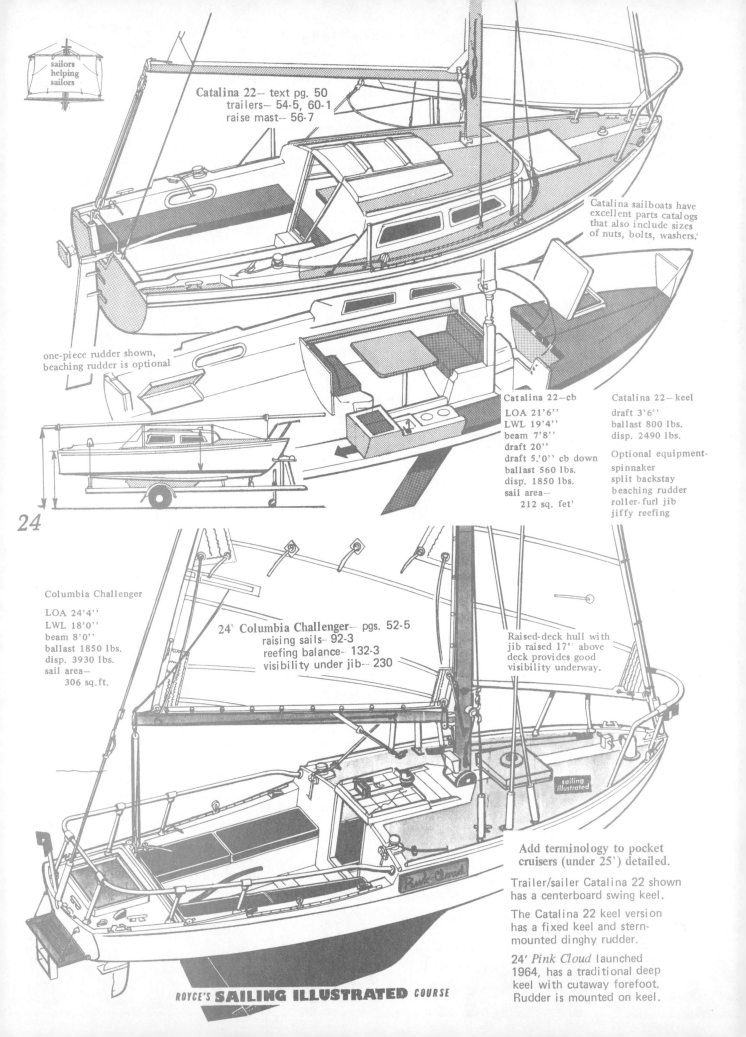

Catalina 22– text pg. 50
trailers– 54-5, 60-1
raise mast– 56-7

Catalina sailboats have
excellent parts catalogs
that also include sizes
of nuts, bolts, washers.

one-piece rudder shown,
beaching rudder is optional

Catalina 22–cb
LOA 21'6''
LWL 19'4''
beam 7'8''
draft 20''
draft 5.'0'' cb down
ballast 560 lbs.
disp. 1850 lbs.
sail area–
    212 sq. fet'

Catalina 22– keel
draft 3'6''
ballast 800 lbs.
disp. 2490 lbs.

Optional equipment–
spinnaker
split backstay
beaching rudder
roller-furl jib
jiffy reefing

24

Columbia Challenger

LOA 24'4''
LWL 18'0''
beam 8'0''
ballast 1850 lbs.
disp. 3930 lbs.
sail area–
    306 sq.ft.

24' Columbia Challenger– pgs. 52-5
    raising sails– 92-3
    reefing balance– 132-3
    visibility under jib– 230

Raised-deck hull with
jib raised 17'' above
deck provides good
visibility underway.

sailing
illustrated

**Add terminology to pocket
cruisers (under 25') detailed.**

Trailer/sailer Catalina 22 shown
has a centerboard swing keel.

The Catalina 22 keel version
has a fixed keel and stern-
mounted dinghy rudder.

24' *Pink Cloud* launched
1964, has a traditional deep
keel with cutaway forefoot.
Rudder is mounted on keel.

ROYCE'S **SAILING ILLUSTRATED** COURSE

sailors helping sailors

The downwind dead-stick landing has many potentials with a good crew.

the best method to leave your dock or mooring.

weathercock the bow

wind vane weathercock

① ②

downwind helm

wind direction

topping lift supports boom

downwind stability desired / downwind helm

weathercock the stern

① ②

upwind helm

upwind stability desired

topping lift is hardened

topping lift is eased

sail lowering directional stability

wind vane weathercock

① ②

downwind helm

wind direction

downwind stability desired / downwind helm

weathercock the stern

① ②

upwind helm

upwind stability desired

sail raising directional stability

topping lifts hardened

upwind helm

release painter

back jib

Leaving slip downwind—

ROYCE'S **SAILING ILLUSTRATED** COURSE

A big sailboat is a big dinghy. The sail raising and lowering sequence shown applies equally to a Snipe and a 100' schooner with more masts and sails. The basic difference is the amount of inertia to start the vessel sailing so it will respond to the rudder, and to run out of inertia to stop at a mooring or dock.

Lowering sails upwind— text page 87. The ketch goes head to wind with all sails luffing, as sails become air brakes to stop at its mooring. Drop genoa, main, then mizzen so hull rides peacefully to its mooring.

Downwind dock.— ketch, medium wind. Harden topping lifts, then drop mizzen and main while on a reach. Drop to beam or broad reach, and drop genoa. A **jib downhaul**—text page 59, is required in medium to heavy winds, so jib can't lift and fill causing erratic steering problems.

Splice a **dock snubber brake**— text page 172, with one eye secured to a dock cleat. Pick up the eye on the other end, and put it on a winch or cleat on your sailboat, which will stop it correctly in the slip.

Dockline markers. When your sailboat is riding normally in its slip or alongside dock tie, *sew dock cleat markers* on docklines left on boat cleats underway. Crew can cleat docklines without making adjustments. If lines are stowed below when underway, add dock markings, then color coding to show corresponding boat cleats.

Downwind deadstick landings— are very practical with a good crew, a snubber line, and docklines with dock cleat markings for your downwind slip or side tie.

docking details—
Homestudy Guide,
pages 48-9

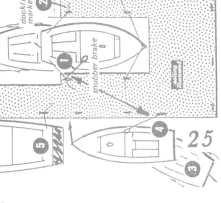

dockline marker

snubber brake

25

Raising sails upwind— text pages 86, 88, 91, 92. The New England weathervane rooster provides the basic theory for the ketch above riding to a single mooring, pointing into a light wind. The same theory also applies to sloops, yawls, cutters, and schooners raising sails riding to a similar single mooring or anchor line.

The aft sail is raised first— *to weathercock the hull so the bow rides peacefully into the wind.*

The mizzen is raised first on the Newporter ketch above, followed by the mainsail, and last the genoa jib as the hull rides peacefully to its mooring.

Backing the jib. It is backed by hand opposite to the desired tack, text pg. 91, and the bow painter is released. After the bow swings to the desired tack, the windward jib sheet is released. The mizzen, main, and jib sheets are taken in and cleated. The Newporter ketch is on course underway.

Raising sails downwind— text pages 86 and 90.
The present slip for our 24' sailboat points into the westerlies, which is left going downwind. At the dock the mainsail cover is removed, and its halyard secured. The jib is raised dockside and dropped into its sail bag to reduce windage.

Leaving slip downwind—
The sailboat drifts downwind on a broad reach. The jib is raised and its halyard cleated. The sheet snap hook is secured to jib clew, the jib trimmed, and the sheet cleated. The boat heads to a reach as the topping lift is hardened, and boom lift released. Mainsail is raised and its halyard cleated. Topping lift is eased, downhaul hardened and cleated; finally, trim both sails.

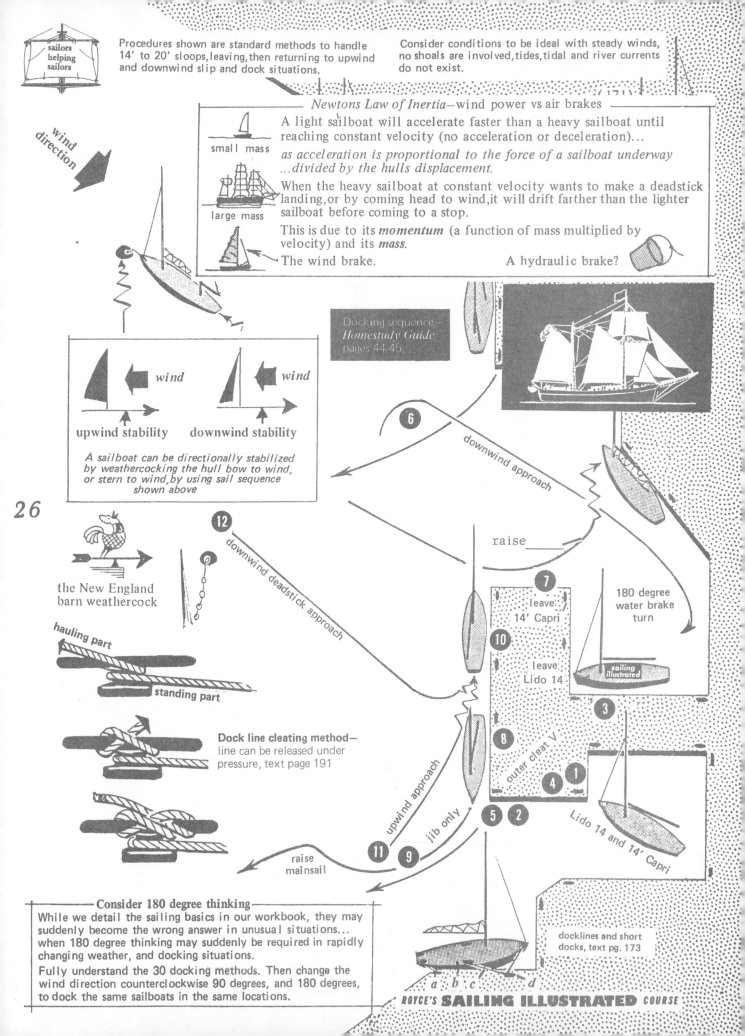

Procedures shown are standard methods to handle 14' to 20' sloops, leaving, then returning to upwind and downwind slip and dock situations.

Consider conditions to be ideal with steady winds, no shoals are involved, tides, tidal and river currents do not exist.

wind direction

Newtons Law of Inertia—wind power vs air brakes

small mass

A light sailboat will accelerate faster than a heavy sailboat until reaching constant velocity (no acceleration or deceleration)...

as acceleration is proportional to the force of a sailboat underway ...divided by the hulls displacement.

large mass

When the heavy sailboat at constant velocity wants to make a deadstick landing, or by coming head to wind, it will drift farther than the lighter sailboat before coming to a stop.

This is due to its **momentum** (a function of mass multiplied by velocity) and its **mass**.

The wind brake.   A hydraulic brake?

Docking sequence— *Homestudy Guide* pages 44-45.

wind   *wind*

upwind stability   downwind stability

A sailboat can be directionally stabilized by weathercocking the hull bow to wind, or stern to wind, by using sail sequence shown above

6

downwind approach

26

raise

12

downwind deadstick approach

the New England barn weathercock

7

leave 14' Capri

180 degree water brake turn

10

leave Lido 14

sailing illustrated

hauling part

standing part

3

8

outer cleat V

Dock line cleating method— line can be released under pressure, text page 191

upwind approach

jib only

4 **1**

5 **2**

Lido 14 and 14' Capri

11 **9**

raise mainsail

Consider 180 degree thinking

While we detail the sailing basics in our workbook, they may suddenly become the wrong answer in unusual situations... when 180 degree thinking may suddenly be required in rapidly changing weather, and docking situations.

Fully understand the 30 docking methods. Then change the wind direction counterclockwise 90 degrees, and 180 degrees, to dock the same sailboats in the same locations.

docklines and short docks, text pg. 173

a b c   d

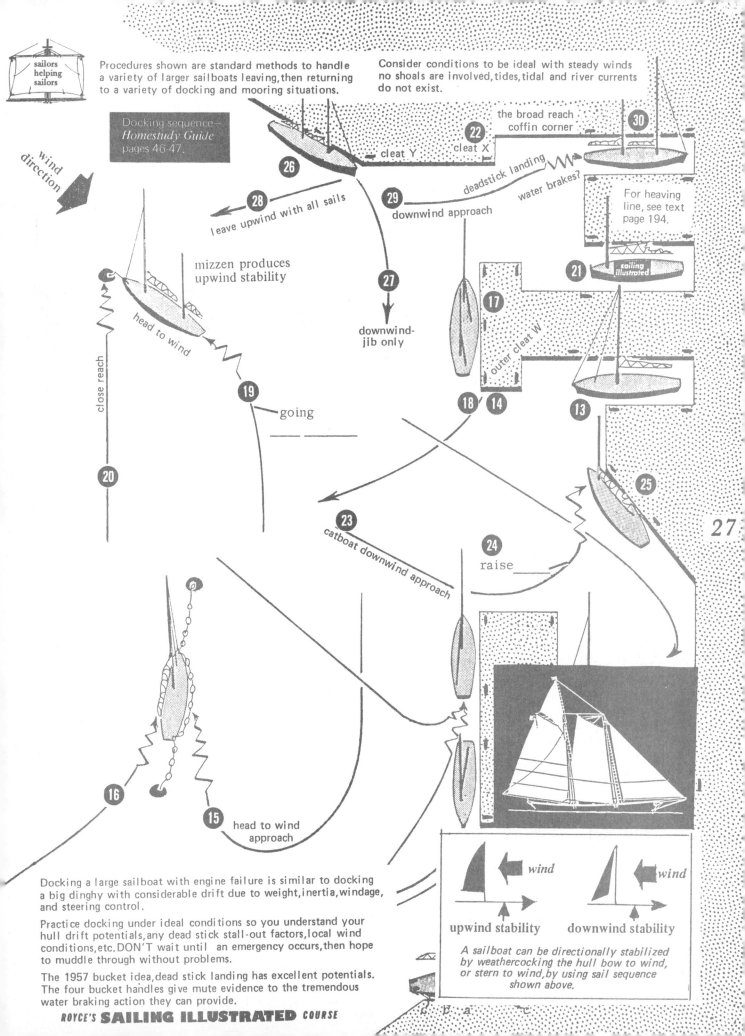

sailors helping sailors

Procedures shown are standard methods to handle a variety of larger sailboats leaving, then returning to a variety of docking and mooring situations.

Consider conditions to be ideal with steady winds no shoals are involved, tides, tidal and river currents do not exist.

wind direction

Docking sequence— *Homestudy Guide* pages 46-47.

the broad reach coffin corner

30

cleat Y   cleat X

26

deadstick landing   water brakes?

28   leave upwind with all sails

29   downwind approach

For heaving line, see text page 194.

mizzen produces upwind stability

27

21   sailing illustrated

downwind- jib only

17

close reach

head to wind

19   going

outer cleat W

18   14   13

20

23

25

catboat downwind approach

24   raise

27

16

15   head to wind approach

Docking a large sailboat with engine failure is similar to docking a big dinghy with considerable drift due to weight, inertia, windage, and steering control.

Practice docking under ideal conditions so you understand your hull drift potentials, any dead stick stall-out factors, local wind conditions, etc. DON'T wait until an emergency occurs, then hope to muddle through without problems.

The 1957 bucket idea, dead stick landing has excellent potentials. The four bucket handles give mute evidence to the tremendous water braking action they can provide.

wind   wind

upwind stability   downwind stability

A sailboat can be directionally stabilized by weathercocking the hull bow to wind, or stern to wind, by using sail sequence shown above.

ROYCE'S SAILING ILLUSTRATED COURSE

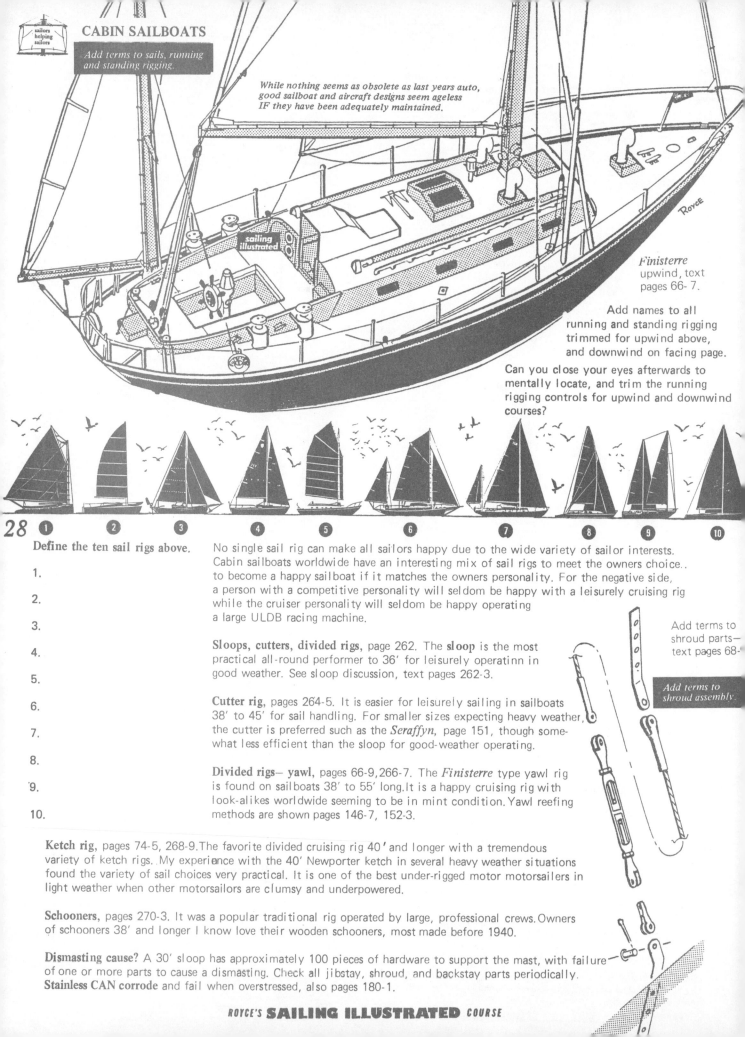

Add terms to sails, running and standing rigging.

While nothing seems as obsolete as last years auto, good sailboat and aircraft designs seem ageless IF they have been adequately maintained.

sailing illustrated

Royce

Finisterre upwind, text pages 66- 7.

Add names to all running and standing rigging trimmed for upwind above, and downwind on facing page.

Can you close your eyes afterwards to mentally locate, and trim the running rigging controls for upwind and downwind courses?

28 ① ② ③ ④ ⑤ ⑥ ⑦ ⑧ ⑨ ⑩

Define the ten sail rigs above.

1.
2.
3.
4.
5.
6.
7.
8.
9.
10.

No single sail rig can make all sailors happy due to the wide variety of sailor interests. Cabin sailboats worldwide have an interesting mix of sail rigs to meet the owners choice.. to become a happy sailboat if it matches the owners personality. For the negative side, a person with a competitive personality will seldom be happy with a leisurely cruising rig while the cruiser personality will seldom be happy operating a large ULDB racing machine.

Sloops, cutters, divided rigs, page 262. The **sloop** is the most practical all-round performer to 36' for leisurely operatinn in good weather. See sloop discussion, text pages 262-3.

Cutter rig, pages 264-5. It is easier for leisurely sailing in sailboats 38' to 45' for sail handling. For smaller sizes expecting heavy weather, the cutter is preferred such as the *Seraffyn,* page 151, though somewhat less efficient than the sloop for good-weather operating.

Divided rigs— yawl, pages 66-9, 266-7. The *Finisterre* type yawl rig is found on sailboats 38' to 55' long. It is a happy cruising rig with look-alikes worldwide seeming to be in mint condition. Yawl reefing methods are shown pages 146-7, 152-3.

Add terms to shroud parts— text pages 68-

Add terms to shroud assembly.

Ketch rig, pages 74-5, 268-9. The favorite divided cruising rig 40' and longer with a tremendous variety of ketch rigs. My experience with the 40' Newporter ketch in several heavy weather situations found the variety of sail choices very practical. It is one of the best under-rigged motor motorsailers in light weather when other motorsailers are clumsy and underpowered.

Schooners, pages 270-3. It was a popular traditional rig operated by large, professional crews. Owners of schooners 38' and longer I know love their wooden schooners, most made before 1940.

Dismasting cause? A 30' sloop has approximately 100 pieces of hardware to support the mast, with failure of one or more parts to cause a dismasting. Check all jibstay, shroud, and backstay parts periodically. **Stainless CAN corrode** and fail when overstressed, also pages 180-1.

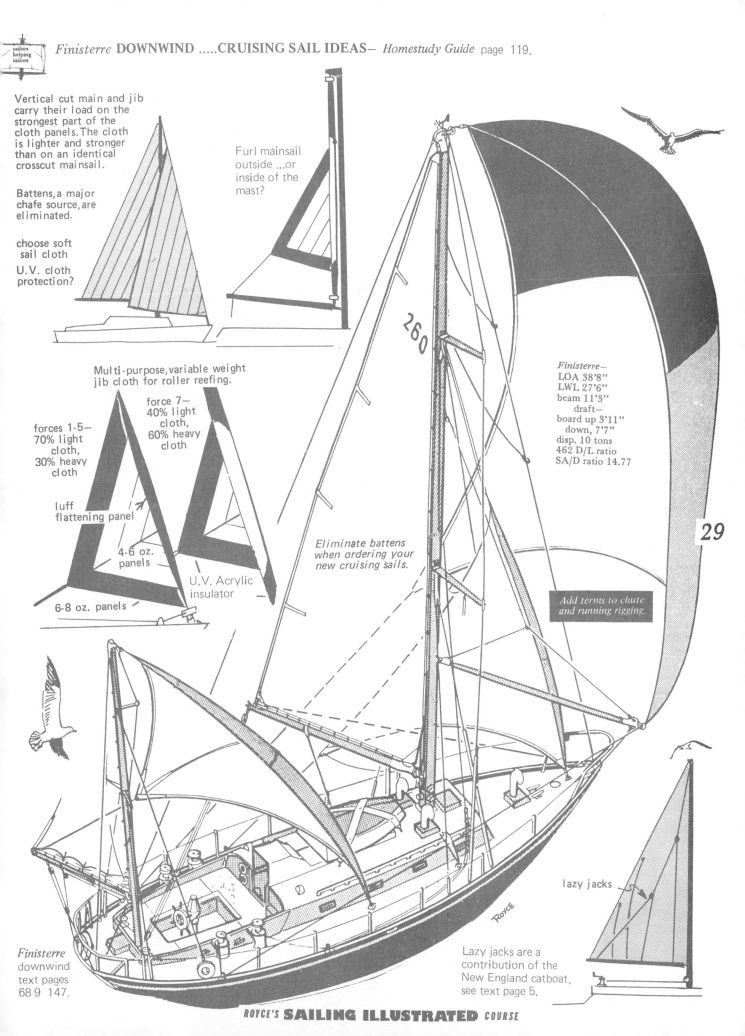

Vertical cut main and jib carry their load on the strongest part of the cloth panels. The cloth is lighter and stronger than on an identical crosscut mainsail.

Battens, a major chafe source, are eliminated.

choose soft sail cloth

U.V. cloth protection?

Furl mainsail outside ...or inside of the mast?

Multi-purpose, variable weight jib cloth for roller reefing.

force 7— 40% light cloth, 60% heavy cloth

forces 1-5— 70% light cloth, 30% heavy cloth

luff flattening panel

4-6 oz. panels

U.V. Acrylic insulator

6-8 oz. panels

260

Finisterre— LOA 38'8" LWL 27'6" beam 11'3" draft— board up 3'11" down, 7'7" disp. 10 tons 462 D/L ratio SA/D ratio 14.77

29

Eliminate battens when ordering your new cruising sails.

Add terms to chute and running rigging.

Finisterre downwind text pages 68-9 147.

lazy jacks

Lazy jacks are a contribution of the New England catboat, see text page 5.

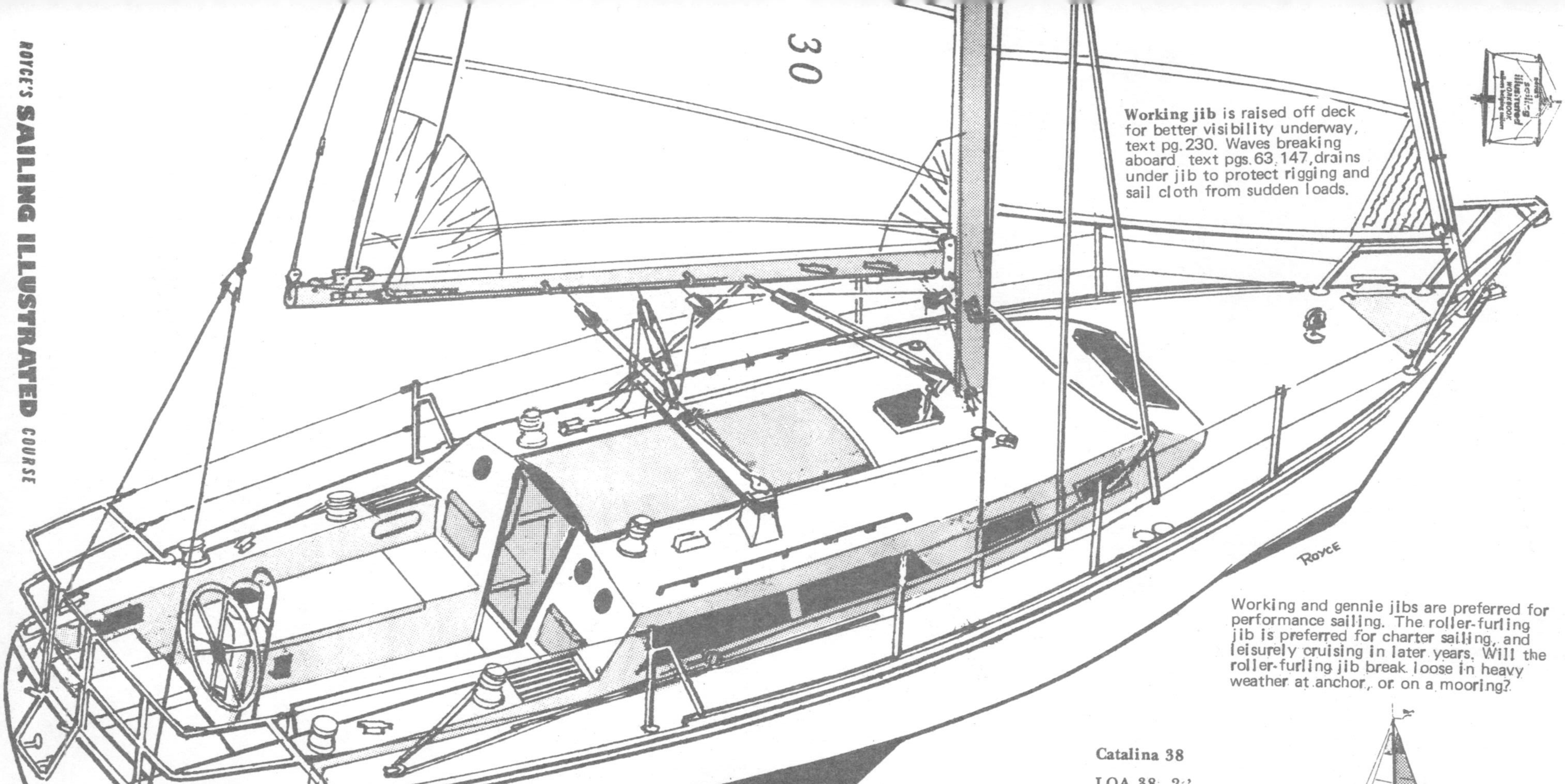

Working jib is raised off deck for better visibility underway, text pg. 230. Waves breaking aboard text pgs. 63, 147, drains under jib to protect rigging and sail cloth from sudden loads.

Working and gennie jibs are preferred for performance sailing. The roller-furling jib is preferred for charter sailing, and leisurely cruising in later years. Will the roller-furling jib break loose in heavy weather at anchor, or on a mooring?

160% genoa

headsail sloop rig

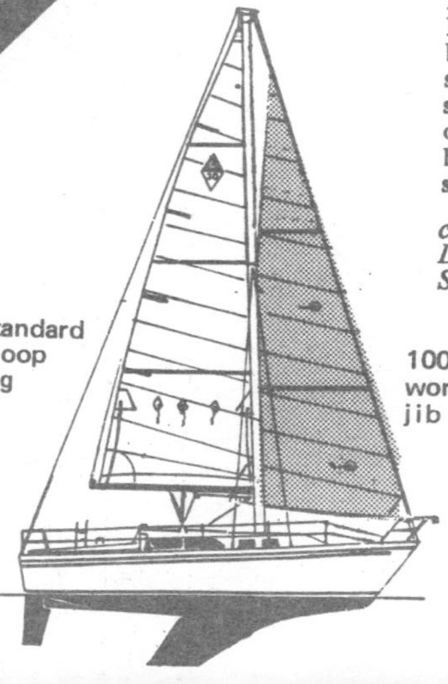

Catalina 38

LOA 38' 2''
LWL 30' 3''
beam 11' 10'
std draft 6' 9'
shoal draft 4' 11''
displacement 15,900 lbs.
ballast 6850 lbs.
std sail area 639 sq. ft.

conservative Catalina 38
D/L ratio— 257
Sail/Disp. ratio— 16.2

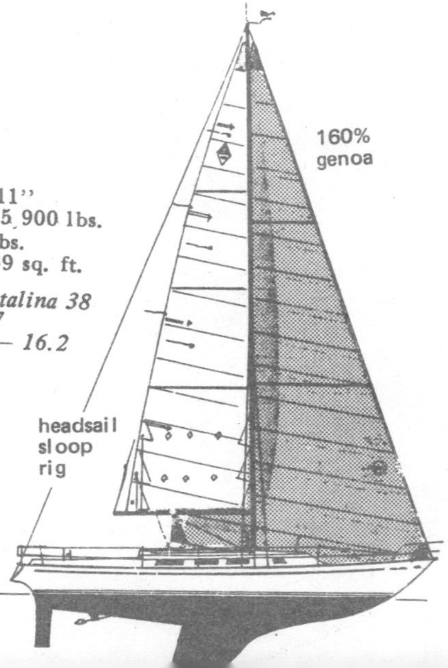

100% working jib

standard sloop rig

30

Earlier Catalina 30s had tiller steering. Later models used wheel steering that required a different cockpit seating arrangement.

Catalina 30

LOA 29' 11''
LWL 25' 0''
beam 10' 10'',
std draft 5' 3'',
shoal draft 3' 10''
displacement 10,200 lbs.
ballast 4200 lbs.
std sail area 446 sq. ft.

standard keel, D/L— 291
standard rig SA/D— 15.2
tall rig Sail/Disp.— 17.2

The Catalina 30 sailing since 1970, is the most popular 30 footer worldwide. It undergoes periodic engineering improvements topside and below to improve operational efficiency.

decksweeper gennie jib

31

Windseeker

sailing illustrated

..."We were rolling along..."

The *blooper*—IOR boats on a run had rolling tendencies with a large chute on one side, and a small main on the other. This was dampened by adding a full-bellied jib opposite to the chute.

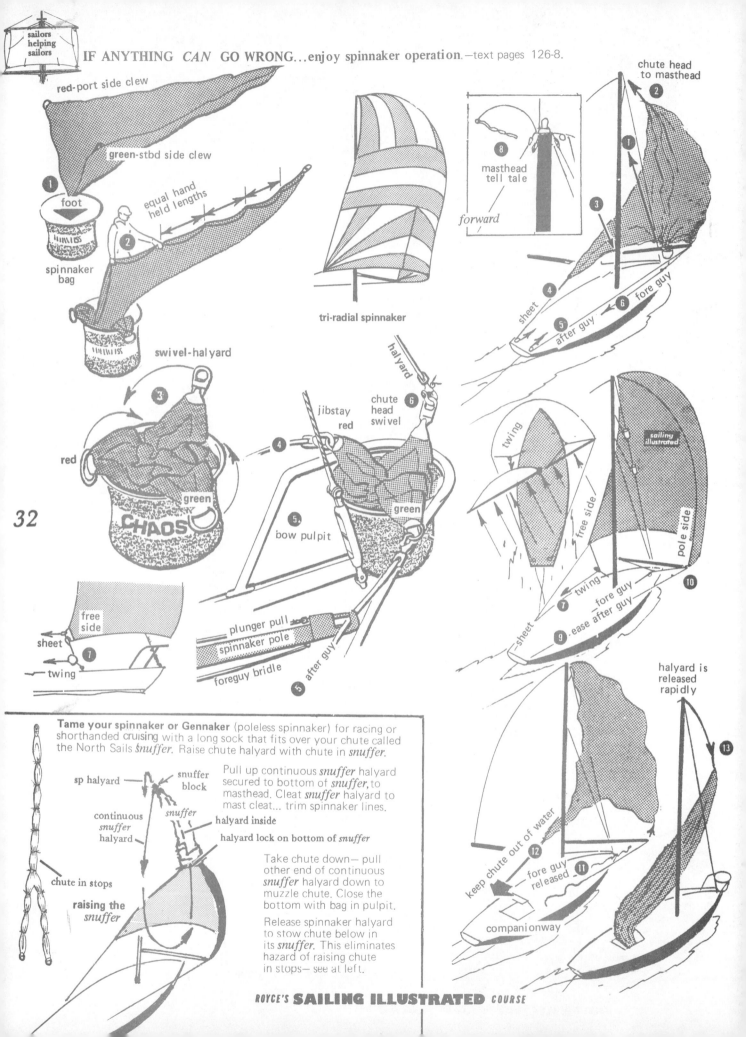

sailors helping sailors

red-port side clew

green-stbd side clew

① foot

equal hand held lengths

②

spinnaker bag

swivel-halyard

③

red

green

CHAOS

tri-radial spinnaker

jibstay red

④

⑤ bow pulpit

halyard

chute head swivel ⑥

green

free side

sheet

⑦

twing

plunger pull
spinnaker pole
foreguy bridle

after guy ⑤

chute head to masthead ②

①

③

④

sheet

after guy ⑤

fore guy ⑥

masthead tell tale ⑧

forward

twing

sailing illustrated

free side

pole side

⑦ twing

sheet

fore guy

⑨ ease after guy

⑩

halyard is released rapidly

⑬

keep chute out of water

⑫

fore guy released ⑪

companionway

Tame your spinnaker or Gennaker (poleless spinnaker) for racing or shorthanded cruising with a long sock that fits over your chute called the North Sails *snuffer*. Raise chute halyard with chute in *snuffer*.

sp halyard

snuffer block

continuous *snuffer* halyard

snuffer

halyard inside

halyard lock on bottom of *snuffer*

chute in stops

raising the *snuffer*

Pull up continuous *snuffer* halyard secured to bottom of *snuffer*, to masthead. Cleat *snuffer* halyard to mast cleat... trim spinnaker lines.

Take chute down— pull other end of continuous *snuffer* halyard down to muzzle chute. Close the bottom with bag in pulpit.

Release spinnaker halyard to stow chute below in its *snuffer*. This eliminates hazard of raising chute in stops— see at left.

32

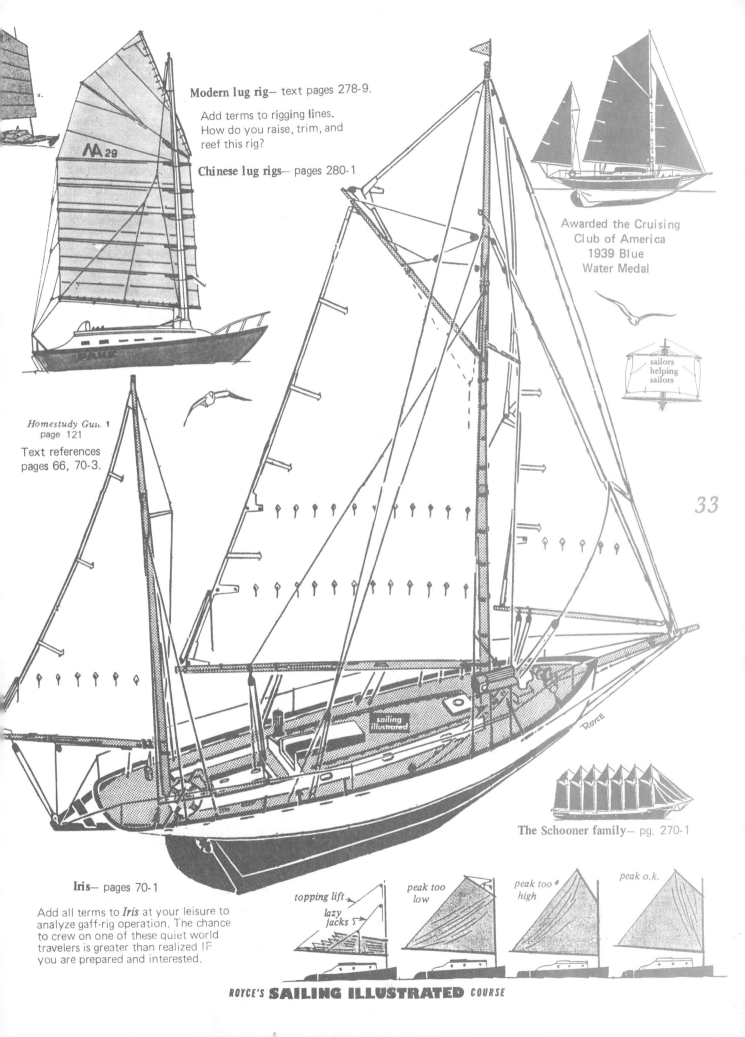

Modern lug rig — text pages 278-9.

Add terms to rigging lines.
How do you raise, trim, and
reef this rig?

Chinese lug rigs — pages 280-1

Homestudy Guide
page 121
Text references
pages 66, 70-3.

Awarded the Cruising
Club of America
1939 Blue
Water Medal

sailors
helping
sailors

33

The Schooner family — pg. 270-1

Iris — pages 70-1

Add all terms to *Iris* at your leisure to
analyze gaff-rig operation. The chance
to crew on one of these quiet world
travelers is greater than realized IF
you are prepared and interested.

topping lift
lazy jacks

peak too low

peak too high

peak o.k.

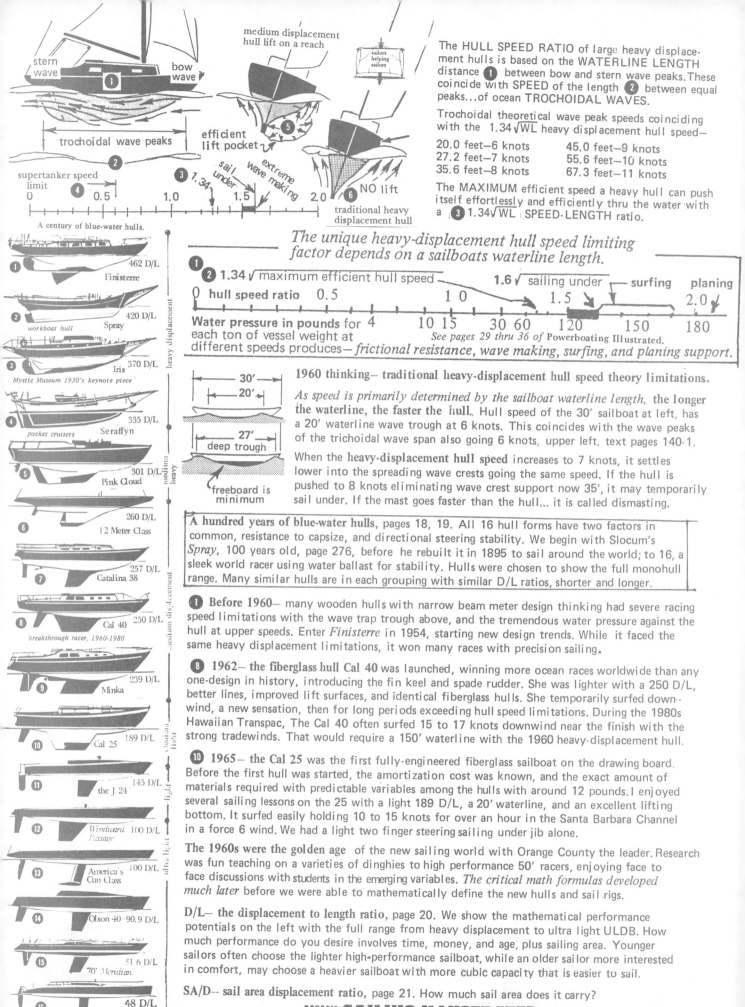

The HULL SPEED RATIO of large heavy displacement hulls is based on the WATERLINE LENGTH distance ① between bow and stern wave peaks. These coincide with SPEED of the length ② between equal peaks...of ocean TROCHOIDAL WAVES.

Trochoidal theoretical wave peak speeds coinciding with the $1.34\sqrt{WL}$ heavy displacement hull speed—

20.0 feet—6 knots   45.0 feet—9 knots
27.2 feet—7 knots   55.6 feet—10 knots
35.6 feet—8 knots   67.3 feet—11 knots

The MAXIMUM efficient speed a heavy hull can push itself effortlessly and efficiently thru the water with a ③ $1.34\sqrt{WL}$ SPEED-LENGTH ratio.

medium displacement hull lift on a reach

sailors helping sailors

stern wave ①   bow wave
trochoidal wave peaks
efficient lift pocket
extreme wave making
sail under
NO lift ⑥
traditional heavy displacement hull

supertanker speed limit ④
0   0.5   1.0   1.34 ③   1.5   2.0

A century of blue-water hulls.

462 D/L Finisterre
①

420 D/L Spray
② workboat hull

370 D/L Iris
③ Mystic Museum 1930's keynote piece

335 D/L Seraffyn
④ pocket cruisers

301 D/L Pink Cloud
⑤

260 D/L 12 Meter Class
⑥

257 D/L Catalina 38
⑦

250 D/L Cal 40
⑧ breakthrough racer, 1960-1980

239 D/L Minka
⑨

189 D/L Cal 25
⑩

145 D/L the J 24
⑪

100 D/L Windward Passage
⑫

100 D/L America's Cup Class
⑬

90.9 D/L Olson 40
⑭

51.6 D/L 70' Meridian
⑮

48 D/L
⑯

heavy displacement
medium heavy
medium displacement
medium light
light
ultra light

The unique heavy-displacement hull speed limiting factor depends on a sailboats waterline length.

① ② $1.34\sqrt{}$ maximum efficient hull speed $1.6\sqrt{}$ sailing under   surfing   planing

0   hull speed ratio   0.5   1.0   1.5   2.0

Water pressure in pounds for each ton of vessel weight at different speeds produces—   4   10 15   30 60   120   150   180

See pages 29 thru 36 of Powerboating Illustrated.

frictional resistance, wave making, surfing, and planing support.

1960 thinking— traditional heavy-displacement hull speed theory limitations.

30'   20'
27' deep trough
freeboard is minimum

As speed is primarily determined by the sailboat waterline length, the longer the waterline, the faster the hull. Hull speed of the 30' sailboat at left, has a 20' waterline wave trough at 6 knots. This coincides with the wave peaks of the trichoidal wave span also going 6 knots, upper left, text pages 140-1.

When the heavy-displacement hull speed increases to 7 knots, it settles lower into the spreading wave crests going the same speed. If the hull is pushed to 8 knots eliminating wave crest support now 35', it may temporarily sail under. If the mast goes faster than the hull... it is called dismasting.

A hundred years of blue-water hulls, pages 18, 19. All 16 hull forms have two factors in common, resistance to capsize, and directional steering stability. We begin with Slocum's *Spray*, 100 years old, page 276, before he rebuilt it in 1895 to sail around the world; to 16, a sleek world racer using water ballast for stability. Hulls were chosen to show the full monohull range. Many similar hulls are in each grouping with similar D/L ratios, shorter and longer.

① **Before 1960—** many wooden hulls with narrow beam meter design thinking had severe racing speed limitations with the wave trap trough above, and the tremendous water pressure against the hull at upper speeds. Enter *Finisterre* in 1954, starting new design trends. While it faced the same heavy displacement limitations, it won many races with precision sailing.

⑧ **1962—** the fiberglass hull Cal 40 was launched, winning more ocean races worldwide than any one-design in history, introducing the fin keel and spade rudder. She was lighter with a 250 D/L, better lines, improved lift surfaces, and identical fiberglass hulls. She temporarily surfed downwind, a new sensation, then for long periods exceeding hull speed limitations. During the 1980s Hawaiian Transpac, The Cal 40 often surfed 15 to 17 knots downwind near the finish with the strong tradewinds. That would require a 150' waterline with the 1960 heavy-displacement hull.

⑩ **1965—** the Cal 25 was the first fully-engineered fiberglass sailboat on the drawing board. Before the first hull was started, the amortization cost was known, and the exact amount of materials required with predictable variables among the hulls with around 12 pounds. I enjoyed several sailing lessons on the 25 with a light 189 D/L, a 20' waterline, and an excellent lifting bottom. It surfed easily holding 10 to 15 knots for over an hour in the Santa Barbara Channel in a force 6 wind. We had a light two finger steering sailing under jib alone.

The 1960s were the golden age of the new sailing world with Orange County the leader. Research was fun teaching on a varieties of dinghies to high performance 50' racers, enjoying face to face discussions with students in the emerging variables. *The critical math formulas developed much later* before we were able to mathematically define the new hulls and sail rigs.

D/L— the displacement to length ratio, page 20. We show the mathematical performance potentials on the left with the full range from heavy displacement to ultra light ULDB. How much performance do you desire involves time, money, and age, plus sailing area. Younger sailors often choose the lighter high-performance sailboat, while an older sailor more interested in comfort, may choose a heavier sailboat with more cubic capacity that is easier to sail.

SA/D— sail area displacement ratio, page 21. How much sail area does it carry?

ROYCE'S **SAILING ILLUSTRATED** COURSE

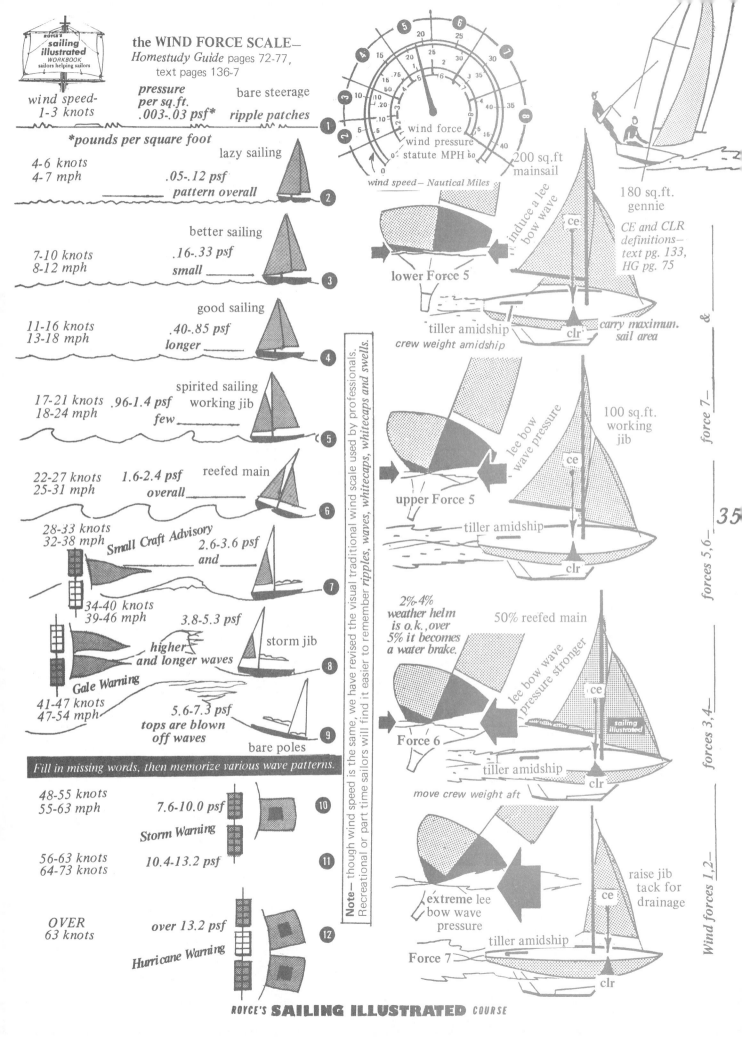

the WIND FORCE SCALE—
Homestudy Guide pages 72-77,
text pages 136-7

wind speed-
1-3 knots

pressure
per sq.ft.
.003-.03 psf*

bare steerage
ripple patches

①

*pounds per square foot

4-6 knots
4-7 mph

lazy sailing
.05-.12 psf
pattern overall

②

7-10 knots
8-12 mph

better sailing
.16-.33 psf
small _____

③

11-16 knots
13-18 mph

good sailing
.40-.85 psf
longer _____

④

17-21 knots
18-24 mph

.96-1.4 psf
few _____

spirited sailing
working jib

⑤

22-27 knots
25-31 mph

1.6-2.4 psf
overall _____

reefed main

⑥

28-33 knots
32-38 mph

Small Craft Advisory

2.6-3.6 psf
and _____

⑦

34-40 knots
39-46 mph

3.8-5.3 psf

higher and longer waves

storm jib

⑧

Gale Warning

41-47 knots
47-54 mph

5.6-7.3 psf
tops are blown off waves

bare poles

⑨

Fill in missing words, then memorize various wave patterns.

48-55 knots
55-63 mph

7.6-10.0 psf

Storm Warning

⑩

56-63 knots
64-73 knots

10.4-13.2 psf

⑪

OVER
63 knots

over 13.2 psf

Hurricane Warning

⑫

wind force
wind pressure
statute MPH

wind speed— Nautical Miles

200 sq.ft
mainsail

180 sq.ft.
gennie

*CE and CLR definitions—
text pg. 133,
HG pg. 75*

induce a lee bow wave

ce

lower Force 5

tiller amidship
crew weight amidship

clr

carry maximum sail area

Note— though wind speed is the same, we have revised the visual traditional wind scale used by professionals. Recreational or part time sailors will find it easier to remember *ripples, waves, whitecaps, whitecaps and swells.*

100 sq.ft.
working jib

lee bow wave pressure

ce

upper Force 5

tiller amidship

clr

2%-4% weather helm is o.k., over 5% it becomes a water brake.

50% reefed main

lee bow wave pressure stronger

ce

sailing illustrated

Force 6

tiller amidship

clr

move crew weight aft

extreme lee bow wave pressure

raise jib tack for drainage

ce

tiller amidship

Force 7

clr

& ___
force 7 ___
forces 5,6, ___
forces 3,4, ___
Wind forces 1,2 ___

35

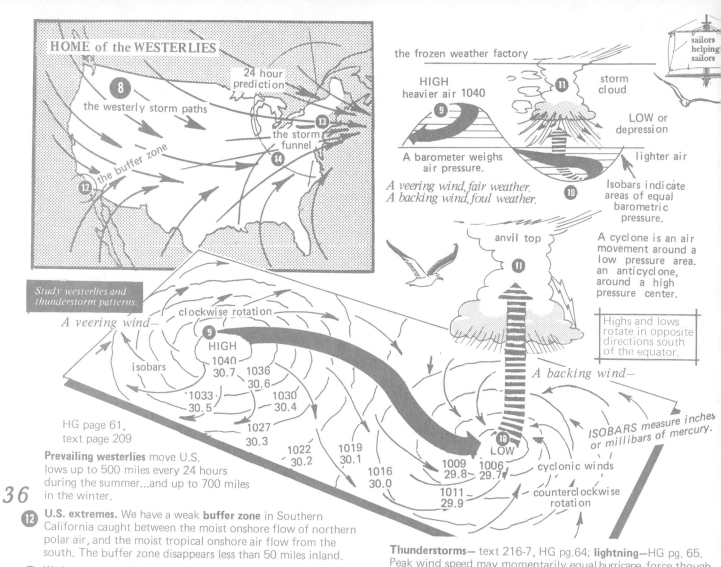

HOME of the WESTERLIES

⑧ the westerly storm paths

24 hour prediction

⑬ the storm funnel

⑭

the buffer zone

⑫

the frozen weather factory

HIGH heavier air 1040 ⑨

A barometer weighs air pressure.

⑪ storm cloud

LOW or depression

lighter air

A veering wind, fair weather.
A backing wind, foul weather.

⑩

Isobars indicate areas of equal barometric pressure.

anvil top

⑪

A cyclone is an air movement around a low pressure area. an anticyclone, around a high pressure center.

Highs and lows rotate in opposite directions south of the equator.

Study westerlies and thunderstorm patterns.

A veering wind—

clockwise rotation

⑨ **HIGH**
1040
30.7
isobars

1036
30.6
1033·
30.5
1027
30.3

1030
30.4
1022
30.2
1019
30.1
1016
30.0

A backing wind—

ISOBARS measure inches or millibars of mercury.

1009
29.8
LOW
1011
29.9

1006
29.7

⑩ cyclonic winds

counterclockwise rotation

HG page 61,
text page 209

Prevailing westerlies move U.S. lows up to 500 miles every 24 hours during the summer...and up to 700 miles in the winter.

36

⑫ **U.S. extremes.** We have a weak **buffer zone** in Southern California caught between the moist onshore flow of northern polar air, and the moist tropical onshore air flow from the south. The buffer zone disappears less than 50 miles inland.

⑬ We have a **storm funnel** on the east coast with lows flowing up the Mississippi Valley then turning right, to westerlies flowing across the U.S., plus lows coming from Canada.

Storm funnel sailors need considerable awareness to prepare for storms moving in to minimize potential damage.

Thunderstorms— text 216-7, HG pg.64; **lightning**—HG pg. 65. Peak wind speed may momentarily equal hurricane force though approximately 20 minutes in passing...will others also follow? Why are sailboats out of control with downdrafts?

What flow patterns do thunderstorms have in your area... are tall hills blocking visibility as they move in. What is a clear air **duster**? How can you predict thunderstorms and dusters?

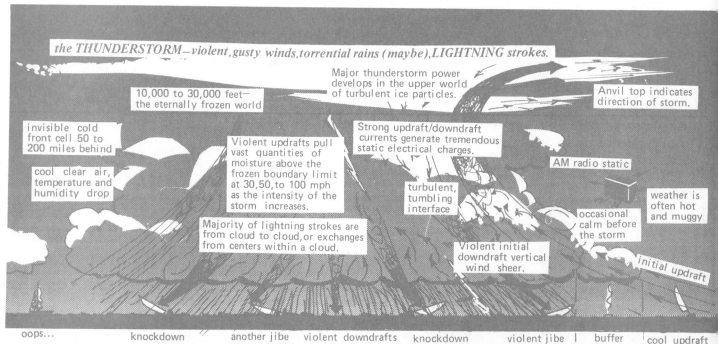

the THUNDERSTORM—violent, gusty winds, torrential rains (maybe), LIGHTNING strokes.

Major thunderstorm power develops in the upper world of turbulent ice particles.

Anvil top indicates direction of storm.

10,000 to 30,000 feet— the eternally frozen world

invisible cold front cell 50 to 200 miles behind

Strong updraft/downdraft currents generate tremendous static electrical charges.

AM radio static

cool clear air, temperature and humidity drop

Violent updrafts pull vast quantities of moisture above the frozen boundary limit at 30,50, to 100 mph as the intensity of the storm increases.

turbulent, tumbling interface

weather is often hot and muggy

Majority of lightning strokes are from cloud to cloud, or exchanges from centers within a cloud.

occasional calm before the storm

Violent initial downdraft vertical wind sheer.

initial updraft

oops...   knockdown   another jibe   violent downdrafts   knockdown   violent jibe   buffer   cool updraft

THE CAPSIZE...plus the UNEXPECTED SWIM — text pages 144-5.

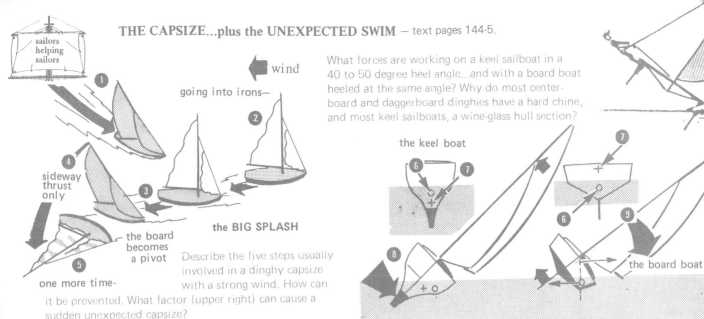

sailors helping sailors

1 ← wind

going into irons—

2

4

sideway thrust only

3

5

the board becomes a pivot

one more time-

it be prevented. What factor (upper right) can cause a sudden unexpected capsize?

the BIG SPLASH

Describe the five steps usually involved in a dinghy capsize with a strong wind. How can

What forces are working on a keel sailboat in a 40 to 50 degree heel angle...and with a board boat heeled at the same angle? Why do most centerboard and daggerboard dinghies have a hard chine, and most keel sailboats, a wine-glass hull section?

the keel boat

6 7 7

6 9

8 the board boat

+o

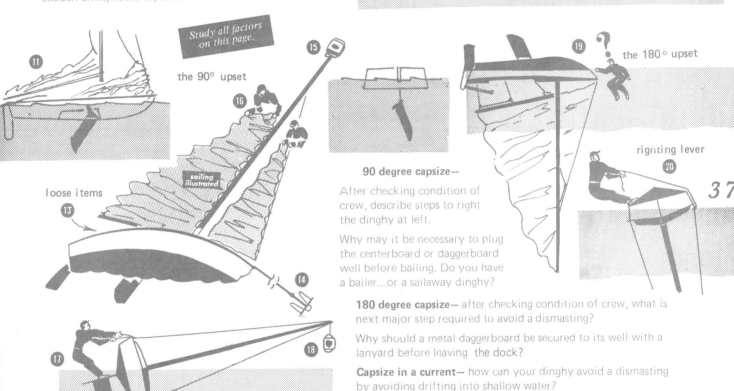

Study all factors on this page.

11

the 90° upset

15

16

sailing illustrated

loose items

13

14

17

18

19 ? the 180° upset

righting lever

20

37

90 degree capsize--

After checking condition of crew, describe steps to right the dinghy at left.

Why may it be necessary to plug the centerboard or daggerboard well before bailing. Do you have a bailer...or a sailaway dinghy?

180 degree capsize— after checking condition of crew, what is next major step required to avoid a dismasting?

Why should a metal daggerboard be secured to its well with a lanyard before leaving the dock?

Capsize in a current— how can your dinghy avoid a dismasting by avoiding drifting into shallow water?

A 180 degree recovery may be faster and easier to make than a 90 degree recovery.

Swim requirements— text page 228; *can you easily swim 100' in normal conditions?* A capsize is a surprise to a person who can swim as he is comfortable in the water. He can systematically follow the procedures shown to prepare a sailboat for righting.

The nonswimmer may panic in a capsize becoming a hazard to himself and to crew members. The nonswimmer is a questionable risk to have aboard in a spirited wind.

Preservers— text page 227. Bulky, clumsy ones are seldom tested for practical use until a person is in the water. The best way to test a preserver is to swim wearing one for 100 yards in good conditions...so you know what to expect in harsh conditions with wave action.

Cabin sailboats— text page 229. Can a person in the water, climb back aboard under his or her own power?

SCUBA diving— text page 228. It is the next requirement for sailors with courses that can be taken during the winter months or evenings...in swimming pools at least 13' to 15' deep to continually practice clearing the ears.

If you never use a tank afterwards, the training will be excellent to check an anchor, dive for an object falling overboard, or to snorkel on a warm lazy afternoon enjoying underwater scenery.

P.S.— the competent sailor is still able to enjoy sailing on days when everything goes wrong.

TILT

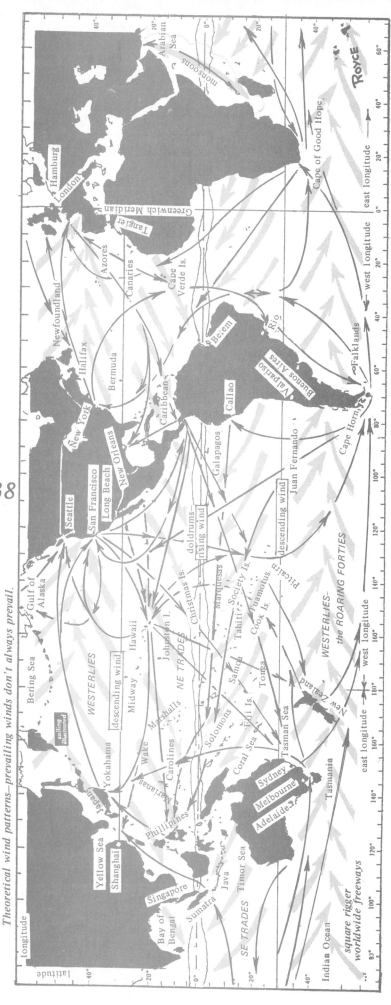

Theoretical wind patterns—prevailing winds don't always prevail.

38

Square rig sailing heritage has been my hobby since grade school. Regardless of much research for our sailing books, the key was missing. I finally drew the sailing routes on a map of the world I had studied for many years, hoping to find the missing answer. The result wasn't what had been anticipated as it produced more questions.

Prevailing wind patterns were drawn on an identical size map of the world. It was put on top of the sailing routes, and the pieces of the jigsaw puzzle began to fall into place. Many sailing routes fell into patterns for cargo vessels to make the best time port to port. Some required more research to find their answers while questionable routes were soon easy to sort out.

The shortest route from New York to Rio puzzled skippers till USN Lt. Maury in 1847 recommended a course 3 times as long as the straight or rhumb line. A BOC single-handed racer studying our new chart shook his head. For the first leg of his New York to Capetown race, he followed the rhumb line or shortest route. He arrived in Capetown SIX days after his main competitor who sailed east almost to mid Atlantic before slowly turning south. What better test could our chart have even for modern ocean racers?

Variables. El Nino has been the scourge of sailors for centuries when ocean winds and currents periodically reverse themselves. Even the name is new. For the first time it was fully researched and reported in the Feb. 1984 issue of *National Geographic*.

New York to San Francisco on a 1850 square rigger was added to our 1988 edition, pages 210 to 213 of *Sailing Illustrated*. We felt it was the best way for readers to analyze weather patterns for best port to port sailing time. Readers then realized a totally different return route can go to Hawaii, to Papeete, to Cape Horn and the Carolinas to discharge and pick up new cargo for New York. Readers understand how cargo can be picked up for Halifax, and/or sail to Europe with a following wind taking the northern route to deliver cargo.

Square rigger types, rigging, and sails. Add names to the sails of *Cutty Sark* and *USCG Eagle* while studying the eight basic traditional rigs on page 40. This will provide a foundation to build on, plus methods to raise, trim, and furl square sails, pages 288-9 in *Sailing Illustrated*. Trim lines vary considerably among square riggers, while the end result is the same, with similar methods still used today.

Wind machines move with wind pressure. Pages 136-7 of our text show the *wind force scale* reefing sequence shown for *Cutty Sark*. The wind pressure/ wave action scale is just as practical with modern sailboats. It is difficult for new sailing students to understand wind pressure instead of Miles per Hour which is of little value.

Square rig history. Our four workbook pages provide an excellent basis for readers. Many excellent books have been written in the past, listed in our book for older traditional craft beginning with Alan Villers. New books such as the 1988 edition of *The Rediscovery of America's Maritime Heritage*, have a tremendous number of oil painting reproductions by John Stobart, one of the best sailing artists in history.

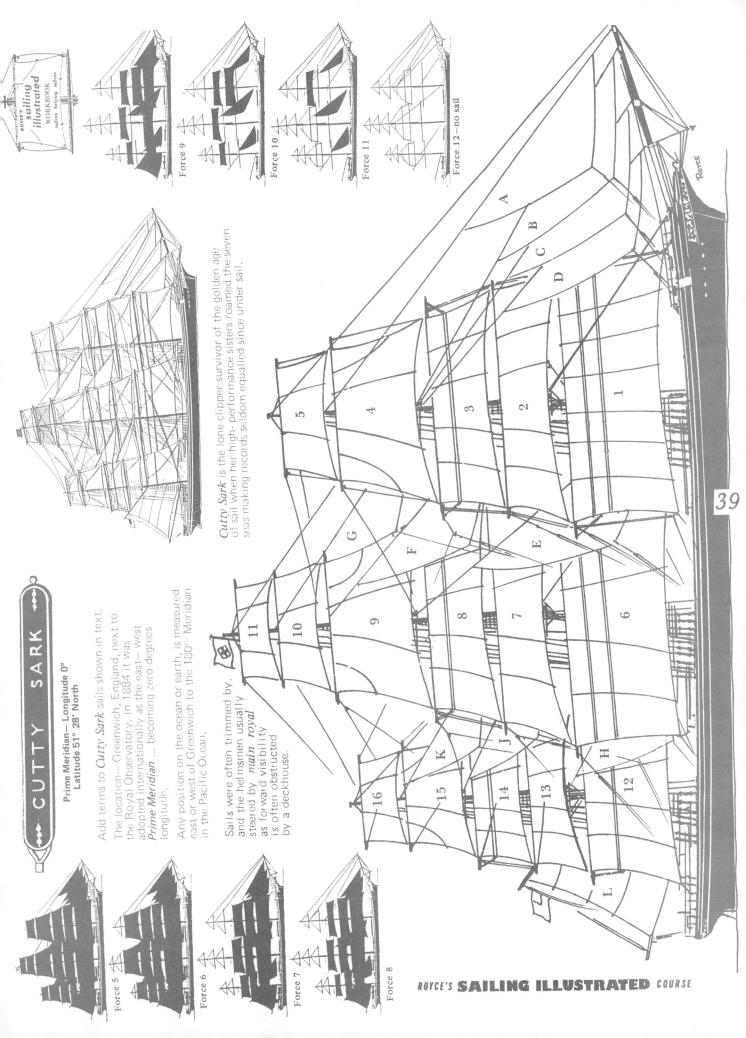

Force 9

Force 10

Force 11

Force 12 – no sail

Cutty Sark is the lone clipper survivor of the golden age of sail when her high- performance sisters roamed the seven seas making records seldom equalled since under sail.

CUTTY SARK

**Prime Meridian— Longitude 0°
Latitude 51° 28' North**

Add terms to *Cutty Sark* sails shown in text.

The location— Greenwich, England, next to the Royal Observatory. In 1884 it was adopted internationally as the east— west *Prime Meridian* ... becoming zero degrees longitude.

Any position on the ocean or earth, is measured east or west of Greenwich to the 180° Meridian in the Pacific Ocean.

Sails were often trimmed by, and the helmsmen usually steered by *main royal* as forward visibility is often obstructed by a deckhouse.

Royce

39

Force 5

Force 6

Force 7

Force 8

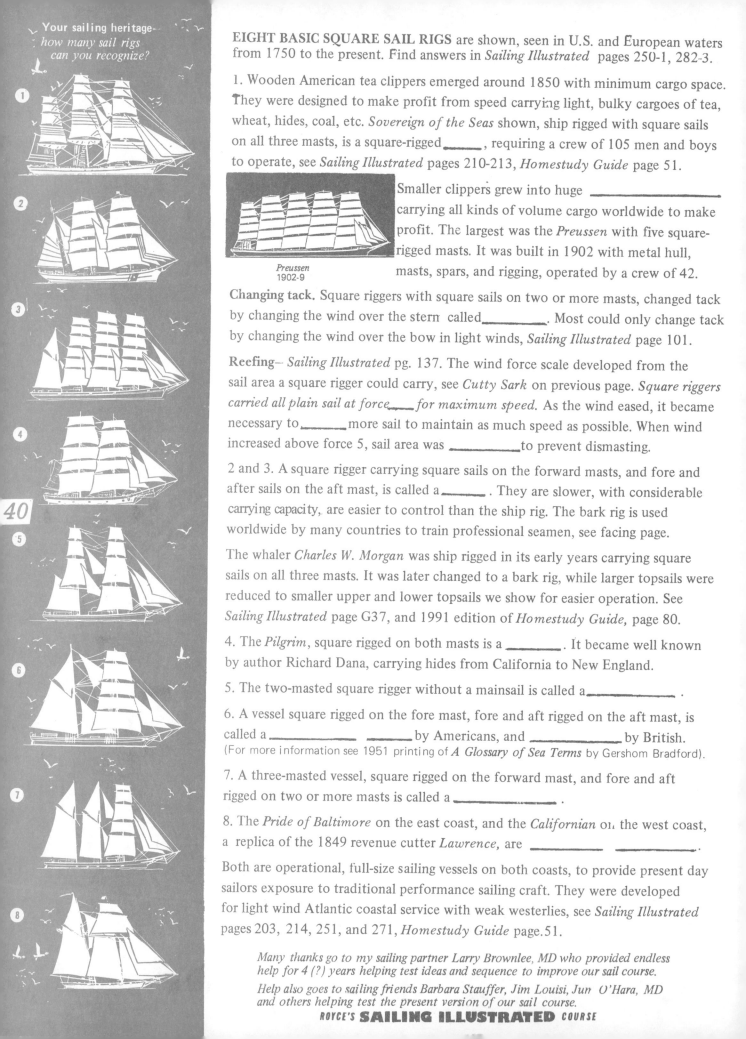

Your sailing heritage—
how many sail rigs
can you recognize?

EIGHT BASIC SQUARE SAIL RIGS are shown, seen in U.S. and European waters from 1750 to the present. Find answers in *Sailing Illustrated* pages 250-1, 282-3.

1. Wooden American tea clippers emerged around 1850 with minimum cargo space. They were designed to make profit from speed carrying light, bulky cargoes of tea, wheat, hides, coal, etc. *Sovereign of the Seas* shown, ship rigged with square sails on all three masts, is a square-rigged _____, requiring a crew of 105 men and boys to operate, see *Sailing Illustrated* pages 210-213, *Homestudy Guide* page 51.

Smaller clippers grew into huge _____ carrying all kinds of volume cargo worldwide to make profit. The largest was the *Preussen* with five square-rigged masts. It was built in 1902 with metal hull, masts, spars, and rigging, operated by a crew of 42.

Preussen 1902-9

Changing tack. Square riggers with square sails on two or more masts, changed tack by changing the wind over the stern called_____. Most could only change tack by changing the wind over the bow in light winds, *Sailing Illustrated* page 101.

Reefing— *Sailing Illustrated* pg. 137. The wind force scale developed from the sail area a square rigger could carry, see *Cutty Sark* on previous page. *Square riggers carried all plain sail at force____ for maximum speed.* As the wind eased, it became necessary to_____more sail to maintain as much speed as possible. When wind increased above force 5, sail area was _____to prevent dismasting.

2 and 3. A square rigger carrying square sails on the forward masts, and fore and after sails on the aft mast, is called a_____ . They are slower, with considerable carrying capacity, are easier to control than the ship rig. The bark rig is used worldwide by many countries to train professional seamen, see facing page.

The whaler *Charles W. Morgan* was ship rigged in its early years carrying square sails on all three masts. It was later changed to a bark rig, while larger topsails were reduced to smaller upper and lower topsails we show for easier operation. See *Sailing Illustrated* page G37, and 1991 edition of *Homestudy Guide,* page 80.

4. The *Pilgrim*, square rigged on both masts is a _____. It became well known by author Richard Dana, carrying hides from California to New England.

5. The two-masted square rigger without a mainsail is called a_____ .

6. A vessel square rigged on the fore mast, fore and aft rigged on the aft mast, is called a _____ _____ by Americans, and _____ by British.
(For more information see 1951 printing of *A Glossary of Sea Terms* by Gershom Bradford).

7. A three-masted vessel, square rigged on the forward mast, and fore and aft rigged on two or more masts is called a _____ .

8. The *Pride of Baltimore* on the east coast, and the *Californian* on the west coast, a replica of the 1849 revenue cutter *Lawrence*, are _____ _____.

Both are operational, full-size sailing vessels on both coasts, to provide present day sailors exposure to traditional performance sailing craft. They were developed for light wind Atlantic coastal service with weak westerlies, see *Sailing Illustrated* pages 203, 214, 251, and 271, *Homestudy Guide* page.51.

Many thanks go to my sailing partner Larry Brownlee, MD who provided endless help for 4 (?) years helping test ideas and sequence to improve our sail course.

Help also goes to sailing friends Barbara Stauffer, Jim Louisi, Jun O'Hara, MD and others helping test the present version of our sail course.

ROYCE'S SAILING ILLUSTRATED COURSE

HALF THE WORLD'S TONNAGE WAS STILL UNDER SAIL BY 1880.

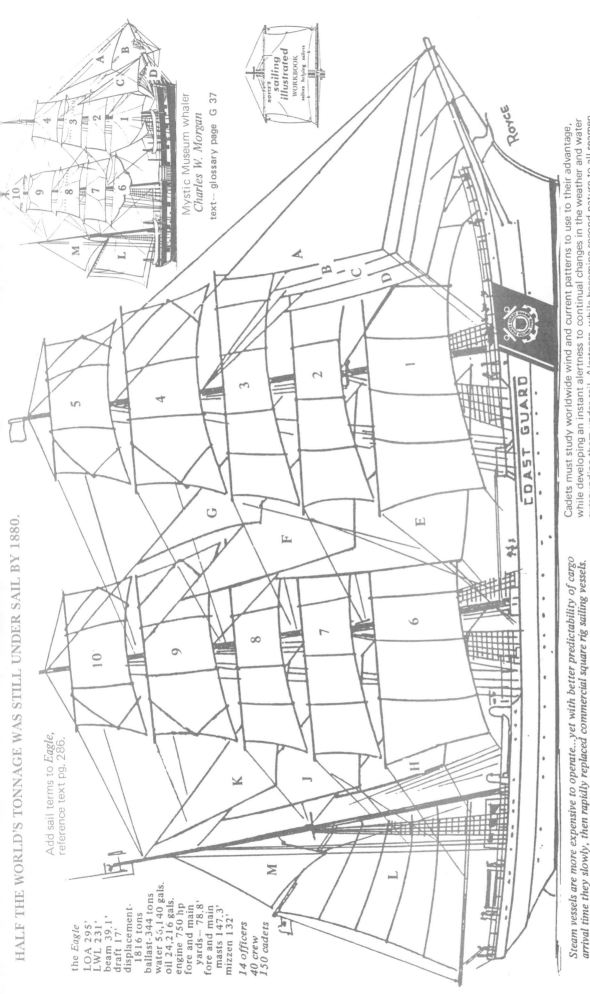

Add sail terms to *Eagle*, reference text pg. 286.

Mystic Museum whaler
Charles W. Morgan
text-- glossary page G 37

the *Eagle*
LOA 295'
LWL 231'
beam 39.1'
draft 17'
displacement-
  1816 tons
ballast-344 tons
water 55,140 gals.
oil 24,216 gals.
engine 750 hp
fore and main
yards-- 78.8'
fore and main
masts 147.3'
mizzen 132'

14 officers
40 crew
150 cadets

ROYCE
COAST GUARD

41

Steam vessels are more expensive to operate...yet with better predictability of cargo arrival time they slowly, then rapidly replaced commercial square rig sailing vessels.

Professional seamanship training begins on land, then on training vessels. Those only with training on steam vessels or motor ships, have a limited background at sea especially facing heavy weather variables of wind and wave action.

Leading navies of the world use sailing training vessels to fill this void while cadets develop team work, character building, alertness, and leadership. Russia has several sailing training vessels used by their fisheries and navy.

Cadets must study worldwide wind and current patterns to use to their advantage, while developing an instant alertness to continual changes in the weather and water surrounding them under sail. Alertness, while becoming second nature to all seamen on sailing vessels small to large to avoid trouble, must also be applied when operating small powerboats to large freighters, aircraft carriers, and tankers.

The 295' USCG *Eagle* using over 200 lines in a major maneuver, has 20 miles of rigging, and 21,350 square feet of sail. Her sister ships-- *Gorch Fock*- West Germany, *Sagres II*- Portuguese, *Mircea*- Romanian, & *Tovarishch*-Soviet Union. Other countries with training barks are Denmark- *Danmark*, Ecuador- *Guyas*, Mexico- *Cuauhtemoc*, and Colombia- *Gloria.*

The last sailor— 150 minute video, narrated by Orson Welles, is a must for all sailors to watch. It covers the dying breed of sailing vessels paying their way by fishing and hauling freight.It shows open ocean operation, to coastal areas of Chile and the Bay of Bengal, plus inland sailing craft from the Nile to Bangladesh. *Ferde Grofe Films-- 3100 Airport Ave., Santa Monica, CA 90405*

ROYCE'S **SAILING ILLUSTRATED** COURSE

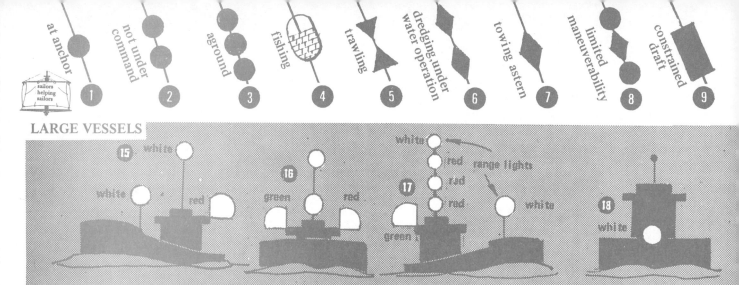

at anchor **1**
not under command **2**
aground **3**
fishing **4**
trawling **5**
dredging, under water operation **6**
towing astern **7**
limited maneuverability **8**
constrained draft **9**

sailors helping sailors

LARGE VESSELS

15 white
white red
16 green red
17 white red red range lights red green
white
18 white

Color running and range lights above on supertanker.

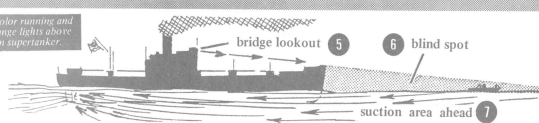

bridge lookout **5**   **6** blind spot

suction area ahead **7**

Lookout— if you can't see the lookout behind the masts and rigging, can he see you? **Propeller suction** may be from ½ to 3 times ahead of the vessel, to fill the void created by the propeller.

Vessels underway— six powerboats moved in close to see a large freighter which had stopped outside of Long Beach harbor to pick up a pilot. When the freighter started moving, its propeller suction pulled the boats under the stern counter. They were hard to see though fortunately seen by a freighter seaman off watch. He reported the situation to the wheelhouse, and the propellers were put in neutral so the powerboats could break loose.

Propeller suction distance greatly increases in shallow water especially when getting underway, as the same volume of water has to be pulled in from a greater distance.

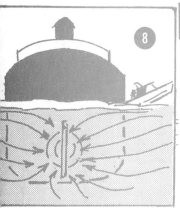

42 Keep clear of tugboats with tows particularly when they are going downstream. They will have stopping problems in an emergency

9

stern light
aft range light   **VLCC—Very Large Crude Carrier over 200,000 tons
***ULCC—Ultra Large Crude Carrier over 400,000 tons
green starboard light
aft range light?
forw ran lig

If you are uncertain of it's action and the risk of collision exists— contact the large vessel on Channel 16 at sea, or Channel 13 *in port only*.

Ships are the largest moving monsters designed, built, and operated by men— text pages 240-244. Much instructor information is found in *Homestudy Guide* pages 143-149.

While only 20 harbors worldwide can handle supertankers, the only one in the U.S. is the LA/Long Beach harbor area able to handle small supertankers to 1150' with 65' draft. While both harbors have endless small to large commercial vessel traffic, Long Beach Harbor also handles the largest battlewagons and carriers with its naval base.

Some sailors may never encounter a large vessel in their lifetime, sailors in the LA/LB harbor areas face small to large commercial vessel traffic almost every day...and every night they go sailing.

Where will the daytime signals be displayed on this supertanker?

Basic patterns are shown, text page 241, for rapid identification to know if a large vessel is underway, at anchor, or preparing to be underway and out of control.

Rapid identification is required— color the supertanker running lights above to know its course at night. This is needed to know the type of commercial vessel operation, speed, maneuverability or lack of... and how to keep out of its way. While we show standard signals, considerable variables exist in how they will be displayed.

Complex recognition lights and signals— text pages 242-3, are shown in a small size. We provide large, four color, laminated 8½ x 11 charts for rapid identification of commercial vessel lights and signals used worldwide.

a Bantry Bay Class Supertanker   maximum draft—81 ½'
38'   105'   **1**

Universe Ireland— a Bantry Bay Class
LOA 1135' beam 174'
326,000 tons with a capacity of 2,513,588 barrels of oil

An hour would be required for the *Universe Ireland* to run her way off and come to a stop with engines on stop...*NOT full astern.*

*T 2 tanker—LOA 523'6'', beam 68'
15 knot normal cruising speed*

USS America LOA 1047'
252' beam   speed 30 knots
79,724 tons   four 22' dia. props

ROYCE'S **SAILING ILLUSTRATED** COURSE

A sailboat becomes a powerboat when the engine is turned on...even when the sails are up. How will other vessels nearby know it changes to a powerboat?

Crossing Situation, Rule 15 (a)—

When two power-driven vessels are crossing *so as* to involve risk of collision, the vessel which has the other on her _____ side shall keep out of the way and *shall...* avoid _____ of the other vessel.

Rule 16. Give-Way Vessel...shall... keep well _____...R.17(a)(i) Stand on Vessel—keep _____ and _____

stand-on

give-way

DANGER ZONE
red stop—
green go

DANGER ZONE
red stop—
green go

Head-on Situation, Rule 14 (a). When two power-driven vessels are _____...*so as to involve risk of collision, which shall alter her course to _____ so that each shall pass on the ____ side of each other.*

TOOT

TURN to RIGHT

TOOT

Fill in missing words.

TOOT
TOOT

—————— River/Tidal CURRENTS ——————

Exceptions to above rule: Inland Rule 9 (a)(ii)— a power-driven vessel...with a _____ current shall have the right-of-way over an _____ vessel, *shall..._____...the signals...It is applied under International with Rule 18 (a)(ii).*

Inland Rule 15 (b)...a vessel _____ a river shall keep out of the way of a power-driven vessel _____ or _____ the river.

Rule 32 (b)..short blast..about __ ____ duration. R. 32 (c)..prolonged blast.._ to _____ duration.

TOOT
TOOT

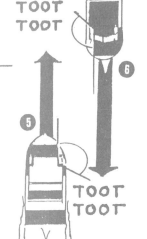

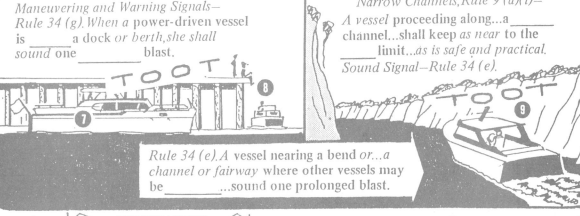

Maneuvering and Warning Signals—
Rule 34 (g). When a power-driven vessel is _____ a dock or berth, she shall sound one _____ blast.

TOOT

Narrow Channels, Rule 9 (a)(i)—
A vessel proceeding along...a _____ channel...shall keep as near to the _____ limit...as is safe and practical. Sound Signal—Rule 34 (e).

TOOT

Rule 34 (e). A vessel nearing a bend or...a channel or fairway where other vessels may be _____...sound one prolonged blast.

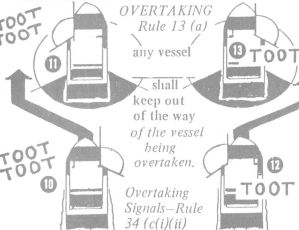

TOOT
TOOT

OVERTAKING
Rule 13 (a)

_____ any vessel

_____ shall keep out of the way of the vessel being overtaken.

TOOT

TOOT
TOOT

Overtaking Signals—Rule 34 (c)(i)(ii)

TOOT

Rule 34 (a)(i)— three short blasts .."I am operating _____ propulsion".

TOOT
TOOT
TOOT

TOOT TOOT TOOT TOOT TOOT

Warning Signals, Rule 34 (d). When vessels ...in doubt...to _____ collision...the vessel in doubt...giving at least ____ short *and* rapid blasts *on the whistle... may be* supplemented by a _____ signal *of at least five short and rapid blasts.*

ROYCE'S **SAILING ILLUSTRATED** COURSE

USCG NAVIGATION RULES International—Inland
Become THE expert by carrying the official 211 page rulebook aboard and refer to it continually. The official long number is COMDTINST M16672.2A.

Buy your copy from a marine dealer, GPO bookstore, or Superintendent of Documents, U.S. Government Printing Office, Washington, D. C. 20402.

Fill in the answers and color the lights and shapes for commercial vessel recognition.

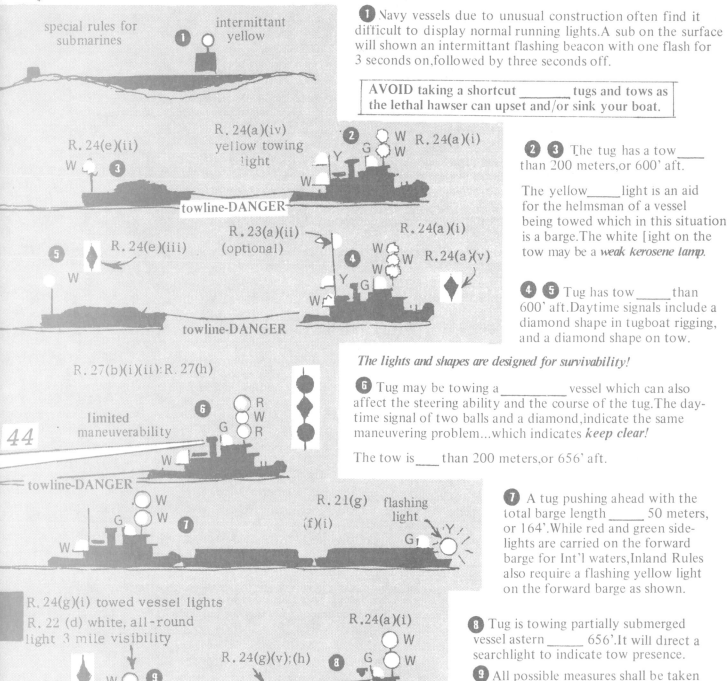

special rules for submarines

intermittant yellow

1 Navy vessels due to unusual construction often find it difficult to display normal running lights. A sub on the surface will shown an intermittant flashing beacon with one flash for 3 seconds on, followed by three seconds off.

AVOID taking a shortcut _____ tugs and tows as the lethal hawser can upset and/or sink your boat.

R. 24(e)(ii)

W

3

R. 24(a)(iv) yellow towing light

2 G W / W R. 24(a)(i)

W

towline-DANGER

2 3 The tug has a tow ____ than 200 meters, or 600' aft.

The yellow ____ light is an aid for the helmsman of a vessel being towed which in this situation is a barge. The white light on the tow may be a *weak kerosene lamp.*

5 R. 24(e)(iii)

W

R. 23(a)(ii) (optional)

4 W / W / Y / G / W R. 24(a)(i) R. 24(a)(v)

towline-DANGER

4 5 Tug has tow ____ than 600' aft. Daytime signals include a diamond shape in tugboat rigging, and a diamond shape on tow.

The lights and shapes are designed for survivability!

6 Tug may be towing a _____ vessel which can also affect the steering ability and the course of the tug. The daytime signal of two balls and a diamond, indicate the same maneuvering problem...which indicates *keep clear!*

The tow is ____ than 200 meters, or 656' aft.

R. 27(b)(i)(ii): R. 27(h)

6 R / W / R G

limited maneuverability

44

towline-DANGER

7 W / W G W

R. 21(g) (f)(i)

flashing light

Y / G

7 A tug pushing ahead with the total barge length ____ 50 meters, or 164'. While red and green sidelights are carried on the forward barge for Int'l waters, Inland Rules also require a flashing yellow light on the forward barge as shown.

R. 24(g)(i) towed vessel lights

R. 22 (d) white, all-round light 3 mile visibility

R. 24(g)(v);(h)

9 W

8 W / W G R.24(a)(i)

towline-DANGER

8 Tug is towing partially submerged vessel astern ____ 656'. It will direct a searchlight to indicate tow presence.

9 All possible measures shall be taken to light the ____ object...or to indicate its presence.

10 G / W G R

R. 26(b)(i)

under 20 meters

11 R / W G R

R. 26(c)(i)

10 The green over white light at night... double cones daytime, indicate a vessel engage in ____

11 The red over white light at night, or daytime basket in the rigging indicates a vessel ____ with nets or lines ____ than 150 meters, or 492' astern.

NO maneuverability...and LIMITED maneuverability means KEEP CLEAR.

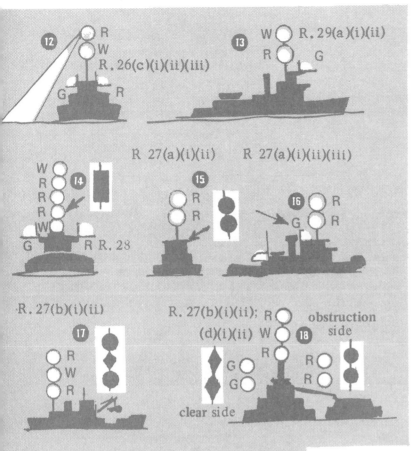

12 The vessel is _____ with nets or lines _____ than 150 meters (492') away.

Additional signals may be shown when fishing near other vessels.

13 Lights of pilot vessel on _____ duty _____ at night...its name is painted on the vessel for daytime identification.

14 A vessel _____ under International Rules which is constrained by its draft... **Inland Rule, is silent.**

15 This is a vessel ____ under command.

16 This is a vessel _____ but ___ under command.

17 The ____ _____ which is not underway has limited maneuverability...note the distinctive daytime signal.

18 The vessel at anchor is _____ or is involved in _____ _____ .

The ____ **side** is indicated by two green lights at night, and two diamonds by day for the side another vessel may pass.

The _____ or **obstruction side** is indicated by two red lights and two black balls.

ROYCE'S **SAILING ILLUSTRATED** COURSE

45

19 Two vertical red lights and a white light forward in the rigging at night....and three vertical balls in the rigging with one forward daytime, indicate a vessel _____.

20 Naval vessels have special missions with special signals such as the vessel shown engaged in _____...with three green lights at night and three black balls in the rigging when underway in the daytime. This indicates it is dangerous to approach closer than 500 meters (1940') to either side... and 1000 meters (3280') astern...to avoid the cutting paravanes with their wire rope tows.

21 A vessel ____ than 50 meters (164') long is at anchor.

22 A vessel _____ than 50 meters at anchor: vessels over 100 meters may illuminate with working lights, Rule 30(c).

23 All vessels 7 meters (23') and longer, Rule 30(c), will show a _____ _____ forward in the rigging during daytime at anchor; exception, special anchorage areas, Rule 30(g).

Expect tremendous variables in location and use of these lights. For example—

Time 2300, low visibility. We saw lights on a vessel towing a net more than 150 meters aft, anticipated speed 2 knots. We were easily clearing its bow, BUT—

The vessel was making 14 knots on a collision course with us. The operator had taken in the nets forgetting to turn off those special lights.

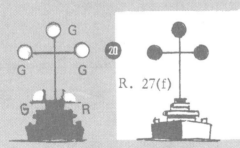

What do ancient sailor weather proverbs predict... that may be just as useful to modern sailors

Proverbs are listed on page 56 in our *Sailing Illustrated Homestudy Guide.*

Names of the cloud formations are shown on page 204 of the reference text *Sailing Illustrated.*

Mackerel sky and mare's tails...

When wind shifts against the sun, trust it not for back it will run...

When clouds appear like rocks and towers...

If clouds look as scratched by a hen...

At sea with low and falling glass...

But when the glass is high and rising...

Short warning, soon past.

Long foretold, long last!

Quick rise after a low...

While rise begins after a low...

A red sky in the morning...

A red sky at night....   46

A light bright blue sky...

A dark, gloomy blue sky...

A pale yellow sky...

A bright yellow sky...

The moon, governess of the floods....

Wooly fleeces deck the heavenly way...

Seagull, seagull sit on the land...

When the sea hog jumps?????

Static becomes the sailors best friend, resulting from upper level disturbances of an incoming storm.

Static on an inexpensive AM radio sometimes 3 to 5 hours ahead rapidly increasing, is the best method to predict a storm moving into your area.

the weather factory

sailing illustrated

sailors helping sailors

Sailors still need to return to traditional weather predictions for self reliance... and self protection.

In less than a century our nation changed from a rural farm economy to city living. Many of us live in air-conditioned environments with little need to analyze changing weather conditions. instant TV weather reports are relayed from outer space, a technology a short ten years old.

The science of radio weather prediction is a short 60 years old. Before that especially on the ocean, sailors were their own weather experts to move cargo from one port to another in minimum time, and for survival. As weather predictions cover large areas, sailors still have to predict rapidly changing conditions in their own immediate area for spirited sailing... or survival. Learn the names and functions of cloud patterns where nature sends its warnings, text pages 204-9.

With practice you can soon predict when a good wind will develop for spirited sailing, or it is better to mow the lawn with weakening breezes. A basic AM radio provides the best method to predict an *incoming thunderstorm* on the water under sail, providing ample time to return to the dock, or be snugged down at anchor in a protected cove, text pages 216-7.

Little publicized *clear weather, blue-sky dusters,* also predicted with a basic AM radio, can be almost as violent as thunderstorms. They are common in the summer on our plain states from Montana south to Texas, and eastward to the Mississippi. Dusters move in with the westerlies. They can be seen a long distance away on the flat plains from the southwest to northwest.

ROYCE'S **SAILING ILLUSTRATED** COURSE

Sailboat steering balance is best defined as simplicity with complexity... and complexity with simplicity.

Balance factors of *sail plan* **and** *hull lateral resistance* **seem confusing.**

CE— sail Center of Effort

CLR— hull Center of Lateral Resistance

Monohull *LEAD* is shown in a vertical position with combined CE designed ahead of hull CLR.

The LEAD is designed to disappear as a sailboat heels called *swinging moment* bringing both CE and CLR into balance for self steering.

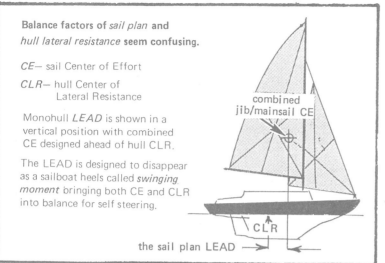

combined jib/mainsail CE

CLR

the sail plan LEAD →

A big sailboat is just a big dinghy. Steering balance factors are obvious on a 24' keel sailboat in an increasing wind. Practice is required to develop similar sensitivity on large sailboats as identical balance factors develop slowly by comparison in the same increasing wind.

A well balanced, well-maintained sailboat is a joy to sail. The author however remembers only two sailboats with perfect balance on his first sail aboard... requiring **tuning** to bring many sailboats into steering balance.

Excessive weather helm, excessive lee helm— text pages 133-5. Sailboats are clumsy to steer, while their heavy weather action behavior can be cranky and unpredictable.

A slight mast rake aft— text page 113. It has been sufficient to improve steering rudder balance on some sailboats, and occasionally, a slight mast rake forward is necessary.

Sailboat ends are weight sensitive. A 40' sailboat came into balance when 300' of heavy chain in the bow was increased to 900', Changing 300' of heavy chain to 300' of light nylon, was the answer for another sailboat.

Wind forces 1 & 2— *ripples.* **Lee-bow wave pressure** has to be increased by crew weight on the low side, with the underpowered sailboat carrying a large genoa. Text page 131— a sailboat on the water is a sensitive **teeter totter** requiring crew weight forward in the cockpit.

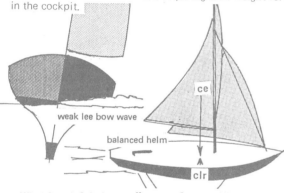

weak lee bow wave

ce

balanced helm

clr

Wind forces 3 & 4— *small waves.* Crew weight starts to move to the high side and slightly aft in the cockpit to balance the complex rudder-helm forces.

Force 5— *longer waves with some whitecaps.* Time to change from genoa to working jib.

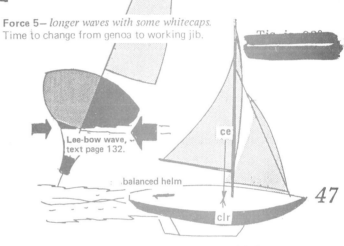

Lee-bow wave, text page 132.

ce

balanced helm

clr

47

Excess heel causes weather-helm drag— text page 134. Crew weight on high side is no longer able to minimize heel forces. Change to working jib so self-steering rudder balance returns.

Force 6— *many whitecaps!!!!*

Excessive weather-helm drag results from too much heel and strong lee-bow wave... requiring a mainsail reef.

Close all overboard valves.

ce

balanced helm

clr

Raise jib tack off deck— text pages 133, 147, and 153-7. Waves breaking aboard have to drain easily overboard to eliminate sudden shock loads on jib and jibstay caused by waves breaking aboard, hitting foot of a low-tacked jib.

Shock-cord steering is possible sailing upwind, force 2 and above, on many well-balanced sailboats when weight distribution, heel, and sail trim fall into rudder balance. The same factors help wind vane and autopilot steering.

Wind-force pressures— text pages 136-7. Wind is the *action*, producing an identifiable wave pattern *reaction*... indicating amount of sail area for various wave pattern wind pressures.

Force 7— *whitecaps and swells.* **Excessive lee-bow pressure** must be compensated for by dropping mainsail to bring CE & CLR forces into balance. This is necessary to reduce tremendous weather-helm drag pressures on rudder.

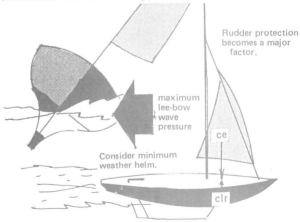

Rudder protection becomes a **major** factor.

maximum lee-bow wave pressure

ce

Consider minimum weather helm.

clr

Move crew weight aft in cockpit to balance sailboat rudder.

Keep hull on its fore and aft lines to avoid the bow digging in causing a hazardous broach— text page 153.

Coming about in a force 7 is spooky. Since the turning point balance moves forward of the mast... expect the stern to swing across a much wider arc from one tack to another.

skipper—

phone—

address—

city—   zip—

The **Sailing Illustrated Course** introduces the first quality, multi-purpose sailing workbook with lecture material. It is designed for public use by any organization, as well as for private lessons. The seven 2½ hour lecture sequence with much testing since 1960 in the classroom, and on the water, provides a well-rounded sailing foundation with flexibility.

Language is the major barrier to sailing. A missing word is added to a statement, and terms to illustrations, to learn the new, unique sounds of the international sailing language.

add lecture dates

Lecture I— **terminology**, workbook pages 2-5, sail rigs, hull, sail terms. *Homework*— add terms to the dinghies, pages 6-8 with contrasting red or black pen.

Lecture II— **underway**, tacks and courses page 10, Right-of- Way, page 11, sail trim closehauled, reaching, running pages 12-15, tacking, jibing, page 17. *Homework*— color U.S. buoyage system page 9.

Lecture III— **metals, corrosion forms** page 19, marine hardware pages 20-23. *Homework*— review hardware terms; add standing/running rigging terms to sailboats pg. 24. Find corrosion forms in your home, boat, car.

Lecture IV— **raise/lower sails** page 25, docking methods pages 26-27. *Homework*— cabin sailboats pages 28, 29, 30, 31, 33. Add running/standing rigging terms to minimum of 3 or 4 sailboats, or all cabin sailboats.

Lecture V— **spinnakers** page 32, wind force page 35, tide, current, fog page 18, capsize/ recovery page 37. *Homework*— thunderstorms/dusters, text pages 216-7, positive ion behavioral factor ?, text page 219.

Lecture VI— **powerboat rules** page 43, commercial vessel operation page 42, commercial vessel signals and lights pages 44-45. *Homework*— add sail terms to *Cutty Sark* page 39, and to *USCG Eagle* page 41. Study text pages 210-211 of the 1850 square rigger sailing from New York to San Francisco, with a different return route back to New York.

Lecture VII— **worldwide weather sailing patterns** page 38. 1700-1900 square rig and schooners page 40.

Lecture VIII (optional). Review highlights of lectures that best fit your sailing area and student interest. *Homework*— go sailing!

Marlinspike seamanship homework requirements page 16 are assigned at each lecture to cover basic knots, whipping, 3-strand splice for each student. Marlinspike page numbers—

square knot, page 192	*cleating dock line, page 191*
bowline, page 192	*heaving line, page 194*
sheet bend, page 189	*coil 3 strand, page 193*
whipping, page 200	*eye splice, page 201*

Send orders to-- **Royce Marketing, 28210 N. Ave. Stanford, Valencia, CA 91355-1111 USA**
phone (805) 499-3053   FAX (805) 257-3867